The Independent Scholar's Handbook

The Independent Scholar's Handbook

Ronald Gross

TEN SPEED PRESS
Berkeley, California

For permission to reprint copyrighted material the author is grateful to the following publishers and copyright proprietors:

CROWN PUBLISHERS, INC.: *From Buckminster Fuller: At Home in the Universe* by Alden Hatch. Copyright © 1974 by Alden Hatch. By permission of Crown Publishers, Inc.

HARPER & ROW, PUBLISHERS, INC.: From *Before the Sabbath* by Eric Hoffer. Copyright © 1979 by Eric Hoffer.

HOLT, RINEHART AND WINSTON, PUBLISHERS: From "Two Tramps in Mud Time" from *The Poetry of Robert Frost* edited by Edward Connery Lathem. Copyright © 1969 by Holt, Rinehart and Winston. Reprinted by permission of Holt, Rinehart and Winston, Publishers.

LITTLE, BROWN AND COMPANY, PUBLISHERS: From *The Ascent of Man* by J. Bronowski. Copyright © 1973 by J. Bronowski.

CHARLES SCRIBNER'S SONS: J. L. Barkas, *Victims*. Copyright © 1978 by J. L. Barkas. Reprinted with the permission of Charles Scribner's Sons.

THE COLLEGE ENTRANCE EXAMINATION BOARD: Reprinted with permission from *Expand Your Life* by Allen Tough. Copyright © 1980 by College Entrance Examination Board, New York.

E. P. DUTTON, INC.: Reprinted by permission of E. P. Dutton, inc. from *This Way Out: A Guide to Alternatives to Traditional College Education* by John Coyne and Tom Hebert. Copyright © 1972 by John Coyne and Tom Hebert.

TEN SPEED PRESS: From *Finding Facts Fast* by Alden Todd. Copyright © 1972 and 1979 by Alden Todd and Julian Bach Literary Agency, Inc. Reprinted by permission of Alden Todd.

SATURDAY REVIEW, INC.: From *What I Have Learned: A Collection of 20 Autobiographical Essays by Great Contemporaries from the Saturday Review*. Published by Simon and Schuster. Copyright © 1966, 1967, 1968 by Saturday Review, Inc. Reprinted with permission from Saturday Review, Inc.

FOUNDATION CENTER: "Foundation Center Cooperating Collections—Free Funding Information Centers."

TEN SPEED PRESS
P.O. Box 7123, Berkeley, California 94707

Text design and composition by Ralph Fowler
Cover design by Fifth Street Design

Library of Congress Cataloging-in-Publication Data
Gross, Ronald
   The independent scholar's handbook / Ronald Gross.
      p.   cm.
   Includes bibliographical references and index.
   ISBN 0-89815-521-5
   1. Learning and scholarship.   I. Title
AZ103.G75   1993
001.2—dc20   93-19276
                                   CIP

Printed in the United States of America
   2   3   4   5 — 97   96   95

Dedication

The tragedy of AIDS has been especially grievous in the arts and intellectual life. Independent scholarship is no exception. Many in the field are suffering; many have died. We offer our support, mourn our losses, and treasure our memories.

As this book goes to press, Jim Bennett, one of the brightest sources of light and warmth in this field, is in a hospice in Chicago. He has written wittily, learnedly, and passionately about independent scholarship. His writing has inspired us, his erudition has illuminated our experience, his scathing irony has sometimes infuriated its targets. He has made a difference. Jim's major book on independent scholarship has been awaited keenly by everyone in the field. We wish him well in bringing it to fruition.

In his name, many of us in this sector of creative life have rededicated ourselves to doing what needs to be done to support our friends and colleagues with AIDS.

Without the breath of life, the human body is a corpse;
without thinking, the human mind is dead.
—*Hannah Arendt*

For those who have experienced it,
the hour of the awakening of the passion for knowledge
is the most memorable of a lifetime.
—*Colin Wilson*

The world needs the inspiration of our
undamaged instinctive love for the truth.
—*Buckminster Fuller*

Contents

Acknowledgments

This book asserts that those of us trying to do serious intellectual work outside academe can look to one another for colleagueship. Happily for me, the book also demonstrates how well this worked for one independent scholar. It was strengthened immeasurably by the following colleagues, peers, and masters, most of them fellow "independents":

Marjorie Lightman, Institute for Research in History; Richard Brown, Newberry Library; William Draves, Learning Resources Network; Richard Gummere, Jr., University Seminars (Columbia); Gloria Erlich, Princeton Research Forum; Victor Marrow, Society for Philosophy and Public Affairs; Walter Haines, New York University; Hal Bowser, *Science Digest* magazine; Kenneth Fischer, The Learners' Forum; Susan Spragg, Denver Independent Scholars' Roundtable; Loring Thompson, vice president emeritus, Northeastern University; Philip Gordon, formerly director, Academy of Independent Scholars; Robert McClintock, Teachers College, Columbia; John Walter, independent scholar; John Ohliger, Basic Choices; Allen Tough, Ontario Institute for Studies in Education; Richard Hendrix, Fund for the Improvement of Postsecondary Education; Ruth Weinstock, education consultant; Lydia Bronte, formerly of the Rockefeller Foundation; Tom Adams, independent scientist; Henry Doering, editor; Tom Hebert, Tennessee Valley Authority; William Zeisel, Editors and Scholars.

Julie Klauber has been my chief research and editorial associate on this book, and her contribution has been enormous. She researched and wrote the sections on grants and awards; special libraries and interlibrary loan; and databases. In addition, she conducted innumerable smaller inquiries with unfailing intelligence and energy. If this book benefits independent scholars, much of the credit should go to her.

For sustained intellectual contributions to the book my greatest debts are to Kathleen Spaltro, Chris Wagner, Walter Haines, and Dorothy Welker—four quite different individuals with a common capacity to care for the work of another.

For invaluable opportunities to share parts of this work as it developed, and for providing hospitality and mental nourishment, I gladly thank the Newberry Library, Basic Choices, the University Seminar on Innovations in Higher Education at Columbia, the Institute for Research in History, the Highlander Center, the Fund for the Improvement of Postsecondary Education, the Office of Adult Learning Services at the College Board (and its predecessor there, Future Directions for a Learning Society), the Free University Network (now Learning Resources Network), the Ontario Institute for Studies in Education, the National Adult Education Conference, U.S. Department of Education, Modern Language Association, and the American Library Association.

Prologue: Encounters with Four Mentors

At certain moments in our lives, mind seems to whisper to memory: "*Print* this." Those moments stay with us: whether as words, perceptions, or the presence of a person. Occasionally we fail to realize their significance at the time. Dramatic moments that we assume will loom large fade with the years, while cruxes are contained in moments that occur unheralded, but stick and stay with us. Four such moments spurred this book.

The first occurred two days after my college graduation—but in retrospect it seems as if *it* was the moment when my higher education really began. It was a balmy spring evening and I was sitting on the porch of Cornelius Hirschberg's house in New Jersey, listening to his latest "report from the front"—the intellectual front in my friend's ever-exuberant battle for understanding. A salesman by trade, "Neil" has also been a learner for most of his adult life.

Since the last time we had talked, he reported, he had faced squarely up to one of life's problems, one that most of us successfully avoid: He had read no great poet outside the English language. "That's no way to go to the grave," he said. "Since I sought a writer worth years of work, and Goethe can be appreciated in translation, I was left with Dante."

Neil already had worked his way (with dictionaries and critiques) through the *Inferno* and the first twenty-two cantos of the *Purgatorio*. "A few days ago, I read an entire canto at first sight and got the general meaning right off. Within two years, I should be able not merely to read, but to *feel* Dante."

At this point Neil paused, and I asked an impertinent question. "Neil, it's always thrilling to hear you talk about this, and you obviously relish it as an experience—but what's it all *for*?" He looked puzzled at first, and I tried to explain. "I mean, does it have a practical *use*, over and above the immediate enjoyment?"

My friend sipped his lemonade thoughtfully, then answered slowly. "Ronald, I have always made a respectable living. But I have not been willing to give up my life to getting the kind of money with which you can *buy* the best things in life. I am stuck in business and routine and tedium; I must live as I can. But I give up only as much as I must; for the rest, I have lived, and always will live, my life as it can be lived at its best, with art, music, poetry, literature, science, philosophy, and thought. I shall know the keener people of this world, think the keener thoughts, and taste the keener pleasures, as long as I can and as much as I can. That's the real practical use of self-education and self-culture. It converts a world which is only a good world for those who can win at its ruthless game into a world good for all of us. Your education is the only thing that nothing can take from you in this life. You can lose your money, your wife, your children, your friends, your pride, your honor, and your life, but while you live you can't lose your culture, such as it is."

The sun had set by now, but Neil's eyes still glowed in a special way that I have since seen in other people's. Whenever I have seen it, this glow has taken me back to that darkening porch and my first glimmer of what real learning is like.

The second such moment occurred on the first day at my first job. I had obtained a position as the lowest of the low at a New York publishing house, Simon and Schuster. Max Schuster, the cofounder of the firm, was a publisher of the old breed, in the days before conglomerates consumed book companies for breakfast.

I had barely found my way to and from the men's room when the summons came to wait upon Max in his vast book-lined office-study. For a young man fresh to the world of work this was an awesome assignation. I found myself sitting in a armchair in what was referred to as the "Inner

Sanctum"—an armchair that had been occupied by Bertrand Russell, Albert Einstein, Bernard Berenson, Will Durant, and hundreds of other writers, philosophers, historians, novelists, and poets.

Max Schuster was not a man to mince words or to warm you up with small talk. His words were well honed; he obviously had delivered this message before and knew exactly what he wanted to say and how he wanted to say it. Fixing me with a firm eye over the glistening mahogany desktop, he declared: "I have one piece of advice for you—not just for success in this business, but personally. Begin *at once*—not today, or tomorrow, or at some remote indefinite date, but right now, at this precise moment—to choose some subject, some concept, some great name or idea or event in history on which you can eventually make yourself the world's supreme expert. Start a crash program immediately to qualify yourself for this self-assignment through reading, research, and reflection." In his librarylike office, such a program did not seem impossible, as a generous slice of the world's wisdom was within arm's reach.

Max knew perfectly well that the path to such expertise was no smooth slide, so he followed these imperious injunctions with a warning: "I don't mean the sort of expert who avoids all the small errors as he sweeps on to the grand fallacy. I mean one who has the most knowledge, the deepest insight, and the most audacious willingness to break new ground.

"Such a disciplined form of self-education," he assured me, gesturing at the photos of famous authors that adorned his desk, "will give you prestige, eminence, and worldwide contacts. You'll enjoy correspondence and fellowship with other people interested in the same specialty. It will add a new dimension and a new unity to your entire education. It will give you a passionate sense of purpose. The cross-fertilization of ideas will become an exciting and unending adventure that will add a new total perspective to your entire life."

I would like to be able to report that this advice changed my life, setting me on the course that has culminated in this book. I cannot. Max's advice fell on deaf ears. I was too young, still too convinced that *college* was the place where one did serious learning, still too fixated on getting started in a career in the "real" world. I did not get the point. Yet the words *had* registered—something within me said softly, "Print this." And later, on other occasions in very different settings, the practicality of Max Schuster's advice became manifest.[1]

Years later, at the other end of the continent, I walked along a California coastline at sunset to watch "fish dancing on the beach under the full moon," as the native Indians had described them to the Spaniards. The fish were grunions. The females come up and lay their eggs above the high-tide mark burying themselves tail-first in the sand, while the males gyrate around them to fertilize the eggs. These eggs then develop without being disturbed by the waters again for the nine or ten days after the full moon.

For me on that evening, however, it was an *idea* that started to develop. It was suggested by my companion, the late Jacob Bronowski, one of those notable independent scholars from whom I feel I have gained what education I have. Mostly, that education came from his remarkable television series, *The Ascent of Man*, from which so many have benefited as I did. But on this occasion I had the privilege of spending an hour or so with him. While the grunions spawned at our feet, we talked mostly about our mutual association with the Salk Institute (he as a distinguished Fellow, I as merely one of many board members of the Institute's main support at that time, The National Foundation). Something set him to speaking about some fellow scientists he had known who, in the years leading up to Hiroshima, had become enamored of their association with political and military power. (Bronowski had turned away from mathematics and the physical sciences, and toward the life sciences, after the bomb.)

"We must somehow figure out how to be a democracy of intellect," he said. "Knowledge must sit in the homes and heads of people with no ambition to control others, and not up in the isolated seats of power." He believed that, only if the adventure of knowing and understanding were shared as widely as possible, would our scientific civilization remain viable. In the end, he contended, it is not an aristocracy of experts, scientific or otherwise, on whom we must depend, but on them and *ourselves*. "The personal commitment of a man to his skill, the intellectual commitment and the emotional commitment working together as one, has made for our true progress as a species. Every man, every civilization, has gone forward because of its engagement with what it has set itself to do. Knowledge is our destiny."

The grunions spawning that night were gone in a season; Bronowski is gone now too. But the ascent of the human mind, as he conceived it, continues. Participation in it, to the degree that our personal endowments permit, is self-declared. Each of us should be warmly welcomed to make the finest contribution our talent and effort can fashion.[2]

The fourth incident occurred in as different an ambience as you could imagine. I was scrunched into a phone booth at Chicago's O'Hare Airport, which was socked in by fog. At such times the only relief, for me, is to catch up with friends around the country by telephone. Trapped in the impersonality of the airport culture, which is the same everywhere, one can at least play another technology against it, the more "congenial" one as Ivan Illich would call it, and feel some contact with real human beings.

I found the futurist Hazel Henderson at her desk, catching up on correspondence after taking a quick trip to Nairobi to attend—and typically, confront—a government-sponsored conference on energy. (I introduce Hazel and her works later in this book, so will not describe her here.) At one point, something she said made me remember the point Max Schuster had made in his office, years before. I quoted it to her, and she responded: "I admire the kind of personal commitment he was urging, but we've got to go beyond rugged individualism, if everyone's to have a fair chance to make their contribution. We've got to invent collaborative organizations for the life of the mind, to give us the mutual support we need. The universities have become intellectual museums. Meanwhile, outside academe, networks in each new field are learning together what we need to know about ecology, disarmament, agribusiness, and the multinational corporations. We need each other to do this kind of essential research and thinking."

Independence of mind and spirit may well depend on *interdependence*. The nurturing of intellectual enterprise requires social support. Although the individual commitment that Max Schuster had urged was indeed crucial, social change is necessary too. Hazel Henderson's words also made me realize why I had not gotten the point of Max Schuster's advice twenty years before. The time had not yet been right.

Independent scholars have always existed—indeed, as I will contend below, have been the mainstream of Western culture—but their widespread visibility perhaps had to await the arrival of a largely college-educated population, including many people with strong intellectual interests sparked by their higher education. It had to await the widespread availability of quality paperback books, of a vast repertoire of musical masterpieces readily available on records and tapes, of the availability of cultural experiences made accessible through cheap and convenient means of transportation. It had to await an era in which the personal aspirations of Americans would begin to turn away from material acquisitions, toward the cultivation of inner resources.

The day of the independent scholar also had to wait for the decline of certain myths about the who, why, where, and how of serious intellectual work. Thirty years ago, our view was clouded by what David Riesman and Christopher Jencks called "The Academic Victory." It was the heyday of higher education. Academe had assumed a dominant role in our culture and society. That dominance blinded us to independent scholarship, to that vast amount of intellectual work that goes on, and has always gone on, outside the academy.

The apotheosis of the professor overshadowed, for a historic moment, the great tradition of Sigmund Freud, Karl Marx, John Stuart Mill, Charles Darwin, Albert Einstein, and such contemporary figures as Edmund Wilson, Barbara Tuchman, Lewis Mumford, Mortimer Adler, and Paul Goodman, all of whom achieved intellectual preeminence without benefit of a faculty position. Forgetting them, we assumed that doing serious intellectual work entailed being a professor. Academe seemed the sole source of significant scholarship.

Now, as the lights dim in the universities and much of the most exciting intellectual activity goes on outside academe, the time seems right to recognize, celebrate, and encourage independent scholarship. Fresh thinking and more broadly based research and experimentation is needed in virtually every field. What Max Schuster suggested as a personal project has become a cultural necessity.

These four moments, years apart, stirred in my mind four perceptions about independent scholarship. Neil Hirschberg revealed the inner incentives for living the life of the mind. Max Schuster pointed to the need for committing oneself to the quest. Jacob Bronowski declared the need to democratize knowledge. Hazel Henderson affirmed our need for one another in using intellect to solve common problems.

But I learned even more than this from them. From each such teacher we learn not just what we are told, but also what the person *is*. Each of these people was doing serious intellectual work outside academe. A salesman, a publisher, a scientist, a social critic—none of them was a professor. Yet each was deeply involved in significant intellectual pursuits. Each was making a distinctive contribution to our shared world of culture or science. Each was using to the utmost those ways to find out and think straight that constitute the methodologies of the humanities, the sciences, and social inquiry.

So beyond what each of these mentors taught me, I learned this from their lives: Serious intellectual work can be pursued outside academe. Together, these strong spirits gave me what we get whenever we encounter any fully realized person, namely a glimpse of one distinct human possibility. In this case, that possibility was independent scholarship.

PART ONE

Starting Out

CHAPTER ONE

Risk Takers of the Mind

This is a book about taking risks of an unusual kind: risks in the realm of the mind. It invites you to make good your impulse (without which you would not have picked up this book) to make the joys of the intellect a significant part of your life. I do not know how much you have already nurtured and cultivated that impulse. You may be just beginning, as each of us must, even those who become notable in their fields. You may have chosen or are compelled to work at a job that does not challenge your mental capacities as much as you would like. Perhaps you have found a way to earn your living through intellectual activity of one kind or another, as so many do in our increasingly knowledge-based society, but have other interests that you would like to explore outside of work. You may even have advanced academic training in a chosen field of study, but find that there are simply no faculty positions available.

Clearly, your position on this continuum will determine which parts of this book you find most useful and congenial. I have started with basic matters that we all have to master when we begin. One of my strong convictions is that the life of the mind should be open to all who want to commit themselves to the time and energy it demands. If you have already mastered the basics, you may want to turn at once to some of the remaining chapters, which have proven useful even to quite sophisticated scholars.

All of us share, however, a certain frame of mind, a certain temper, that is worth evoking at the start. We are all, novices and sophisticates, people "for whom the life of the mind has a preponderant place, regardless of their profession," as the late French psychotherapist Ignace Lepp put in his helpful *L'Art de vivre de l'intellectual.*

> There are many [such] among doctors, lawyers, engineers, the clergy, and even among ordinary men and women who have never gone to a university. Many workingmen are self-taught intellectuals. They devote their free time to serious reading and discussion. Their limitations stem more from a lack of method than a lack of intelligence. By comparison with such self-taught intellectuals who have a real passion for knowledge there are university professors who are scarcely more than barbarians. Outside of their narrow specialization their reading runs to detective stories and their conversation more to automobiles and racing than to matters intellectual. (ibid)

A "real passion for knowledge" is, I believe, the step beyond those inchoate forms of "self-fulfillment" that have swept through our culture. Those who have tried everything from est to Esalen, many have indeed found an enlargement of spirit. But at this point such vague, personality-centered quests are proving unsatisfactory.

I first discerned the change while conducting Life Planning workshops at New York University several years ago. I noticed how much satisfaction some people got out of going beyond *self*-discovery to discovery of something important or beautiful or powerful or fascinating about the world. For thousands of such people, *self*-fulfillment consists of finding and filling their "hole in the world," as I have come to call it. These individuals are moving beyond the infatuation with the self to a more mature engagement with the world outside. By placing their quest for fulfillment in an intellectual framework, they find support and direction for their efforts. By accepting the bracing demands of a disciplined mode of inquiry, they join a community of searchers that sustains them. Such people have discovered a particular question, problem, issue, person, task, or puzzle that is *theirs*. It intrigues them, it challenges them, it amuses them, it enchants them, it bedevils them—and they love it.

Listen to a few of them talk about how it feels to find and fulfill your own intellectual quest.

> Acting as intellectual entrepreneur in a field like this gives me access to a realm where people, ideas, theory, and practice can interact—a place where a

janitor can work with editors and authors and professors because we're all intensely concerned with the way this literary genre reflects today's social realities, and tomorrow's.

> —Phil Kaveny, who is a janitor by occupation and a science
> fiction critic, lecturer, and conference-organizer by avo-
> cation

It's a first-hand, direct experience with the universe. Nothing relaxes me better after my work in computer programming than to see these things the average person will never see. And the occasional solar eclipse! There's literally nothing on earth you can see that rivals the moment when, over the profile of the lunar mountains, the corona of light shoots out the sun. It's fantastic!

> —Charles Kapral, who helps investigate "lunar transient
> phenomena" through a worldwide network of amateur
> astronomers

We have felt exhilarated and energized by our new knowledge. Finding out about our bodies and our bodies' needs, starting to take control over that area of our lives, has released, for us, an energy that has overflowed into our work, our friendships, our relationships with men and women, and for some of us, our marriages and our parenthood.

> —The Boston women whose pursuit of the truth about
> their own physical and mental health as women led to
> the groundbreaking book they wrote together in 1971,
> *Our Bodies, Our Selves*

My hankering for history keeps me from living in the past.

> —Esther Kelly Watson, who at eighty-four completed and
> published a book recounting the ninety-year history of
> the Westminster Presbyterian Church, a publication that
> was honored as a significant addition to the history of
> her native city of Portland, Oregon

I had lived among these people as a boy, and nothing in my life has given me as much satisfaction as learning something of the elegance with which their oral language was constructed and the mellifluous quality of its sounds.

> —Coy Eklund, the president of one of the nation's largest
> life insurance companies; he researched and wrote a
> Chippewa language workbook so that this threatened
> Indian language would not be forever lost to future
> generations

You sense a special kind of personal power from pure intellectual achievement. It's completely separate from that which comes from your occupation or material possessions or any other source. Nothing else in my life gives me quite the sense of accomplishment as finding a rare species of protozoa in a puddle next to a shopping center.

> —Tom Adams, a microscopist interested in the life forms
> found in a pond near his home in New Jersey

I've scratched my head for a long time to figure out why I like caves. I guess it's just that there's always more to discover both physically and psychologically each time I explore a cave.

> —William Halliday, a doctor in Seattle whose lifelong
> hobby, exploring caves, has led him to worldwide travel,
> conservationist activism, and the writing of three books,
> one of which is regarded as the bible of spelunking

I've rescued legions of brave men from undeserved oblivion. I'm never happier than when I'm on the trail of some lost data—taking notes, putting the pieces together, making history!

> —John Walter, whose research on military engagements
> in the Civil War is so valuable to his fellow historians and
> to universities, libraries, and historical societies that they
> purchase his "capsule histories"

You may have experienced similar feelings back in your college days, or you may be experiencing them right now if you are presently in college. You may have tasted a subject or a field or a particular topic that turned you on, intellectually. Perhaps you caught the enthusiasm by contagion, from a professor whose passion for the subject sparked your own enthusiasm. You suddenly got a glimpse of what pursuing such a field would be like and saw that it would be one of the most exciting, rewarding, enjoyable things you could do.

But then, the course moved along to the next topic or ended. (Formal education is driven by the syllabus, not by our enthusiasms.) The midterm, the final, the grade, the credits, the diploma—somehow your spark of intellectual excitement got lost in the shuffle. You may have concluded, without even realizing it, that perhaps that sort of thing is only for professors; that having chosen not to enter academic life, you have no business pursuing such impulses.

As more and more Americans in each generation get a taste of higher learning in college, they are, however, increasingly inclined to continue some serious intellectual pursuits throughout their lives. Loring Thompson, who as vice president for planning at one of the nation's largest private universities, is a veteran observer of campus trends, reports that

> increasingly, college graduates are making some kind of serious inquiry a part of their life plans. People now have the freedom to select important interests and devote much of their lives to these interests regardless of employment opportunities; they can choose an academic life-style even though they are not earning their living that way.
>
> Future college students may be motivated to be professional or avocational academicians. They will study the subject matter of greatest interest to them. If the employment market offers attractive opportunities, they may earn their living in that field; they are prepared to earn their bread at another occupation if necessary, and to continue to devote their creative interests to their chosen field.
>
> In other words, these people will be selecting an academic way of life: a life involving abstract thinking, intellectual analysis, perceptivity, and creativity. The fact that they may not be paid for doing this will not deter them. The achievements of avocational academicians in the past portend a bright future for this living pattern.[1]

Is this sort of life for you? It may be, if you have kept your mind active in the years since you were in college but have an uneasy feeling that you have rarely, if ever, stretched it to anything like its limit; if you have read, but widely rather than intensively, never having homed in on something so absorbing that you wanted to get into it deeply; if you have taken courses occasionally—but found them superficial; if you have wondered, when encountering someone who seemed to have found an engrossing intellectual pursuit, if there might not be a field that would do that for you.

"But I don't have the *talent*." That's the most frequent reaction I get from people attracted to making such projects a part of their lives. "I don't seem to have a distinct drive in any one direction, or a fascination with any particular field or subject. The people who do this sort of thing all must have that."

There's truth to this—but it is a half-truth. Those who have looked closely at the lives and work of individuals who have found their "hole in the world" have realized that talent is not simply "given" or found. Maurice Gibbons, the senior member of the Self-Education Study Team at Simon Fraser University in Canada, concluded, after a study of lives of people who, on their own, became acknowledged experts in their fields, that "talent may be a product people *create*, rather than a gift they receive. . . . Talent may be the retrospective acknowledgment that a person has identified and intensively pursued his or her work."

After examining autobiographies and biographies extensively, Gibbons and a team of analysts discerned a significant pattern in the way in which these independent scholars achieved their expertise. (I will draw from these findings later in this book.) They concluded that "any person can discover and develop the unique potential for talented behavior which each of us possesses." The secret seems to be to "focus on the field of activity that [you] find compelling and . . . relate all [your] random experience to it. [This] leads to accomplishment, expertise, self-education and recognition as [being] talented."[2]

Few of us ever find such a field. One reason is our assumption that such intellectual adventuring is the exclusive domain of professors. Those who live the life of the mind outside academe are usually invisible; their presence is not signaled by tree-lined campuses, ivy-covered buildings, and academic titles. They are easily overlooked, and there are few role models to remind us that leadership in the life of the mind is often exercised by independent scholars.

Yet once we cast a fresh eye over the intellectual landscape, we find that serious inquiries are being pursued outside academe far more frequently than we might have imagined. Taken together, these inquiries constitute much of what is most exciting in our cultural life. For the people conducting those inquiries, their research is not merely a "job," it is a passion that they have developed into a vocation. Their basic motivation is not to make a living, but to know, understand, and communicate. Scholarship is their joy, and not *merely* their job.

Consider a few such figures whose works played a powerful role in contemporary life:

Susan Sontag, *Beyond Interpretation*
Frances FitzGerald, *The Fire in the Lake*
Marilyn French, *Shakespeare's Division of Experience*

Victor Navasky, *Naming Names*
Justin Kaplan, *Samuel Clemens and Mark Twain*
Tom Peters, *Thriving on Chaos*
Gary Null, *The Complete Handbook of Nutrition*
Edward De Bono, *Serious Creativity*
Margo Adler, *Calling Down the Moon*
Thomas Friedman, *From Beirut to Jerusalem*
Gilbert Brim, *Ambition*
Jean Houston, *The Hero and the Goddess*
David McCullough, *The Path Between the Seas*
George Lock Land, *Grow or Die*
Kirkpatrick Sale, *Human Scale*
Susan Brownmiller, *Against Our Will*
William L. Shirer, *The Fall of the Third Reich*
Arthur Koestler, *The Act of Creation*
Philippe Ariés, *Centuries of Childhood*
Theodore H. White, *The Making of the President*
Alvin Toffler, *Future Shock*
Frances Moore Lappé, *Diet for a Small Planet*
E. F. Schumacher, *Small is Beautiful*
Lewis Mumford, *The City in History*
Edmund Wilson, *To the Finland Station*
Paul Goodman, *Gestalt Therapy*
Henri-Louis de la Grange, *Mahler: A Biography*
Lady Antonia Fraser, *Royal Charles*
Judy Chicago, *The Dinner Party*

These people are merely pinnacles in an intellectual landscape teeming with unaffiliated researchers, investigators, theorists, inquirers, data collectors, and intellectuals. There are thriving "amateur wings" in hundreds of fields. The Canadian sociologist Robert Stebbins has found that "around the world amateurs are conducting projects and gathering data that are valuable contributions to their particular disciplines. Amateurs were chiefly responsible for observations of the lunar occultations that helped establish more accurately the location of the moon, thereby making it possible to land on it. Amateur ornithologists, especially women, conduct much of the leg-banding research in bird migration. In entomology, amateurs do most of the mapping and enumerating of insect populations in various localities. In several fields, the amateurs preceded the professionals, establishing and developing those fields to the point where full-time work could be carried out in them."[3]

Whole fields are dominated by knowledge-seekers working on their own: biographers, inventors, freelance writers, explorers and students of frowned-upon or new fields such as psychic phenomena, radical ideology, innovative therapies, American political assassinations, and women's and environmental studies.

Not only can you join in the search for new truth in whatever *field* appeals most to you; you can also choose from among quite diverse *activities*. Independent scholars are not confined to poring over volumes in hushed libraries, although some thrive on that. They can choose to operate deeply over a broad range of related disciplines. They can be advocates or activists. They can align their researches with their jobs or careers, or pursue their researches as an avocation.

I am defining "scholarship" broadly and unconventionally—that will be clear already. The usefulness of the idea of independent scholarship, for me, is to open before us a wide range of possibilities for using the mind. Some of those possibilities are as highly focused—as "narrow," if you will—as the specialized researches of many academic scholars. There are people whose chief enthusiasm in life is the pursuit of everything that can be found out about such subjects as elvish language, big bands, Armenian lace making, bonsai, medieval Dutch architecture, Southwest Indian ceremonies, hibiscus culture, Model T restoration, World War II ballooning, Richard III, J. F. K., numismatics, samurai swords, Polish paper cutting, biblical coins, gunslingers of the Old West, Dracula, Dorothy Sayers, horse-drawn vehicles, transient lunar phenomena.

There is even an expert on these experts. Henry Doering became so captivated with these people's enthusiasm and zest that he called up a few hundred of them on the phone and talked with them about their special fields. "We started the project at my office [Doering is an editor for *The World Almanac*] because we'd gotten irritated with ourselves. It seemed like the more leisure time we have, the less we do with it. We thought that if we could talk to a group of individuals who live life to its fullest, and find out what spurred them into action, that it just might prove contagious."

The interviews resulted in a delightful book with a delightful title: *The World Almanac Book of Buffs, Masters, Mavens and Uncommon Experts.*[4] The above list comes from it, for Doering found leading experts in each of those fields. After completing the book, Doering felt he had only lightly touched on the range of such people in the United States.

"There are easily twenty experts out there for every one I've contacted," he says. His conclusion after talking with probably more such people than anyone had before: "I enjoy these people's enthusiasm. They have something to tell us about how to live a full life."

At the opposite extreme are those independent scholars whose interests are much broader than would be condoned in academe. You may choose to be interdisciplinary or innovative in your studies, pursuing a subject that transcends academic departments and disciplines, or that even defines a new discipline.

The "Socratic amateur" is a model of independent scholarship articulated by Vincent Kavaloski of Madison, Wisconsin, who developed it as part of his research on the history of the Great Books movement.

The Socratic amateur is the classical antithesis to the professional purveyor of knowledge. Socrates distinguished himself from the Sophists of his day, who set themselves up as possessors of knowledge, and would teach students whatever they wanted to know, for whatever purpose, good or bad. Socrates insisted that he did *not* have wisdom—that he merely loved it, and hence should be called not a sophist but a *Philo*-sopher, a mere lover of wisdom. The Socratic amateur isn't afraid to be a generalist, and tackles the biggest and most complex problems without reducing them to techniques, seeking to share and spread understanding, rather than to control and possess knowledge. The tradition was exemplified by the wandering scholars of the twelfth century whose allegiance was to learning, not to any temporal power, and by the medieval universities, which arose out of the struggles of such scholars and their students with the Church.

Later, when the universities which they founded had in turn become moribund and "academic," once again it was independent scholars—in this case, the founders of modern science like Galileo, Kepler, and Boyle—who founded "learned societies" outside of the universities, to explore new ideas and new ways of knowing which the universities refused to entertain.

Independent scholarship always arises as a challenge to the dangerous myth that serious thinking only goes on in established, orthodox institutions, and that learning is the exclusive possession of the professoriate. In our own day of excessive bureaucratization and professionalism in learning, the Socratic amateur is an urgently needed voice.

This type of thinker is often called an intellectual, a term defined by Charles Kadushin as "an expert in dealing with high-quality general ideas on questions of values and esthetics and who communicates his judgments on these matters to a fairly general audience." Despite our assumption that most such people are professors, Kadushin discovered that over half of the nation's best-known intellectuals are "independents." Among them are such mainstays of our cultural life as Dwight Macdonald, Mary McCarthy, Norman Mailer, Robert Silvers, Susan Sontag, Norman Podhoretz, John Gardner, Pauline Kael, Murray Kempton, John Simon, James Reston, and Wright Morris. "The alleged domination of the intellectual elite by academics is . . . a mistaken impression," he concludes. "High-quality generalized commentary on economic, social, political, ethical, and esthetic problems of contemporary life is not necessarily found among the ranks of university scholars. The university, with its publish-or-perish dictum, tends to reward specialized expertise rather than generalized commentary."[5]

Confirmation of this finding was provided when Richard Kostelanetz, the noted literary critic and cultural commentator, surveyed the American intellectual landscape to choose the fourteen "masterminds" profiled in his book of that title. Of the outstanding thinkers, investigators, and creators he selected, well over half were *not* academics and only four had pursued academic careers. So even at the uppermost reaches, such intellectual commentary on our culture and society is quite open to the nonacademic thinker. This is good news for such thinkers, and also good news for the nation. Matters of such moment, involving our basic values and principles, are too important to be left to the academics.

Another important kind of independent scholar is the activist or advocate—the person who applies the skills of scholarship to some issue or cause about which he cares deeply. Take the case of I. F. Stone, whose career perfectly illustrates the activist use of scholarly skills in a field that most people refuse to see as true scholarship because it pertains to contemporary affairs.

The example is particularly telling because Stone later used those same skills in a project that *is*, as everyone can really see, scholarly.

For decades, Stone published his *Weekly*, in which he rigorously documented and analyzed U.S. policy and practices, providing much of the intellectual ammunition of the anti-Vietnam War movement. Stone regularly exercised his scholar's ability to find the relevant facts in the original documents, albeit not classical papyri, to connect fragmented pieces of evidence and to draw significant conclusions from thousands of pages of hearings before the Senate Foreign Relations Committee. Those researches resulted in data, information, and understanding about the real roots of the U.S. role in Vietnam, research that significantly affected our nation's politics in that period.

From the time of his retirement until his death in 1989 at the age of 81, Stone was able to use many of the same skills he had mastered in researching the *Weekly* on a fresh project: a history of fifth-century Athens, including a "scoop" in the story of Socrates' trial. He began it by mastering Greek in order to be able to read the documents in the original. To see this latter project of historical research and writing as scholarship is easy. But, by my definition, the earlier Stone, the editor of the *Weekly*, was just as much an independent scholar.

Inquiries that use the skills and tools of scholarship to develop materials vitally important to the nation are rarely encompassed by university-based scholarship. This lack has been deplored from within academe. Professor Maurice Hungiville of Michigan State University noted that

> the scholar, by temperament and training, is most comfortable with dead people. Many graduate departments, in fact, discourage dissertations on anyone who is not dead and safely embalmed in a biography.
>
> The scholar's contempt for the present and the journalist's indifference to the past leave a great gap, a whole range of unexamined events that are no longer news but not yet history. Some scholars and journalists ought to be encouraged to venture into this unfamiliar, booby-trapped terrain. What they bring back may be neither journalism nor scholarship, but it just might be indispensable.[6]

Other kinds of independent scholars, the synthesizer or popularizer and the practical or professional among them, compel me to define scholarship rather broadly. Each of these types will be described in the chapters that follow. Like the scholars in the categories I have described above, these scholars share certain basic, defining characteristics. They are all:

> involved in a serious project of extended duration
> studying organized bodies of knowledge
> using original sources or direct experience
> applying humanistic or scientific methods
> intending to produce results that can be examined and evaluated by others

The great mining companies still rely on independent prospectors to find some of the best new sources of ore—the land masses to be explored are so vast that no company's own organized effort could cover them. Professional astronomers have long relied on amateurs to monitor celestial phenomena of various kinds—simply because the heavens are too immense to permit the few observatories to gather more than a fraction of the needed data. Those who study the sea encourage divers and serious beachcombers to submit notes of observations and samples of marine life through the American Littoral Society—the seas, too, are simply too large for the professionals in the field to be able to obtain all the materials and observations they need. Social scientists have begun to realize that "this country is so big, so varied, so almost unencompassable, that social research cannot have enough observers who will break down its momentary generalizations and open up new views," in the words of David Riesman.

The earth, sky, sea, and society are powerful metaphors for the breadth of those natural and human phenomena that scholarship and science confront. Each of those realms is simply too vast to be investigated adequately by a small professional cadre.

A bright future beckons to each of us who feels the urge to "do the utmost with his [or her] mind, no holds barred," as the physicist Percy Bridgeman once characterized the essence of science. For each of us, the doors to the house of intellect are as open as is this book. We are invited to enter, look around, acquaint ourselves with its vast number of rooms, and choose the place in it where we find ourselves most at home.

Emily Taitz and Sondra Henry:
A Quest for Women "Written Out of History"

Once we saw that gap in Jewish history, we just knew
we had to do something about it. So we set out to
find those missing women.

Emily Taitz

Most of the basic problems you will encounter in your initial work as an
independent scholar were faced and overcome by Emily Taitz and Sondra
Henry in their effort to recover the lost legacy of Jewish women. Their
book brings back to vibrant life thirty centuries of women who were *Written Out of History* (New York: Bloch, 1978), as the book's title puts it.[7]

The findings are fascinating in themselves and, by rectifying generations
of neglect of women in Jewish culture, Henry and Taitz have added significantly to the contemporary reevaluation of women in history, a field of enquiry that has developed largely from the work of independent scholars.
They have, moreover, opened up a large area for further research.

But to us their example has an additional significance. For whatever your
field, you probably will confront some of the same problems as they did,
problems of

> ➤ conceiving your project in specific terms and deciding that it is
>   worth doing
> ➤ finding leads in a field virtually devoid of prior work
> ➤ tracking down and gaining access to obscure collections of needed
>   materials
> ➤ winning the respect and help of senior scholars
> ➤ securing volunteer help
> ➤ finding the time and sustaining the energy to persist in an extended
>   task of research
> ➤ writing up the results of your research to reach as large an audience as possible

➤ finding and dealing with a publisher for a book of independent scholarship

Like many independent scholarship projects, this one began almost casually. Asked to prepare a pamphlet on the subject for their temple, the authors found a dearth of materials. "Women were written out of Jewish history, it seemed," says Taitz. "It was as if [they] never existed at all. You can read page after page, book after book, and not find any mention of women. Once we realized this, we just knew that we had to do something about it. So we set out to find these missing women."

"Our original goal was modest," recalls Henry.

> We thought in terms of a pamphlet. But once we got rolling, and material started to accumulate rapidly, it became apparent that a book would be needed to present it.
>
> We were kept fueled for the task by the excitement and stimulation of the idea. Once you commit yourself to a quest like that, which means so much to you, it generates its own momentum. Each woman we found had her own story to tell, sometimes in her own words, sometimes only in documents left by others. These women began to haunt us as though demanding, finally, to be recognized.

Henry and Taitz started with the biblical women, such as Sarah, Rebecca, Rachel, and Deborah. But after the Bible the sources left an enormous gap up to the nineteenth century where they found Henrietta Szold and then Golda Meir. They knew there must have been other women who made a contribution to Jewish life. To find them, the researchers began with only a handful of footnotes and items in bibliographies. Yet the first law of independent scholarship—that one thing leads to another—carried them forward.

"Finding leads was never a problem once we began," Taitz recalls. "We were never at a loss as to where to go next. Rather, it was a matter of tracking down and collating clues—like a detective searching for a lost or missing person.

"For example, we saw a three- to four-line mention of a sixteenth-century woman scholar, Rebecca Tiktiner, who had written a book called *Meneket Rivka*. It took dozens of phone calls, letters, and searching card catalogues till we located the rare manuscript itself at the Jewish Theological Seminary's rare book collection and were able to have part of it photographed for us.

> Another example was locating actual letters, written in the 1500s by a rabbi's wife in Kurdestan. We knew the originals existed since they were referred to and paraphrased in a book of letters. We tracked them down at the archives of the Hebrew-Union College–Jewish Institute of Religion in Cincinnati, prevailing upon the curator to locate one letter for us, to actually piece it together from torn fragments, and to have it photocopied for our book.

Slowly, figures emerged from the mists of the past: Beruriah, a noted scholar during the Talmudic era, Gluckel of Hamelin, who wrote her memoirs in the seventeenth century, and a few women who were prominent during the Italian Renaissance. These, in turn, led to others. Sifting through historical reports, papers, court proceedings, and letters, Henry and Taitz discovered great and powerful women who influenced the course of Jewish history: property owners, traders, philanthropists, lecturers on Jewish law, printers, writers, martyrs—women who demonstrated without a doubt that the Jewish woman was a vital force in the life of her people.

How did academic scholars respond to these two independents entering their domain? Quite well, Henry reports, because she and Taitz approached them in the way that proves effective in most fields. "We formulated the questions as precisely and specifically as we could, so that they understood that we had done our preliminary work and were not just "picking their brains" or trying to take advantage of their knowledge without making it clear what we had already done and where we were going."

Nevertheless, they faced some formidable challenges, as most independent scholars do, in figuring out exactly how to relate to the establishment in their field.

> Had we realized the prominence of some of the people we contacted, we would have been intimidated. We wrote what we now realize was a rather impudent letter to Dr. S. D. Goitein, a noted Arabist and Judaic scholar at the Institute for Advanced Studies in Princeton, asking why no women were included in his collection of medieval letters. He graciously replied and referred us to his extensive mention of women in his then-forthcoming work, *The Family* (one of a three-volume work on the Mediterranean Society from the ninth to the

thirteenth century). He also referred us to a published pamphlet which listed all of his own works in print. Our correspondence included several other early requests for information, and Emily subsequently had a meeting with him at which time they discussed additional sources. He seemed genuinely pleased with our book and our acknowledgments to him in it.

Independent scholars often need volunteer help, and in this case the documents being used had to be translated from Hebrew, Yiddish, Italian, German, and Arabic—a task that would challenge the resources of many a college campus. Yet Henry and Taitz could not pay for this work. "We enlisted people through our enthusiasm for the project," explains Taitz.

> Since we were doing it as a labor of love, not something to advance our careers, people seemed to respond altruistically. Their only payment was a thank-you on the acknowledgments page and a copy of the book. Today, having been published, [when] lecturing and teaching this material, we feel more like professionals in the field, and might feel obligated to offer some fee for the same services.

Being a team helped Henry and Taitz to deal with the time problem all independents face: How do you squeeze out enough hours from the rest of your life to pursue an extended research project?

> We worked together, buoyed up each other at low points, even supplementing each other's energies and covering one another when we had other obligations.
>
> Two people studying together is in the Talmudic tradition. Although our families cooperated (we are each married: I have four children and Sondra has three), they were definitely an added distraction. At one time we wryly thought of dedicating the book: "To our families, without whom this book would have been finished a year earlier." We probably cut out all extraneous activities (down to priorities) without even realizing it.

Throughout, the scholarly partners added to each other's strength. (The formation of partnerships is discussed in detail on pages 82–88.) "As a team, we seemed to 'click' intellectually from the very beginning," according to Henry. "Emily was more involved with the creative writing and literary style, while I did much of the initial research and like to double-check sources. We did not realize at first how monumental a task it would become, but even after we did, it never occurred to us that we couldn't do it. Each of us, however, felt that we could not have done it alone. We each had distinct sources of information and felt comfortable approaching different types of people."

Arduous as it is, research is only half the job of scholarship. Presenting the results is the other half. "This was the most trying aspect of the project," Taitz reports, "having to go over and over the work, revising and rewriting. Our goal was to try to make the book lively and readable, while at the same time providing scholarly footnotes, thorough references, and an index for those interested in pursuing the subject in depth."

They began by exchanging several drafts of each chapter. Then the final draft went to Taitz who wrote it up "in a more graceful manner." They discussed and corrected each chapter together.

"For us, finding a publisher was luck," says Taitz.

> Our manuscript was accepted on the first try, but only after a recommendation to the publisher by a respected personal contact. We recommend that an independent scholar who thinks she may have a "hot" topic should approach the bigger publishers first and not settle too quickly. (If we had it to do over, that's what we would do now.) The fact that Sondra is a lawyer gave us some advantage in dealing with the publisher. But we also talked to friends in the publishing field to find out exactly what a good contract should contain.

What have been the rewards of their labors—over and above that of bringing to vivid life again a whole tradition of important human beings? Since publication of the book, Henry and Taitz have taught related courses at Hofstra University and at adult education programs throughout their region. "Our decision to launch the project began a growth process for both of us which is still continuing," they affirm.

The authors know that their work has merely opened a door on a whole new area of scholarship. "The more we worked, the more we became aware of the endless amount of material that we did not yet know or could not locate," they write at the end of their book. Their example should stimulate independent scholars in other fields. Working independently, with virtually no extant literature in their chosen field, these two investigators found and gained access to the original sources they needed, enlisted the help of advanced, respected scholars as well as volunteer translators, marshalled the resources to sustain the project, both financially and psychologically, and presented their findings in a published book that won critical commendation and a broad readership.

CHAPTER TWO

From "Messy Beginnings" to the Fruits of Research

The potential in you is new in nature,
and no one but you can know what you can do,
nor will you know until you have tried.

Dr. Ari Kiev (after Emerson)

Rarely do researchers or writers "let their hair down," revealing that they started where each of us must start: with mere infatuation for a subject. The messy beginnings of all serious inquiries are hidden from our view in that "foul rag-and-bone shop of the heart" where, as W. B. Yeats asserted, "all the ladders start." Established researchers rarely portray the faltering steps by which they came to pinpoint their purposes, choose their subject, sharpen their skills. By the time the work of a scholar or scientist comes to our attention, it is usually well packaged as a finished monograph, a carefully crafted article, a well-honed paper, a polished book, a museum-worthy collection or display, a documentary on film or videotape, or as some other finished work. This final product seems to have sprung full-grown from the author's head. So we tend to get a misleading picture of how intellectual and creative projects get started.

In this section we will trace that process through some of its chief stages, through steps you can start taking at once. By doing so, you will be on your way to finding those subjects that connect with something within you, releasing the energy to shape a first project of inquiry. The four steps are:

1. Start your own intellectual journal.
2. Reconnoiter new realms of knowledge.
3. Enter a field.
4. Develop your first "projects."

Note: Readers who have already identified the subject or project they want to pursue may wish merely to skim this chapter, review the list on pages 35–36, and proceed directly to Part Two.

Step 1: Start Your Own Intellectual Journal

"What would happen if I forced myself over a period of several months to sluice my mind the way I sluiced dirt in my gold-hunting days, using a diary as a sluicebox to trap whatever flakes of insight might turn up?" Eric Hoffer asked himself that question in his journal on November 26, 1974. He did not expect a happy outcome.

> I . . . had the feeling that I had been scraping the bottom of the barrel, and . . . doubted whether I would ever get involved in a new, seminal train of thought. It was legitimate to assume that at the age of seventy-two my mind was played out. . . . Would it be possible to reanimate and cultivate the alertness to the first, faint stirrings of thought?

In due course, Hoffer was able to report that the experiment had succeeded reasonably well.

> It is more than six months since I started this diary. I wanted to find out whether the necessity to write something significant every day would revive my flagging alertness to the first, faint stirrings of new ideas. I also hoped that some new insight caught in flight might be the seed of a train of thought that could keep me going for years. Did it work? The diary flows, reads well, and has something striking on almost every page. Here and there I suggest that a new idea could be the subject of a book; but only one topic, "the role of the human factor," gives me the feeling that I have bumped against something which is, perhaps, at the core of our present crisis.[1]

Keeping an intellectual journal is the best way to cultivate your own "alertness to the first, faint stirrings of thought." Virtually every important writer and thinker has kept such a diary, whether they called it a notebook, daybook, or something more personal. "Every intellectual used to keep a journal," Abraham Maslow pointed out, "and many have been published and are usually more interesting and more instructive than the final formal perfected pages which are so often phony in a way—so certain, so structured, so definite. The *growth* of thought from its beginnings is also instructive—maybe even more so for some purposes."

The most ambitious log kept by any individual in our time, so far as I know, is Buckminster Fuller's Chronolog.[2] It contains "any and every scrap of paper that was written by him, about him, or to him," according to one of his biographers, Athena Lord. He was encouraged in the practice by his first boss, the chief engineer of his factory: "For your own sake and knowledge, you should keep a sketchbook of your work."

"Flushed with happiness, Bucky followed his advice," Lord writes. "The sketchbook . . . made a kind of mental bank account from which he drew all his life. . . . From a shoe box full of paper, the collection has grown to six tons of records now stored in the Science Center in Philadelphia."

The charming *Morning Notes* of that remarkable amateur in psychology, philosophy, and biology, Adelbert Ames, Jr., suggest how freewheeling and personal the style of such writing can be. (Ames was the pioneering psychologist who created the Perception Demonstration Center at Princeton and whose work revealed how dramatically our perceptions are shaped by our expectations, purposes, and habits.) His friend and editor, Hadley Cantril, describes the method:

> He had the habit of putting a problem to himself in the evening just before he went to bed. Then he "forgot" it. The problem never seemed to disturb his sleep. But he often "found" the next morning on awakening that he had made progress on the problem. And as soon as he got to his office he would pick up his pencil and pad of paper and begin to write. He always said he didn't know just "what would come out," and dozens of times he would call me at Princeton in the middle of the morning, ask, courteously, if I had a few minutes, and say, "Hadley, listen to this. I'm surprised at the way it's turning out and I think it will interest you." It was almost as though he himself were a spectator.[3]

You will gradually find your own best method of generating thoughts. The crucial thing is to *start*. As with so many other aspects of independent scholarship, it is the *doing* that teaches us *how*. You will want to draw from a wide range of sources for your "sluicing" and, perhaps, follow the suggestions of Dr. Ari Kiev:

> You might start by clipping and pasting newspaper articles that interest you for the next thirty days. At the end of that time, see if there isn't some trend suggestive of a deep-seated interest or natural inclination. Keep alert each day to the slightest indications of special skills or talents, even when they seem silly or unimportant to you. Take note of the remarks of friends and relatives when they say that something is "typical of you." Perhaps as a child you had certain leanings that you never developed.[4]

To get yourself started on your own intellectual diary, you might want to leaf through a few examples of the genre:

Eric Hoffer, *Working and Thinking on the Waterfront*
Adelbert Ames, Jr., *The Morning Notes*
Paul Goodman, *Five Years*
John Robben, *Coming to My Senses*
Jessamyn West, *Hide and Seek*
Charles Darwin, *Diary of the Voyage of HMS Beagle*
André Gide, *The Journals of André Gide*
Andy Warhol, *The Philosophy of Andy Warhol (From A to B and Back Again)*
Anaïs Nin, *A Woman Speaks: The Lectures, Seminars, and Interviews of Anaïs Nin*
Henry Thoreau, *The Journal*
Christopher Isherwood, *Kathleen and Frank*
Suzanne Mitchell, *My Own Woman: The Diary of an Analysis*

If you would like to sample a variety of logs, you might want to look through *A Treasury of the World's Great Diaries* (edited by Philip Dunaway and Mel Evans) or *Revelations: Diaries of Women* (edited by Mary Jane Moffat and Charlotte Painter), or select a few that look especially interesting from Jane DuPree Begos's *Annotated Bibliography of Published Women's Diaries*. Or try the notebooks and diaries of any important intellectual in whom you have an interest, such as Leonardo da Vinci, Abraham Maslow, Franz Kafka, Leo Tolstoy, Fyodor Dostoyevski, Françoise du Maurier, Eugène Delacroix, William Gibson, Paul Gauguin, John Steinbeck, or Gertrude Stein.

Letters are also rich stores of insight into the workings of keen minds. Two premier examples are *The Born-Einstein Letters* and the correspondence between Lewis Mumford and Van Wyck Brooks. In each of these, a pair of master minds in their fields shared their thoughts and work, in steps small enough so that we can easily follow. Just as important, they shared the trials and triumphs of using the mind at its utmost.

Step 2: Reconnoiter New Realms of Knowledge

We have all browsed—in a bookstore or library or through a dusty bookcase in a house we rented for the summer. I am going to suggest an enhanced style of browsing that you can use as a way of finding new subjects of interest. (If you are already interested in a subject, you may want to skip this step, though even the most advanced scholars often find that wandering through the stacks of a library, dipping into a book here and there as the spirit moves them, offers a serendipitous intellectual stimulation that is unavailable any other way. For this reason, many leading scholars and librarians are dubious about the so-called benefits of transferring library holdings to computers—a practice that will preclude this kind of browsing—though it may make new forms possible.)

By making the process of browsing a bit more self-conscious, you can conduct your own informal reconnaissance of the terrain of learning. All you have to do is follow three rules:

> Pick the best places.
> Keep moving.
> Keep a list.

By picking the best places, I simply mean the best library or bookstore or collection of other resources that you can find for your purposes. Follow F. Scott Fitzgerald's advice: "Don't marry for money—go where money is, then marry for love." Go where the richest resources *are*, then you can let serendipity take its course. In a less rich environment, the items that might best turn you on might simply not be there.

What is the best place for you? It is the best-stocked one within convenient range. Finding it is often a matter of taking some thought and going a little out of your way. For example, most of us have a neighborhood public library, but the central branch of your city's public library is likely to have a far better set of open shelves, and it may only take half an hour to get there. For "super-browsing," go there.

Many cities now have specialized bookstores, study centers, and activist organizations or other agencies in numerous fields, one of which may be the right place for you once you have identified a broad field that you might get deeply interested in—such as military history, astronomy, biblical studies, or environmental research.

Once you are in the right place, follow the remaining rules simultaneously: Keep moving, and keep a list. You are brainstorming, not post-holding. You want to get a comprehensive glimpse and taste of a wide range of works. And you want to keep a log of your discoveries along the way, with notes in case you want to retrace your steps and delve more deeply. You are compiling your "little black book" of intellectual attractions—books, ideas, authors, points of view, realms of fact or imagination with which you want to make a date sometime, get to know better, and perhaps come to fall in love with.

Here's an excerpt from one such log:

➤ *Passionate Amateur's Guide to Archaeology in the U.S.*—guidebook of trips, museums, sites, etc.; how to participate in "digs"; certification as qualified amateur archaeologist offered in several states

➤ "America"—film series by Alistair Cooke; can be borrowed from library

➤ *Amateur Archaeologist*—magazine for, about, and by independent investigators

➤ "Urban and Industrial Archaeology"—field trips in cities to find remnants and artifacts of earlier cultures, especially at sites where new buildings are being excavated; can check with City Building Office

➤ Museum of the American Indian—bookstore with complete collection of materials and study guides. Also has lectures and films

Major intellectual journeys quite often begin with browsing. As a teenager, Joel Cohen was browsing at his local bookstore in Battle Creek, Michigan, some years ago. He began leafing through the pages of *Elements of Physical Biology* by Alfred J. Lotka. "Here's a guy who thinks the way I do," he recalls exclaiming to himself. "Mathematics might be a useful way to make some sense of life." Cohen had been amazed to learn that the degree to which an earthworm turns its head in the direction of light is directly proportional to the logarithm of the intensity of the light. "I has just learned about logarithms in school. This simple organism was behaving in a mathematically lawful way, and it knew logarithms without school! It seemed to me I had better learn some math." Another book, Abraham Moles's *Information Theory and Esthetic Perception,* so captivated the youngster that he wrote the author in France, asking permission to translate the book into English and enclosing his version of the first chapter as a sample. Moles granted the request and Cohen then wrote to the University of Illinois Press, which subsequently published the translation. Neither author nor publisher knew that their translator was sixteen years old. Twenty-five years later, Cohen conducted his research in "biology by the numbers" as head of the laboratory of populations at The Rockefeller University.

As part of your super-browsing, you may want to take a fresh look at some of the important realms of learning, but from your own point of view—a way in which you have probably never scrutinized them before. The exhilarating prospect here is to "come to ourselves" intellectually. After years, sometimes decades, of learning *for someone or something else*—our parents, our teachers, the requirements of getting a diploma—we are now invited to begin using our minds *for ourselves.* We are freed from being told what, why, and how to learn, and we discover at once the first lesson of freedom in any realm: Freedom is far more demanding than taking orders, but also far more rewarding.

Forget about which subjects you have already been told are important or prestigious. Just let each one roll around in your head for a while to see whether it commands your interest. And do not worry about how formidable each one sounds. No one in the world is a complete master of any of these realms! As Allen Tough, the Canadian adult-educator who compiled the following list, points out: "Such an inventory of the length and breadth of human understanding contains much more than any one person could tackle."

> *Economics.* The world of business and industry; economic policy; the world of work and how your own occupation fits into the broader society; finance and credit; international development.
> *Environment.* The natural environment; weather; agriculture; ecology; wildlife; geography; pollution; natural resources and energy.
> *Justice.* Laws; police and courts; crime and delinquency; political repression.
> *International affairs.* Causes and patterns of war—effects of escalation and weapons races; the views of hawks and doves; how a war affects families; refugees; realistic routes to peace. Population growth—poverty; third world; scarcity and distribution of the world's resources; consumption by affluent nations; patterns of economic development in contrasting countries.
> *Social issues.* The major problems of our society today; how governments react to them; major decision making; the future of society; how leaders foresee and cope with major societal problems.
> *Contemporary organizations.* Their growth and decline; organizational development and renewal; the impact of large corporations and governments on their employees and the public.
> *Biography.* Lives of great and interesting individuals working in familiar fields and those working fields new to you—people in other countries and their ways of life.
> *Anthropology.* Lifestyles and living conditions within a ten-mile radius of your home or work; learn or imagine what it's like to be someone else (such as a poor farmer in India, a corporation president in New York City, a student in Japan, a Chicago ghetto resident, a politician, a professional athlete).

➤ *Evolution and history.* The evolution and breakdown of civilizations; current trends and broad changes in society; the long-term future of life on earth; the life of the individual in the year 3000.

➤ *Philosophy.* Why we exist; philosophy of life; your own place in the universe; basic aims in life; religious truth; ethics; philosophy; the vital practices of various religions.

➤ *Science.* Its history and future; scientific methods; recent advances in the physical and biological sciences.

➤ *Human sexuality.* Female/male relationships; sex research, sex-role patterns; socialization of children for their roles in various cultures.

➤ *Psychic phenomena.* Parapsychology; UFOs; mysticism.

➤ *Architecture, Design, Art, Music, Dance, Poetry, Drama.* How they develop and reflect the times. In addition to learning about one of these areas, you might want to learn—or go back to—painting or drawing, a musical instrument, singing or dancing, writing, or acting.[5]

Each of those categories could fill years of study. The point is to realize the wealth from which you can choose and to start modestly to sample one subject or another that especially appeals to you.

Step 3: Enter a New Field

When I first read the list of realms of learning, my initial question was one that may have struck you too. "How would I begin exploring one or another of these subjects?"

The obvious first step would be to pull together the books in your local public library on the subject and thereby get an overview of the scope of the subject. Take astronomy for example. Are you interested in observation or theory—in the composition of meteorites or the origin of the universe? You might want to select the most authoritative and recent comprehensive book to get a taste of the various areas within the field.

At the same time, you might dip into the magazines, both at the library and at a local magazine store, for a stimulating glimpse of what is current and exciting in the field. Such magazines, with their advertisements for the latest books, will also bring your awareness of the literature up-to-date.

A visit to a local center of activity in the field, such as a specialized scientific bookstore or equipment outlet, or a local astronomer's society, will put you in touch with local practitioners and enthusiasts. Usually, such places will have a bulletin board with notices about upcoming events in the field, and one or two of those meetings would give you the flavor of activity in the field in your area.

Thus, with a minimum of time you can dip into a field such as astronomy, get a sense of its scope and current thrust, meet some of the lively local experts, and participate in some interesting activities.

By this time, you would likely have come to some conclusion about your commitment to the field. You might have identified an area you would like to investigate. You will have learned that extensive networks of amateurs participate in organized observation of celestial phenomena ranging from meteorites to lunar transient phenomena to the behavior of vast nebulae. Through these networks you can learn how to conduct scientifically significant observations and how to accumulate them in a useful way.

The means of finding out about a field are many, depending on your own style of learning. Do you like nothing better than to settle down with five or six books on a given subject? Or would you much prefer to listen to a tape cassette of three leading experts discussing the subject? Would you like to meet someone who is knowledgeable in the field and learn more about it face-to-face? Or would you like just to wander around a conference on the subject? Every one of these options is available in virtually any field you choose, so the choice can hinge on your personal preference.

I call the full range of these options "The Invisible University." As I described it in *Peak Learning* (Jeremy P. Tarcher, 1991), this is what universities were before the ivy had centuries to grow: *people learning together*. There is no central quad, since the approach is to learn *everywhere*, from the infinite variety of databases, information sources, and materials that exist.

There is an unlimited number of ways to learn: apprenticeship, tutorials, mentoring, work-study, correspondence, travel, reading, etc. If you want to see learners at IU pursuing their studies, just punch up some bulletin boards on your computer terminal, drop into your local library, or visit a club, association, public-interest group, specialized bookstore, political clubhouse, arts center, or other place where people gather to talk, create, share, help, argue, advocate, or otherwise use their minds.

The resources of the IU are both traditional and cutting-edge, centuries old and newly created. Some examples:

> *Adult and continuing education.* Available in every community; offered by colleges and universities, public school systems, and libraries.

> *Networks.* You can plug into one of the many invisible networks of people learning from one another on a regular basis via mail, phone, computers, and newsletters.

> *Conferences.* A good place to meet people in your field of interest and to take in the most up-to-date issues, ideas, and technologies.

> *Learning groups.* Convening your own group of co-learners is easier then you think.

> *Specialized bookstores.* Whether you visit them in person or via catalog or correspondence, you will find not merely books but people who share your interests.

> *Television.* Making creative choices in your television viewing and following up on what you have seen can add a new dimension to your learning life.

> *Libraries.* Beyond offering books, they can serve learners in unexpected and useful ways that most people have not heard of—and such help is available for the asking.

> *Churches.* These are beehives of free or inexpensive learning options.

> *Magazines and newspapers.* Get the most out of them: challenge yourself to read other points of view and try to get a feel for the major issues, developments, and people in your field, in your community, in your world.

> *Growth centers.* Virtually every community now has places where you can explore yourself, your emotions, and your relationships with other people.

> *Arts centers.* The arts, an ideal way to learn and grow, are burgeoning nationwide.

➤ *Teaching.* It will increase and extend your command of your subject, prompting you to take a fresh overview and forcing you to make sure your knowledge is up-to-date.

➤ *Correspondence courses.* More possibilities here than most people imagine. Would you believe advertising, French cooking, small craft design?

➤ *"Open" programs at colleges.* You can create your own curriculum, study in your own way (instead of attending classes), and get credits and a degree.

➤ *Audiocassettes.* There are cassettes that cover the entire range of college subjects, today's experts, novels, poems, and plays—all of which you can listen to at your own speed.

➤ *Computer online services.* To find out about these, check computer magazines, computer stores, and user groups.

Step 4: Develop Your First Projects

The important thing about your first project is not that it is your first, but that it is *yours.* Because it is your first piece of original research, you do not have to worry about whether or not it succeeds. One of the project's purposes is for you to begin to explore what success means to you in this kind of activity. It is a real experiment that, while it should be enjoyable in itself, is designed for what you can learn from the way it goes.

The course of your project may be irregular, unpredictable, serendipitous, but that is no problem whatever as you are not following a prescribed course of study. Unlike someone taking a course and following a road that has been laid out in advance, you are adventuring. Sometimes there is no way to plot out beforehand how you will proceed as your problem or subject unfolds before you.

As your interests, feelings, curiosity, enthusiasm, and concerns begin to converge on a particular topic, it would be well to draft, purely for your own use at first, a brief statement of your plans. I have never known an independent scholar who did not discover, at the end of an hour or two of work on such a one-page statement, that he or she had sharper goals.

Strangely, even professional academics often neglect this beneficial exercise. The late C. Wright Mills, whose studies of *The Power Elite* illuminated how our society really works, confessed that:

> One of the very worst things that happen to social scientists is that they feel the need to write of their "plans" on only one occasion: when they are going to ask for money for a specific piece of research or "a project." The project is likely to be "presented," rounded out in some arbitrary manner long before it ought to be; it is often a contrived thing, aimed at getting the money for ulterior purposes, however valuable, as well as for the research presented.[6]

Mills rightly frowns on this practice, and your planning can easily help you avoid precisely this pitfall because it is for your eyes only and decidedly subject to change as you and your project grow.

What might your plan look like? Here is one that was drafted for a first project in history, the one that launched John Walter, who was mentioned in Chapter 1, on his lifelong study of the Civil War.

> Like so many Americans, I have long been intrigued by the Civil War as a crucial and thrilling era in our nation's history. But to me, history has always been more than dates and facts and statistics. It's been people—caught up in events which, to them at the time, are the essence of their lives. This conviction has led me to some unanswered questions—simple questions about which men were where, and when.
>
> I want to compile a list of every unit in the Civil War, on both the Federal and Confederate sides, including even those units which served for short periods or on obscure assignments, and therefore don't appear in the supposedly definitive *Official Records of the Union and Confederate Armies*.
>
> My chief source of materials will be obtained at or through major research libraries, plus leads in the literature and additional assistance provided by others in the field.
>
> My larger interest, which this project may lead into, is to collect information on each of these units—where they served, what engagements they fought in, who led them, what commands they were attached to—in order to compile a narrative history of each of them.
>
> I know that there are fellow scholars out there, as well as universities, libraries, and historical societies which would welcome this data. And beyond these peers, there are hundreds of thousands of Americans who will eventually have an even more vivid appreciation of this watershed in our history, if I can bring back to life these legions of our ancestors.[7]

Before you immerse yourself in the "literature of the field," you can and should let your own imagination play and come up with some theories of your own. This sounds presumptuous to most people. We were all taught to believe that you need to learn what other people have found and thought before knowing enough to offer your own ideas. Of course, it makes sense to take full advantage of your predecessors, and your own ideas should eventually take into account what is already known. But imaginative conjectures at an early stage can be exciting, harmless, and occasionally rewarding. By adding this stage to the usual scientific research procedure, Loring Thompson argues, you join the creative vanguard in your discipline rather than merely collect data or absorb the conclusions of other scholars. "By bringing in spontaneous thinking prior to the detailed research, the stage is set for its continuation and fruition in fresh and sound conclusions at the end of the project." Thompson therefore recommends such a step right after your initial assembly of the facts that are obviously most pertinent to the question you are addressing. "Formulate your own best spontaneous solution at that point," he urges. "Then, review and compare your solution with those advocated by others, and assemble whatever additional facts now appear pertinent. Finally, synthesize your own ideas with those of others." [8]

Here is quite a different kind of plan; it is by an amateur astronomer, Charles Kapral.

> Having participated for several years in the Lunar Transient Phenomena (LTP) program sponsored by the Association of Lunar and Planetary Observers (ALPO), I am now planning a detailed study of the sunrise albedo profile* for the crater Gassendi. No one has ever performed such an investigation of how the albedo changes at sunrise or sunset on any feature of the moon.
>
> The project developed in response to a disagreement within the field, as to how the albedo profile of a feature behaves at sunrise. The ALPO-endorsed theory is that the change between sunrise and the normal albedo will only be about 1.5 to 2 steps on the Gray Scale. I believe the range is much greater, depending on the altitude of the sun.
>
> I would welcome collaboration with other trained LTP observers. Our

---

* The *albedo* is the ratio, to the total sunlight received, of the light an object reflects in all directions.

procedure will be [to] calculate when sunrise occurs on Gassendi, then take measurements for the remainder of the night, in fifteen-minute intervals with seeing measures every hour. A year or two of data should establish a fairly good profile of sunrise on Gassendi.

The telescope I'm using is a 2.4-inch Unitron refractor.

Results of this study will be sent to Winifred Cameron, recorder and analyst for the LTP section of ALPO, at the Godard Space Flight Center, and may be written up for the ALPO journal.[9]

Plans can get quite audacious. Here is one by Mark Overland that would entail far-flung exploration.

Mine is a scientific research project involving the underwater encounter with and complete documentation of human divers and free-roaming killer whales. My purpose is threefold: to provide unique essential footage for a feature-length documentary film, to foster further trust and cooperation between humans and wild killer whales, and to provide scientific data on human-orcan interactions for future ethological research with *Orcinus orca* in a natural setting without artificial controls or motivation. . . . .

We now recognize that dolphins and porpoises have an advanced intelligence and social life. Orcas are members of the family Delphinidae and, like all dolphins, they possess highly organized central nervous systems. Surprisingly, the dolphin's neuroencephalization quotient has evolved to a level shared only by humans. Furthermore, certain portions of the dolphin brain are more developed than comparative regions in the human brain. Much of this additional brain development is in the highly convoluted cerebral cortex—an expansion of that part of the brain serving higher intellectual functions as language, perception and thought. In this regard, orcas, with an approximate brain weight of 6,000 grams (human brains weigh around 1,500 grams), present astounding and unique possibilities.

Yet ethological studies relating to *Orcinus orca* have only recently begun, and the bulk of these studies deal primarily with distribution, physiological, and predation analyses. Although orcas are found worldwide, little is known about the movements of any individual groups with respect to distances covered, extent of migrational movements, and so on. Intraspecific relationships, such as the means of communication or signaling, have scarcely been examined. Although there is some information on the structure of orca pods and the culmination of courtship behavior, our knowledge about the social organization of killer whale groups remains scanty. There is great need for further investigations. . . .

Our plan is simple. We intend to dive with wild killer whales and to obtain a film record of that interaction. This will take place in one of several locations in Washington and British Columbia especially selected for this project. (The location ultimately depends on the orcas.) That footage will be incorporated into a forty-five-minute documentary film on the world of killer whales in Washington and British Columbia.[10]

Statements of purpose by the active researchers in a field have more importance than their personal usefulness and the clues they broadcast on how researchers can help one another. They constitute the closest thing to the "state of the art" of on-going research in each field.

From Seed to Fruit:
How an Idea Grows to Become a Product of Research

1. You enter the idea, perhaps only a sentence or two, in your notebook.
2. Deciding it is one worth development, you strengthen it with subsequent thoughts and combine them into a one-page memo to yourself (and possibly some others).
3. Finding that the concept continues to interest you, you fold in further thoughts and possibly reactions from others with whom you have had conversations. This "pre-plan" may have a paragraph on each of the obvious things: the background, the problem or question as you now see it, the objectives of your proposed project, how you plan to go about it, the outcome you would be looking for, the resources you would need for the investigation, how you would present and get feedback on the results, the people who would be most interested in the results, and how they best can be reached.
4. At this point you may want to condense the idea down to one paragraph and enter it on your personal research agenda to see how it relates to your other proposed projects as well as to start circulating it among colleagues for their possible help.
5. Deciding that you definitely want to get started on the project, you draft your plan. The plan is simply an enlarged version of the pre-plan that has been thought through and filled in. You may want or cast it in the form of a proposal to a possible funding source or

agency that could lend assistance in the form of resources, an aegis, and so forth.

6. The plan may go through revisions on the basis of feedback and your own second and third thoughts.

7. You conduct the project, making whatever revisions in the plan are called for by what happens (or does not happen). You may need to change some of your planned procedures, use alternative resources, or even modify the scope or thrust of the objectives in order to overcome difficulties or seize unexpected opportunities.

8. You draft sections of the report as the project proceeds and findings begin to emerge.

9. You draft the entire paper—which may be between five and fifty pages long—and perhaps distribute it to a few people for comments and suggestions.

10. You finalize the paper and disseminate it in whatever ways are appropriate.

Eric Hoffer:
A Passionate Philosopher

> When I got out of the woods and back to town, I had money. First I bought all new clothes and threw the old ones away. Then I went to the Japanese barber where he and his wife not only cut my hair but got way down into my ears and nose to clean them out. Then I got myself a room halfway between the library and the whorehouse. Both were equally important.
>
> Eric Hoffer

No independent scholar's beginnings were messier than Eric Hoffer's. "You might say I went straight from the nursery to the gutter," he confessed readily to an interviewer. At the age of nine, Hoffer was told by the person he trusted the most that, with his short-lived parents' genes, he would definitely not live past the age of forty. "I believed her absolutely. When I was almost twenty, my life was half over, so what was the point of getting excited about anything? I didn't have the idea that I had to get anywhere, that I had to make anything of myself. . . . I made up my mind to go to California because California was the place for the poor. So I bought a bus ticket to Los Angeles, and I landed on Skid Row, and I stayed there for the next ten years."

Yet from those beginnings Hoffer came to exemplify American individualism in matters of the mind. Without academic training or affiliation, this self-educated political philosopher won a large following and critical acclaim in the 1970s.

Hoffer hammered potent and subtle thoughts out of a fertile brain and gritty life-experiences. Completely his own man, utterly dedicated to finding his own truth without regard for the time, cost, or consequences, he showed that serious thinking can be done quite outside the system of supports that most intellectuals enjoy. Moreover, Hoffer's philosophy itself affirmed an axiom of independent scholarship: that mental power, indeed genius, are far more pervasive in our society than we imagine. The life of the mind, he both demonstrated and contended, is available to virtually everyone.

The facts about his life are easy to summarize. He did only manual work: dishwashing, claw-the-earth prospecting, railroading, lumbering, migrant farmwork, and, mostly, waterfront day labor on the San Francisco docks. A loner all his life, he was entirely self-educated. In 1951 his book *The True Believer* gained him an ardent readership, and a broadcast interview with Eric Sevareid on national television in 1967 made Hoffer a cultural hero thereafter. Subsequently he published eight books.

Hoffer's achievement—and the questions it provokes—are evident in this capsule description by his friend James Koerner:

> A common laborer who had been blind in childhood; who had then recovered his eyesight and proceeded to educate himself entirely by his own efforts; whose reading had been broader and deeper than that of many leading intellectuals in the United States and Europe; whose ideas were frequently more penetrating and provocative than theirs; and whose prose style was a monument to economy and precision. Who the hell is Eric Hoffer, I asked myself as I read his books, and how did he happen?

How Hoffer "happened"—how he found his ideas, cultivated them, and did his research—was outrageously unconventional and therefore wonderfully quickening for our own creativity. "I'm not a professional philosopher," said this thinker who had done more to interest Americans in philosophical ideas than any professional philosopher with the possible exception of Mortimer Adler (another independent scholar). "My train of thought grew out of my life just the way a leaf or a branch grows our of a tree." His thinking and writing occurred as a regular part of his life. In one of his books, *Thinking and Working on the Waterfront*, he wrote:

> My writing is done in railroad yards while waiting for a freight, in the fields while waiting for a truck, and at noon after lunch. Now and then I take a day off to "put myself in order." I go through the notes, pick and discard. The residue is usually a few paragraphs. My mind must always have something to chew on. I think on man, America, and the world. It is not as pretentious as it sounds.

It sounds even less pretentious—indeed, it sounds eminently practical—when Hoffer described how a specific key idea came to him out of an immediate experience. For example, one day on the docks he drew as partner the worst worker there, a clumsy and inept man avoided assiduously by everyone.

> We went to work and started to build our load. On the docks it's very simple— you build your side of the load and your partner builds his side, half and half. But that day I noticed something funny. My partner was always across the aisle, giving foreign aid to somebody else. He wasn't doing his share of the work on our load, but he was helping others with theirs. There was no reason to think that he disliked me. But I remember how that day I got started on a beautiful train of thought. I started to think why it was that this fellow, who couldn't do his own duty, was so eager to do things above and beyond his duty. And the way I explained it was that if you are clumsy in doing your duty, you will be ridiculous, but that you will never be ridiculous in helping others—nobody will laugh at you. That man was trying to drift into a situation where his clumsiness would not be conspicuous, would not be blamed. And once I started to think like that, I abandoned him entirely. My head was in orbit! I started to think about avant-garde, about pioneering in art, in literature. I thought that all people without real talent, without skill, whether as writers or artists and so on, will try to drift into a situation where their clumsiness will be natural and expected. What situation will that be? Of course—innovation. Everybody expects the new to be ill-shapen, to be clumsy. I said to myself, the innovators, with a few exceptions, are probably people without real talent, and that's why practically all avant-garde art is

ugly. But these people, the innovators, have a necessary role to play because they keep things from ossifying, they keep the gates open, and then eventually a man with real talent will move in and make use of the techniques worked out by clumsy people. A man of talent can make use of any technique. Oh, I worked and worked on this train of thought; I was excited all day long, and I have a whole aphorism that came about as a result; when I got back to my room all I had to do was write it down. It often happened to me just that way—and all on the company's time!

Hoffer was a voracious reader. He had library cards from virtually every library up and down the California railroad lines. There seemed to be no subject that he was afraid to tackle, no author who intimidated him. Yet he felt no compulsion to pursue, let alone admire, certain authors generally considered essential reading for an intellectual. He freely admitted never to have read Freud and confessed that he "never got anything from Plato. Socrates was supposed to be a workingman, wasn't he? A stonesman or something. But this is not the way a self-taught mason would argue—he would tell stories to illustrate his points. How can you convince anybody by going after him the way Socrates did—another question, another question—showing him how stupid he is."

When he did find authors from whom he could cull grist for his own mill, he culled grandly. His first flash that he might himself become a writer came when, isolated for the winter while prospecting in the mountains, he read Montaigne. "Here was this sixteenth-century aristocrat . . . and I found out that he was talking about nothing but Eric Hoffer! That's how I learned about human brotherhood."

Hoffer did bolster his initial ideas with research, but even his research was unconventional. "I don't know the first thing about research," he admitted.

Listen, suppose you come to San Francisco looking for a person whose address you don't know. You can trace him by research. You look in the telephone directory, you go to City Hall; if he's a workman, you go to the unions; if he's a doctor, you go to the medical association, and so on. This is not my way! My way is to stand on the corner of Powell and Market and wait for him to come by. And if you have all the time in the world and you are interested in the passing scene, this is as good a way as any; and if you don't meet him, you are going to meet someone else. That's how I do research. I go to the library, I pick up the things that interest me, I use whatever comes my way. And I believe that if you have a good theory, the things you need *will* come your way. You'll be lucky. You know what Pasteur said: "Chance favors the prepared mind." Take one of the chanciest things in the world, like war. Both Kitchener and Frederick the Great, when they were considering a general's qualifications, would always ask, "Is he considered lucky?" It was a perfectly legitimate question, because if he was considered lucky, it meant he was prepared to take advantage of chance. I depend on chance to help me find what I need, and most of the time I've been lucky.

Expose yourself to chance. For example, go to a shelf of books and browse in a subject that interests you. Don't consult bibliographies or what somebody else says. Don't adopt any method that will limit chance. One way you limit chance is to get other people's opinions about what the best books on any subject are.

To give his ideas finished form, Hoffer retreated to Golden Gate Park, following a favorite path down to where the park meets the ocean. The walk took him about an hour from where the bus left him at the entrance, and that was just about right for chewing over the concept or problem he had selected for scrutiny. Then, sitting on a bench facing the Pacific, he transcribed the product of his thinking in his notebook, "adding crumb to crumb."

Writing was a way of thinking for Hoffer, as it is for most intellectuals. He has described, better than anyone else, the process by which what one reads becomes part of one's own thinking and then of one's own writing. He *always* took notes and made notes in the form of active responses to what he was reading. "You learn as much by such writing as you do by reading." Then, usually much later, he reviewed whole swatches of his notebooks, picking those items that would be useful, transcribing them onto small cards, "digesting them," transforming them into his own thoughts. "It is like a cow eating grass," he said. "The cow does not become grass, the grass turns into cow. If you want or learn, you have to do it this way. I always knew I could educate myself this way and that nothing would be beyond me. But my great advantage was that I was never rushed."

A final lesson is this: write constantly, freely, and much—but afterward cull, select, and organize, *ruthlessly.*

Sometimes a man writes a thin book and a thick book. Usually in the thin book he tells you what he knows. And in the thick book he tries to cover up what he doesn't know. The thin one is clear and interesting; the thick one is dull. In general, the thin books give you as much as you want to know on the subject. As Keynes said of Marshall, the economist, if you just read the footnotes you would know more about his position than if you read the text. It is a sound principle—the thinnest books by an author are the best.

To point up this virtue Hoffer established a prize of $500 to be awarded to a member of the faculty, staff, or student body of the University of California for the best written essay—limited to five hundred words. When a professor of journalism complained that an essay of that size was utterly impossible, Hoffer observed that his own experience had shown him that any idea could be expressed in two hundred words. "I have therefore given you enough space for two and one half ideas."

Many independent scholars are loners, and Hoffer was the archetype of this species. He always lived alone, had only one or two very close friends in the course of his life, and eschewed the kind of intellectual company on which some writers thrive. About the one woman he once loved, he said: "She had things all worked out. She was going to educate me. She wanted me to become a professor of physics and mathematics. She wanted to throw a rope around me." So Hoffer drew away from her, to continue his solitary journey.

Hoffer's isolation, solitariness, and standoffishness from organized intellectual life, let alone academe, were not merely personal idiosyncrasies. They reflected some basic convictions that illuminate the need for independent thinking.

First of all, Hoffer hated intellectuals. But by the term *intellectual*, Hoffer did *not* mean men and women of the mind who pursue truth and understanding for its own sake—he exemplified that breed. The criterion for intellectual in his lexicon was not a passion for truth but a passion for power, especially power over people. He defined an intellectual as "a self-appointed soul engineer who sees it as his sacred duty to operate on mankind with an ax. . . . I am not venting any personal grievance against the intellectual," he insisted. "They have treated me fine. But anyone who wants to be a member of an elite goes against my grain, and that's what the intellectuals who now make most of the noise really want."

Secondly, Hoffer knew from his own experience that intelligence, perceptiveness, understanding, mental capacity, indeed wisdom are far more widely diffused among people than we usually imagine. "Every intellectual thinks that talent, that genius is a rare exception. It's not true. Talent and genius have been wasted on an enormous scale throughout our history; this is all I know for sure."

Hoffer knew for sure because he developed his own ideas through discussion with the men with whom he worked and spent his leisure time—suggesting that we, too, might find far more intellectual stimulation among such people than we might expect. "I have never felt cut off intellectually, but I have never associated with literary people. I could always talk to the people around me and discuss my ideas with them."

The significance of Hoffer's achievement for independent scholarship is best summed up in one of his own aphorisms. Echoing Pasteur, he wrote: "All experiences are equidistant from an idea if your mind is keyed up." The crucial factor is not the set of circumstances in which we find ourselves, but the "keyed-up mind." Each of us can press our creative inquiries vigorously and successfully, whatever our situation.

Eric Hoffer certainly found those rewards that many people seek when they undertake intellectual projects. But for him those rewards sprang, interestingly enough, mostly from the quest itself rather than from the benefits his books brought him. Even after he published four books, one of which sold half a million copies and became required reading in numerous college political science courses, Hoffer lived essentially the way he always had. He worked on the waterfront most days, lived in a simply furnished room with no phone and a bed that folded into the closet, declined most of the lecture invitations he received, and spent his spare time just as he had before: reading, thinking, writing. "I need little to be contented," he said. "Two meals a day, tobacco, books that hold my interest, and a little writing each day. This to me is a full life." He continued to work on the docks until 1967, writing between assignments. He published more books, lectured at the University of California at Berkeley, wrote a column for the *San Francisco Examiner*, and made many public appearances until 1970, when he withdrew from public life to continue his writing. He died in 1983 at the age of eighty.[11] Clearly, Hoffer did not need his fame or fortune to enjoy the deep satisfaction of using his mind creatively. Clearly, neither do we.

PART TWO

The Practice of Independent Scholarship

Let us call him an autonomous learner, for he directs himself. What he does is to create knowledge. It seems useful to think of him as someone with a certain set of skills. He knows how to formulate problems. He can identify the relevant resources of information or whatever, that are available in his environment. He is able to choose or create procedures and to evaluate his results. . . . Out of all this, he is able to create useful knowledge.

Michael Rossman

My strategy for success in independent scholarship is to divide and conquer.

➤ Divide your problem into manageable pieces.
➤ Identify just those resources you need for your particular intellectual undertaking.
➤ Draw from different sources to meet each of your specific needs.

Such a "loose parts" approach will enable you to accomplish your goals by using institutions on your terms.[1] Your solution will not be just like anyone else's, but such special solutions are easier, more practical, and more effective than any formula. Think of your project as a coat that you are making out of different patches of your own choice, each one attractive to your eyes, each one useful for its particular place in your garment. It may look odd to other people as you walk around, but if for *you*, from the *inside*, it feels just right, if you like what you see when you look in the mirror, and if it keeps you warm, then go with it![2]

Consider what *you* want to do. What specific *activities* do you want to be doing or be involved in? What kind of *environment* do you want and need for those activities? What *resources* are required? What kinds of *people* do you need, and for what particular *purposes*?

There is not likely to be one sole agency that will solve all your problems. But you can put together a package of the resources, services, and support you need from a variety of sources. This method has several advantages, starting with the fact that it is feasible. By taking just a part of what you need from each such source, you can meet your needs without making a substantial demand on any one source—thus making it more likely that you will get what you need from each.

For example, a major college or university in your area is not likely to give you an appointment as a professor by way of solving all your problems at once. But consider these "loose parts," one or more of which would cost such an institution practically nothing, and which many independent scholars have arranged:

➤ Library privileges
➤ Contact with selected faculty
➤ Work space
➤ Courtesy title
➤ Admission to lectures, seminars, and so forth

Examples and details of how to arrange for these and other resources are provided throughout this section. This "loose parts" approach may seem formidable at first glance. "How will I manage to juggle all those balls in the air?," I am often asked when I first suggest it. In practice, the pieces tend to fall together quite naturally as each part meets a pressing need. Consider the case of Dorothy Welker, a scholar in Chicago who, to accomplish her project, the first translation of an important colonist's diary from sixteenth-century Brazil, marshalled the following "loose parts":

➤ Access to scholarly resources—through association with the Newberry Library, one of the major research collections that welcomes independent scholars
➤ Expert advice and assistance—provided by experts on Brazil all over the world
➤ Colleagueship and collaboration—she teamed up with a professor of Spanish and Portuguese at a nearby university.
➤ Sponsorship and help in getting the finished product published—provided by the Newberry Library, which arranged for a publisher

Welker's ardent interest in her subject provided the impetus she needed to put her particular package together.

My subject intrigued me in large part because [the diarist] was a considerable independent scholar himself. He evidently had no university education, but he had read voraciously and he had an inexhaustible curiosity about every phase of Brazilian life. Because he had no special training, he fell victim to some of the perils of the independent scholar: he is sometimes pretentious, he is often inaccurate, he claims sources he didn't really use, he gets hopelessly mixed up in his grammatical constructions, he tries in vain to imitate good literary style. But his endless enthusiasm carries him through, and his work is one of the most valuable sources we have on the Colonial Period in northeastern Brazil.

Sometimes independent scholars have to be even more resourceful in order to overcome even more daunting impediments to their work. As case in point was a project similar to Dorothy Welker's: the endeavor of Ronald Christ and Helen Lane to enable the latter to translate *On Heroes and Tombs* by Ernesto Sábato. The translation was a major work of Latin American literature that, when it finally appeared in 1981, earned a front-page notice in *The New York Times Book Review*. But the road to that rewarding outcome was not smooth, as Ronald Christ recounts.

> When no publisher was able to offer an advance for this translation and no subvention was available from the Center for Inter-American Relations' limited translation program, Helen Lane and I, with the cooperation of the book's author and publisher-to-be, worked out a novel agreement. Helen agreed to translate small sections of the book when she could steal time from better paying projects. Ernesto Sábato agreed to offer consultation when needed, and to go on waiting; Mr. Godine agreed to publish the book no matter how long it might take to complete the translations; and the Center agreed to pay Helen for those translated snippets with proportionally small sums filched from other sources, such as the budget for office supplies. The paperclip fund, we called it.[3]

For even more ambitious projects, an independent scholar's "loose parts" package may be larger and more complex, and the process of putting it together may take many years and cover much ground.

Janet Barkas:
Coming to Terms with a Murder

Janet Barkas exemplified the "loose parts" approach in the dramatic quest that led to her book, *Victims* (New York: Scribner's, 1978). She used a repertoire of investigatory methods, including library research, interviewing, field observation, academic study, teaching and lecturing, activism, correspondence, travel, introspection, and reflection. Throughout, she was driven by the independent scholar's characteristic determination to find the best information and insights, impelling her far beyond the library, the classroom, and the study. She marshalled every means to reach directly to the sources of the knowledge she needed, including, as the end of her account portrays, some sources in herself and her family that proved painful to explore.

The project began with tragic circumstances: Barkas's brother was murdered in a random slaying on a New York street. After the shock, the grief, and the sorrow, Barkas had another reaction: a rage to know, to understand, to master and communicate the truth about what had happened in a way that might be helpful to others.

> I wanted to do something about the conditions that caused my brother's death. But without knowledge, I was helpless. I set about a self-structured program that led to years of travel, interviewing, reading, a master of arts in criminal justice, teaching and lecturing on crime and violence at colleges and universities around the country, and the book. That summer I went to London, Paris, and Amsterdam. I met with police officials, criminologists, and journalists—the "visible" students of crime and violence; they were more accessible and willing, even eager, to share their knowledge and insights with me. Upon my return I attended trials in the criminal courthouses of New York. I met judges, lawyers, assistant district attorneys, and police officers. I went through the training program given by OAR (Offender Aid and Restoration) and began meeting with incarcerated juveniles. I spent Christmas Eve on Rikers Island at a party for the adolescent inmates. I also continued my active participation in Women-to-Women, a volunteer program at Bedford Hills women's prison aimed at easing ex-offenders' reentry into "civilian" life. I published a query in an inmate newspaper and corresponded with almost two hundred offenders imprisoned for violent property and personal crimes.
>
> During the summer of 1975 I traveled throughout Ireland, England, Northern Ireland, and Italy interviewing, observing, and researching wherever I went. But it was not until I visited Belfast, Northern Ireland, that I began to think more about *victims*. In the Irish press, in daily conversations, in the fears of the people, the focus was on the innocent children, mothers, and workers killed by anonymous bombs. Rarely was the criminal mentioned. Without my knowing it, my education so far had "favored" the offender.
>
> I returned to New York confused. On a Saturday afternoon about a week later, my father called to tell me about a television program on crime victims he had just seen. He asked whether I had thought of writing a book about the *victims* of crime. I reflected on the academic volumes on victimology, a subdiscipline of criminology, that were starting to appear. I knew that no one had yet published a study of crime victims for the nonprofessional. About the same time, I had read an article on crime victims by psychiatrist Martin Symonds, a former police officer. I wrote to Dr. Symonds, and he suggested I

sit in on his graduate class at John Jay College of Criminal Justice on the psychopathology of the criminal; in the spring he would be teaching the psychology of the victim.

I placed ads in local and national newspapers and, promising anonymity, asked victims to come forward with their stories. One rape victim I met had seen my notice in our university alumni news. I also selected names and stories at random from the newspapers: If the victim had a phone, I would call. If there was an address and only an unpublished number, I would write. In almost all cases I was granted an interview, perhaps because I knew only too well the double victimization that most crime victims endure. I once drove to upstate New York to talk with a couple whose daughter had been murdered a year before. A sweet, warm, lovely girl, whose former high school boyfriend had shot her to death. When the father pointed to her high school graduation photograph and said, "That's our daughter," I shared their sense of anger and loss. We cried together. I entrusted them with my own grief about my brother, and we spoke with emotions that most others could not comprehend. I wanted *Victims* to reflect my training and education in criminal justice, my interviews with victims, criminals, judges, police officers, and lawyers. I wanted it to be a book by someone with academic and professional credits. I did not intend a personal statement. I was afraid to mention my brother, even though this death was the initial reason I became involved with victims and the criminal justice system. But my publisher questioned my omission. I exploded. "It's not fair to my family. I couldn't do that to them. I won't bring more pain onto them."

Reluctantly, I agree to ask my family how they would feel if I now shared the fact that Seth was murdered. To my astonishment, they said, "If it will help, then tell it." I realized that I was not protecting my mother or my father or my brother's widow. They had survived the tragedy and the years of remembering the sad, undeniable facts; they had lived with it every day. It was I who would now have to face it, privately and publicly.

Barkas's book was published to widespread critical and professional acclaim, and gave her the opportunity to bring what she had learned to thousands of people via lectures, the media, and related articles.

CHAPTER THREE

Resources: Where?
What? Who? How?

Virginia Woolf was right. Whether you call it a den, office, workshop, writing studio, or whatever, you will require your own special environment in order to be able to focus on your research. It is no accident that the quaint old word for independent scholarship, *study*, is also the name of a place. You do not need a great deal of space. One or two hundred square feet will enable you to carve out some privacy and insulate yourself from distracting sights and sounds.

One independent scholar, who successfully turned an eight- by ten-and-half-foot segment of her house into her "dream study," described her labors.

> It took me six months of research in the magazines and at the stores that sell products and equipment. My particular problem—everyone has one—was that not only was this space even smaller than most people have, but it had a toilet in the corner! So I was working with severe limits on the two things you most need to do this right: space, and money. I explored desk surfaces that you can push up flush with the wall and latch closed when not in use, the old door-stretched-over-two-filing-cabinets trick, having the dining room table double as a desk. I also did the manual work myself, including scraping, plastering, and painting the walls, or, in the case of electrical wiring, got volunteer help from handy friends. But the end result is a great support for my work: It's *my* space, designed and constructed by me and just the way I wanted it. It's quite a feeling to have created just the environment you always wanted and needed to work in. To me, it's symbolic of the fact that after all

those years of doing intellectual work for *them*, in *their* spaces (college dorms, libraries), I'm now embarked on doing *my* work, for *myself*, in *my* place.

Even if you are lucky enough to have a commodious house, you probably will have to do some significant revamping to meet your needs. Contemporary houses tend to lack attics, and even basements; garages are giving way to carports, and walls between different areas are often eliminated, making it more difficult to insulate against noise, visual distraction, phones, and random interruptions. Experts in the home-design field predict that most houses of the future will be very big or very small, and that the desire for togetherness within these houses will squeeze out private spaces. Independent scholars will need to forge their own retreats.

The best detailed discussion I have seen of how to go about designing and furnishing a study is the chapter "A Personal Learning Space" in *This Way Out: A Guide to Alternatives to Traditional College Education* by John Coyne and Tom Hebert (New York: Dutton, 1972).

> Look around town for some cheap office space. Ask friends to rent their garage. An apartment is not needed, only a ventilated temperature-controlled space; windows aren't needed.
>
> Move everything out; survey the space you have secured. Don't move anything into it for a day or two. Get acquainted with the form of the room. Let it assert itself. Stand in the middle of the empty space; extend your arms. Stand there a few moments. Walk around the edge of the space, against the wall. These exercises will help you to organize the space; they also will keep you from filling it up with unnecessary furniture. Keep it simple. Perhaps there are partitions that should come down, doors that can be taken off their hinges to open spaces.
>
> Decide upon the basic areas: desk (both sit-down and stand-up types), reading, and conversation. If you have one large space you will want to enclose part of it. This is easily done. At a used-lumber or house wrecking yard buy two or three sheets of one-half-inch plywood in the standard four-by-eight-foot size. Used plywood is cheap. Buy some two-by-fours while you're there. Don't build yet.
>
> The desk. You need a long, clear space. The hollow-core door is still the best. They are six feet six inches long, although you can get smaller closet doors that are useful. A damaged or "factory second" door costs two dollars to four dollars at a used-lumber yard.

There are a number of ways to support the door. The standard desk height is twenty-nine inches. Building blocks will work. Hardware stores carry wrought-iron and wooden legs for doors, but these are flimsy. Two methods that work: obtain two metal and corrugated cardboard file cabinets. . . . Large office supply houses carry them. They come unassembled. With the metal base they raise the door to a normal height. The heavy cardboard is strengthened by the metal frame. The files support five hundred pounds. The door and filing cabinets make a simple, easily movable desk. The second method is to buy four metal sawhorse brackets at Sears, cut two thirty-inch pieces of two-by-four for the top rails and eight twenty-five-inch lengths for the legs, which are inserted in the brackets. Now you have two carpenter sawhorses. Lay the door on them and you have a desk. It instantly disassembles for moving. It looks good. At an office supply store buy some plastic trays for paper and writing materials.

Place the desk facing a wall. No one can concentrate looking out a window.

The chair. Get a comfortable swivel chair; for fifteen dollars at a used-furniture store you can get an adjustable office chair that probably cost seventy-five dollars new.

Visual display. Buy a package of corkboard. It comes [in] four twelve-inch panels to a package, with adhesive backing. Four panels arranged around your desk hold the right amount of paper. Too much tackboard and the eye wearies. The eye is attracted to horizontal movement (lateral scan). The tackboard holds the paper so that it can signal the eye, demand action.

Storage. For file storage get a secondhand two-drawer file cabinet or use the door and file cabinet system described above. Don't get the tall four-drawer model. The top of the two-drawer provides a second work space. Position this at right angles to the desk. Put the phone on it.

For books and other objects go to the shelving department at Sears or a hardware store. Either buy the steel rack shelving which comes unassembled in two-foot, four-foot, and six-foot sections, or buy the "standard and bracket" shelving which is attached to the wall. It is useful to have two shelves right above your desk for files and reference books.

A second work station. Many people like to have a second work station, a stand-up one. A secondhand drafting table is possible or construct one out of plywood and two-by-fours. The leading edge should be about forty-three inches high with a gentle upward slope. The dictionary can go on this table.

Space definition. Returning to the problem of the large open room. Now that you have a sense of the space, start experimenting with the plywood. What size office feels most comfortable? Where are visual screens needed? With these screens you don't need doors. To make them, cut the plywood in the lengths required to partially enclose the space. The screens are to be sixty inches tall; the plywood which is in forty-eight-inch widths must be raised one foot. Cut two-by-fours into three-foot lengths and nail them onto the plywood, two to a section to make legs twelve inches long. Join the sections with large hinges so that they can be shifted. Now paint them.

Acoustics. If the space is large or there is an outside noise source, put a rug on the floor; hang drapes of some sort; keep mood music going on the hi-fi; put up ceiling tile. Put a rug down in any case.

Lighting. An adjustable crane lamp, clamped to your desk is the best. Two will light most study spaces. Avoid "hot-spots" (unshaded lights), and fluorescents (they make everyone look awful).

An alternative to creating such a space as part of your living quarters is to seek it outside. The Writer's Room in New York City is in reality four rooms in an office building across the street from the Forty-second Street Library. The first thing you notice when you walk in is the hum of half a dozen word processors, each one being used by an author. Two large windows overlook the Manhattan skyline, but that is the only possible distraction. The furnishings are minimal and inoffensive: well-worn desks, well-worn carpets, well-worn dictionaries and thesauruses in a well-worn bookcase, a couple of potted plants that seem to thrive on the sound of keyboards. But writers who work there speak of the place as a godsend.

Often, a library will be glad to provide something like the Writer's Room, itself a spill-over from the famous Frederick Lewis Allen Room at the Forty-second Street Library, which proved too restrictive for some writers (you must have a signed nonfiction book contract to use it, and of course the room is only available when the library is open). Your local library may have an unused room or corner with a desk or a carrel that could be made available to you for your research, and where you could be able to leave materials overnight. Many libraries also have work rooms with typewriters that, together with the library's photocopying machines and research materials, may make a better base for at least some of your activities than even the best home study.

Local colleges and even public schools may find themselves with unused space on their hands. Churches and community centers also have given refuge to independent researchers.

Another haven for scholars is The Work Place in Washington, D.C. "We serve a number of independent scholars, usually unaffiliated and committed to remaining independent," says codirector Beverly Nadel.

> Books, articles, and government reports have emerged from this office. The concept of The Work Place was born from the need of my partner, Jean Levin, herself a free-lance writer and researcher. Jean needed a place to work, unencumbered by the distractions of home, but still enabling her to remain independent without an institutional affiliation on a permanent basis.
>
> At this moment, our clients are working on a wide range of projects, including a biography of an English noble family, a book on nutrition, and a political novel. In addition, work that has over the years been produced here includes *The Politics of Pain* by Helen Neal, *Overcoming Math Anxiety* by Sheila Tobias, and a volume on the accident at Three Mile Island.
>
> We think our business reflects some of the significant social developments of recent years: alternative career patterns, open work environments, shared work space, and the emerging role of women in business. By design, our clients represent a spectrum of careers in social science and humanities. Some are in transition, moving from traditional work structures to self-employment. Others are confirmed free-lancers who need the supportive and stimulating environment we offer plus a professional office arrangement. Visiting scholars from universities here and in Canada have frequently used our office as their base of operation while in Washington.
>
> We are unique in Washington and take pride in meeting the needs of independent, unaffiliated people whose needs were not being addressed in the past. While independent research and scholarship is very rewarding (and at times frustrating), the isolation can be a hindrance. Our office helps people to feel less "cut off" and affords them the opportunity to share the satisfactions as well as the frustrations.

Ambitious independent scholars might want to band together to create their own work space. They could pool their funds, buy or rent some suitable space, subdivide it, and create their own studio, a kind of collective of independent scholars. Something much like it already has been done at least once, in San Francisco, where a group of artists, scholars, architects, and others needing work space refurbished an abandoned chocolate factory and warehouse. Jane Jacobs provides an excellent account of what they accomplished in her notable work of independent scholarship, *The Death and Life of Great American Cities*.

Special Library Collections

No matter how specialized your field of interest, there is probably a gold mine of resources somewhere in the country just right for you. With a minimum of digging you may be able to unearth a wealth of materials to make your research as easy and exhaustive as possible. America's libraries house a wealth of specialized, unusual, rare, and otherwise hard-to-come-by materials in virtually every field imaginable. Almost invariably they are free and usually are accessible to anyone. These repositories of knowledge are the homes of scholars nationwide, and finding one that specializes in your field is relatively easy.[1]

> ➤ If your chosen field is mnemonics, remember this: You can find Mark Twain's Memory Builder game and almost five thousand other items relating to this subject, dating from medieval times to the latest cybernetic discoveries, in a small library in New York City.
> ➤ Is life on other planets your kind of encounter? Your tax dollars have paid for a string of NASA research center libraries, including one in California that contains some seventy thousand items on virtually every aspect of extraterrestrial life.
> ➤ Should your ruminations run in Rumanian, you can find twelve thousand volumes of periodicals in that language at the University of Illinois. If it is Portuguese periodicals that you wish to peruse, the University of Wisconsin has twenty thousand volumes of them.
> ➤ If engraving is your avocation, 1,650 autographed letters of seventeenth- and eighteenth-century British engravers can be found in the Free Library of Philadelphia.
> ➤ Those with equestrian interests might wish to gallop off to one of the fourteen libraries that have in-depth collections of materials about horses; those with bugs up their sleeves will find some forty libraries specializing in entomology.
> ➤ If it is minstrels and minstrel shows you are investigating, you can sing your way to one of eight libraries that collect extensive materials in that field.

The examples cited above are from among the thousands listed in *Subject Collections: A Guide to Special Book Collections and Subject Emphases as Reported by University, College, Public and Special Libraries and Museums in the United States and Canada,* compiled by Lee Ash and published by the Bowker Company. New editions are issued regularly. It is available in most large libraries and is very easy to use. The entire directory is arranged alphabetically by subject; under each subject is a listing of libraries that reported special collections in that field, with their addresses, chief librarians, number of volumes, the types of materials they contain (such as manuscripts, maps, microforms, and so on), and notes about their contents.

The Directory of Special Libraries and Information Centers is, as its subtitle indicates, *A Guide to Special Libraries, Research Libraries, Information Centers, Archives and Data Centers Maintained by Government Agencies, Business, Industry, Newspapers, Educational Institutions, Nonprofit Organizations, and Societies in the Fields of Science, Technology, Medicine, Law, Art, Religion, History, Social Sciences, and Humanistic Studies.* It is edited by Margaret L. and Harold C. Young, and published periodically by the Gale Research Center. It lists some fifteen thousand library and information centers whose collections are geared to the special interests of their users. The fifteenth edition was published by Gale Research Center in 1992. The entries are arranged alphabetically by the name of the agency, and include such information as address, telephone number, key staff, founding date, number of staff, subjects, special collections, holdings, subscriptions, services, automated operations, networks and consortia, publications, special catalogs and indexes, and other remarks. A subject index helps the user identify libraries in his or her field of interest in each state and Canada.

These two directories are among the most important guides to special collections in the United States, but there are many others. Some are geared to special collections within a particular geographic area. For example, the *Directory of Long Island Libraries and Media Centers,* issued yearly by LDA Publishers, contains alphabetical listings of academic, public, and special libraries. A brief description of each library is given, including its address, telephone number, personnel, special collections, hours, and access privileges. Also indexed are subject collections, online information systems, equipment for public use, and computers.

Paradoxically, it is often difficult to obtain access to these directories, which were compiled to provide access! "Although I have found such directories in several metropolitan regions over the past few years," reports independent scholar Alden Todd, "they are almost never mentioned to outsiders, and are usually kept at a working librarian's desk. However, if you ask specifically for such a directory, a friendly librarian will often pull forth his or her copy and lend it. It can help you find the unadvertised, out-of-the-way special collections maintained by corporations, trade associations, law firms, research institutes, social agencies, historical societies, and so on."

There are also guides to special collections in particular subject areas. An example of these is the *Directory of American Libraries with Genealogy or Local History Collections*, compiled by William P. Filby, published by Scholarly Resources, Inc. It contains a state-by-state listing of genealogical libraries in the United States, including addresses, telephone numbers, hours, personnel, holdings, numbers of books and manuscripts, and information and interlibrary loan services. A geographic index is included.

Your local library may have many of these regional and subject directories. If not, the librarian can probably determine whether a directory exists for the area or subject you are interested in. He or she should be able to find out whether the directory is available at a nearby library or whether you can obtain it directly from the organization that issues it.

Many special collections are open to the general public, but some may be used by only the members of the association or agency that operates them. Fortunately, this information is noted in virtually all of the directories mentioned here. Sometimes a restricted library will grant access to its collections to nonmembers with special interests. A letter to the chief librarian explaining your needs, especially with supportive references from your own library or from another person or agency whose opinion is likely to be respected, often will help.

"Showing seriousness of purpose, along with a touch of charm, usually is enough to win the courtesy of the house for a published writer, even though the special library may, in principle, be closed to outsiders," advises Alden Todd. "I have used dozens of restricted libraries in my time and have never been turned away."

Are the Rewards Worth the Effort?

If a special collection in your field is convenient to your home, it will probably be well worth the effort to check out its resources. But what good will it do you to learn that there is a one-hundred-thousand-item collection in a library halfway across the country? How can you find out in advance if the collection is worth a special and perhaps costly trip?

Suppose you are interested in Arabian horses. The dozen or so libraries listed under "Horses'" in *Subject Collections*, mentioned earlier, may have literally tons of data on horse husbandry, harness racing, equestrian medicine, and the like. Fascinating, maybe, but probably not worth a plane trip to Pennsylvania or Washington. Fortunately, many of the listings in the above-mentioned sources will give you a very good idea of the specific nature and depth of the collections. As an Arabian horse specialist, you may feel a trip to California State Polytechnic University is worthwhile when you read that its collection is considered

> among the finest Arabian horse collections in the world. Collector's items and rare books are featured in addition to the working materials used in tracing pedigrees or in researching specific problems, such as immunodeficiency disease, which is endemic to the Arab breed. . . . Arabia of the 18th and 19th centuries is also featured in the collection, mainly in books of European and American travelers who incl. descriptions of the "horse of the desert" in their writings. Official studbooks from 22 countries, numerous private studbooks, histories of the Arabian horse, and backfiles of serial publications are also important segments of the collection.

If California is too far away, or if you want more specific information about the particular items in a special collection, you may be able to obtain a printed catalog or list of the library's holdings. Many special libraries publish these, and such publications are usually mentioned in the directories noted above. The listing for the special collection on Arabian horses, for example, indicated that the collection has "a current desiderata list available upon request." *Subject Collections* also notes catalogs of some of the other "horse collections," such as *The Keeneland Association Library: A Guide to the Collection* and *The Dictionary Catalog of the Library of Sports in the Racquet and Tennis Club*.

Interlibrary Loans

What? You're still not ready to travel across country? Perhaps you really do not need an entire special collection in your field, but there are one or two books you would love to get your hands on. Although independent scholars will invariably come across some real treasures it they find that special gold mine, you may have decided that in your case it is just not worth the time, money, or effort. But wait, you still may be able to get hold of those special books. If you have not yet discovered the research bonanza of interlibrary loan, now is the time to do so.

Most libraries, from the very smallest public library to the largest university library or most specialized research center, participate in one or more cooperative networks with other local, state, or national libraries. Through these networks, one library can borrow a book from another library for its own user. The specific arrangements vary widely from library to library and may be as informal as a complex computerized operation shared by major research libraries through a region.

In Nassau County, New York, for example, all of the fifty-four public libraries belong to the Nassau Library System. If a borrower at any one of those libraries needs a book that is not locally available, the librarian will call an online union catalog to get a listing of other libraries in the system that own the book. The librarian will then call those libraries to find one that has the book available, and that library will send the book to the borrower's library on a special truck that makes daily trips to each library in the system. If the book is not available in any of the public libraries, the interloan department puts the request through to the Suffolk Cooperative Library System, the New York State Library in Albany, and to public, academic, and special libraries across the country. The public libraries also may request books individually from libraries in other parts of the country.

To borrow a book on interlibrary loan you may have to request the service specifically. It is a costly operation that some libraries do not like to perform unless asked. In fact, some libraries (but not many) now are charging the borrowing library an interlibrary loan service fee that can be passed on to the user. When requesting this service, you will have to provide the librarian with specific bibliographic data about the book(s) you want: author, title, publisher, edition, date of publication, and your source of information.

An interlibrary loan can save you a great deal of time and money in obtaining a hard-to-find book without ever leaving your own community. But as valuable as it is, it is not a panacea. In the first place, the marvelous serendipitous discoveries that can result from browsing through a special collection are lost because you usually must request a specific book. This drawback can be overcome partially by browsing through the libraries' catalogs, if they are available, or through special subject bibliographies in your field. Whenever you come across the name of a book that looks interesting to you, make a note of its author, title, and so on. Then, if the book is not available in your library, ask the librarian if he or she can obtain it for you on an interlibrary loan.

The other problem with interlibrary loan is that not all libraries will lend their materials, especially rare books, manuscripts, correspondence, artwork, ephemera, and the like. Subject collection directories will usually specify when interlibrary loan is limited or not available. Some directories will specify when interlibrary loan is available. Our Arabian horse enthusiast will find that the collection noted above 'is made available upon request to persons outside the academic community." Some libraries will provide photographic duplications of their materials, sometimes for a fee, depending upon their individual policies, resources, and copyright limitations. Many of the directories mention the availability of this service, but you should always inquire about it.

Sometimes you can be pleasantly surprised. I recently requested via interlibrary loan from my local public library an arcane monograph published in the series of Papers of the Bibliographical Society of America. Obviously, this is not the sort of item frequently requested of a neighborhood public librarian. Moreover, I did not have a complete bibliographical reference for the item. I did not know which issue it had appeared in, though I knew the year. The librarian handled my request with dispatch, found the exact citation and the library in the state that held the series, and had me out on the street in twenty minutes with my order placed to obtain the publication through interlibrary loan. Ten days later a postcard arrived in my mailbox announcing that the material was available; when I asked for the publication at the library, I received a photocopy of the sixty-page monograph at no charge! Apparently, the policy of the library that provided this item is to duplicate copies of such articles rather than to forward the book itself at the risk of losing a hard-to-replace item.

I am told by librarians that this practice is not widespread, but that it and other comparable courtesies often are extended precisely *because* such requests are so rare. Here is one situation in which the independent scholar's minority status works to advantage! These libraries are sensible enough to realize that they can meet the needs of the occasional independent scholar because they do not have to do it for everyone and that those with the initiative to be doing serious research have a legitimate claim on their help, when it can be provided at a manageable cost.

Even after you have done everything you can by the borrow-and-beg method, you may feel compelled to burrow further. At that point, a personal trip to the most promising libraries can yield additional rewards, as one scholar found:

> I have spent four years tracking down the originals of forgotten books by forgotten authors, acquiring microfilms and photocopies at great expense unaided by any foundations or grants, having to rely heavily on correspondence with libraries and archives in Europe and America. Their staffs have been most cooperative. Yet, whenever it became possible to make a visit in person, from Columbia to Copenhagen, from Harvard to Halle, invariably I found on their shelves pertinent and essential books and documents which had been reported nonexistent, not listed in the catalogues, or totally unknown to anyone living.

Access to Databases

We already can discern dimly the end of the centuries-long practice of scholars congregating on one site (a campus) largely because that site houses a massive library essential for their research. Some independent investigators are already liberated from the campus.

Patrick McGrady, one of the nation's premier science writers, lives as he likes in furthest Oregon. Yet he is in instant and complete contact, as he must be to pursue his inquiries, with the state-of-the-art findings in his field. He was the first medical journalist in the nation with on-line computer access to the National Library of Medicine databases. (Hundreds of institutions enjoy this access, most of them universities and hospitals.) The system expanded his horizons quite dramatically. "I became terribly excited about the potential for acquiring fast, accurate, and comprehensive information," he told me.

> For example, I wanted to get abstracts on all the work done by a German physician on a cancer-killing drug named ifosfamide and an agent (rescue factor) that spares the patient the deadly toxicity of this treatment. Within five minutes on the CANCERLIT database, I learned that he had published fourteen papers on cytostatic drugs, most of them on ifosfamide. I was also able to determine from CLINPROT that none of the current American research included use of this rescue factor. (Scandal!) Such information would have taken me literally weeks to discover without my computer.

Databases are computerized indexes of journals and reports in specific subjects. Database searches save researchers time by accomplishing in minutes what would otherwise require days. These searches can provide you with a list of documents tailored to your individual needs, often including abstracts or summaries of the articles listed. They may be broadened to encompass general subject areas or narrowed with specifications of publication date, language, geographic area, and so forth. Database indexes are often more comprehensive than printed indexes are: they are usually updated more frequently than printed indexes can be, and the computer can search for terms and information sources too current to appear in printed indexes. Computer logic can be used to combine related aspects of a problem, such as driving and alcoholism, in order to generate a custom-tailored index, which is impossible with printed indexes. Some databases contain even more information, such as the texts of legal cases, statistical data, and reports of research in progress.

Database searches often are accompanied by document delivery systems, through which the full texts of the articles, reports, or other documents cited in the search are provided to the user. This service is especially valuable for people who cannot easily obtain the actual documents, perhaps because they live far from, or do not have ready access to, the available sources. Document delivery systems enable these people to call, write, telex, or cable their requests and to receive their materials quickly and easily.

The most comprehensive listing of databases can be found in Martha E. Williams's *Computer-Readable Data Bases: A Directory and Sourcebook*, published in 1992 by the American Society for Information Science for Knowledge Industry Publications, Inc. It includes the names and producers of over seven thousand databases worldwide, together with information about the coverage, years of origin, numbers of items, and other pertinent information about each database. There are also several indexes—a two-level subject index, indexes of processors, vendors, and CD-ROM producers, and a database name index—that make finding the information you need easier.

Another useful tool for locating information about databases is *Modem USA: Low Cost and Free Online Sources for Information, Databases, and Electronic Bulletin Boards via Computer and Modem in Fifty States*, by Lynne Motley (Allium Press, 1992). The book consists of thirteen chapters of online information sources, including government, library, and book, environment and nature, science, music, gardening, genealogy, writing, and computers. Within each chapter, entries include name, address, telephone number, and contents and scope of database or bulletin board. Many of the libraries in the library and book chapter offer searchable online catalogs of their holdings for periodicals, books and, occasionally, music. Some holdings may be searched by subject or keyword. There is a section of instruction for the newcomer, as well as a glossary of computer terms. *Lesko's Info-Power*, by Mathew Lesko (Information USA, 1990), is yet another source for database listings. One chapter includes the names, addresses, telephone numbers, contents and contact persons for more than 170 government databases and bulletin boards, with advice to the reader that this is just a sampling of what is available.

Almost seven hundred bibliographic databases, containing more than eighty million references to journal and newspaper articles as well as to other sources, are publicly available. The following are just a few examples of the listing titles in those databases:

Medicine and Health
American Medical Association Journals Online
Cancerliterature
Epilepsyline
Health Planning and Administration
Medline
Toxline

Sciences
AGRICOLA
BIOSIS
Chemical Abstracts
Energy Line
National Technical Information Service

Social Sciences
Drug Information
Historical Abstracts
Psychological Abstracts
Social Sciences Citation Index

Education
Academic Index
ERIC
Exceptional Child Abstracts

Management
ABI Inform
Harvard Business Review
Management Contents

Database searching is available through most large academic and special libraries as well as in numerous private companies. Many public libraries also have databases or have access to them through system, state, or affiliated libraries. A growing number of private information service firms and information brokers specializes in database searching and document delivery systems. These brokers often provide related services, such as information re-search, analysis, and management.

Information brokers charge for their services, as do many of the libraries that offer database searching. Charges range from a flat fee for each search to rates based on professional "person hours" or on the time it takes for the computer to complete and print a particular search, or on some combination thereof. A typical fee for a broker's database search might include a $60 ser-vice charge and $25 for computer and telecommunications time. Document delivery generally ranges from about $4 to $25 per item, depending on source, time, copying, communications, and other costs. More extensive broker services, such as information analysis, are usually billed by the hour. Rates vary from company to company and from broker to broker. Even among libraries the charges range from one end of the scale to the other, with some offering lower rates (or even free searching) to individuals affiliated with them and others offering special subscription rates.

Some public libraries offer database searches free of charge to the general public, but you may have to inquire specifically about them because librari-ans sometimes are reluctant to volunteer information about costly services that might be abused. The New York State Library, for example, makes a lim-ited number of free searches available to public library systems throughout the state, which in turn pass them on to individual public libraries for use by their patrons.

Whether you choose to use the services of a private concern or a public in-stitution may depend on the extent and specialization of your needs, the time you have available, and other factors. If your financial resources are limited and your needs are not very highly specialized, it will probably be worth your while to survey the availability and cost of databases in the various academic, public, and special libraries in your area in order to find relatively inexpen-sive or free sources. Many large businesses and corporations maintain or sub-scribe to database services related to their professional concerns; a friend or relative who works for such an institution might be able to run a search for you.

Barbara Tuchman:
A Quest for Excellence

I don't belong to the academic world at all.
I never took a Ph.D. It's what saved me, I think.
If I had taken a doctoral degree, it would
have stifled my writing capacity.

Barbara Tuchman

Good scholarship is hard work, but it can be hard work of the most gratifying kind. In doing it, independent scholars have some important advantages over academics. That simple proposition is what I want to focus on in Barbara Tuchman's complex career. In an interview once, when I suggested this particular emphasis, she did not object, did not protest (as many intellectuals would) that it would ignore the importance of her opinions on more substantive issues. Throughout her distinguished career and right up to her death in 1989, at the age of seventy-seven, she herself insisted on the importance of hard work in producing excellence.

"I do all my own research," she said, "though reviewers have speculated that I must have a band of hirelings. I like to be led by a footnote onto something I never thought of. I rarely photocopy research materials because, for me, note-taking is learning, distilling. That's the whole essence of the business. In taking notes, you have to discard what you don't need. If you [photocopy] it, you haven't chewed it."

Out of such effort and attention came quality. *A Distant Mirror: The Calamitous 14th Century* was, for example, the product of seven years' work. It won widespread acclaim. One national review set the tone by stating that "any future list of truly great American historians will include the name . . . Barbara Tuchman. . . . Her new book may well reach a larger audience than any other serious work of history published in our time." Thus her work garnered honors: two Pulitzer Prizes, the presidency of the American Academy and Institute of Arts and Letters (she was the first woman to hold the post), and selection as the first woman to deliver the Jefferson Lecture in Washington, the highest honor the government awards for intellectual achievement outside the sciences.

From our point of view, what is most interesting is not where Tuchman ended her career, but where she started. Excellence takes time to cultivate, and she started late, achieving eminence only after the age of fifty. Her first book, *Bible and Sword*, was written over a five-year period because her duties as a mother and wife left her only half-days "at the most" to devote to it. The book was rejected by "I don't know how many publishers" before it finally appeared in 1956. But Tuchman was spurred to further efforts by something more enticing than early success: "The experience of writing history affected me as I suppose heroin does the addict, and from then on I was caught."

Even after having achieved a reputation, Tuchman found that she had to start on her later projects just about where you or I would begin. "I knew nothing about the fourteenth century when I began." Her previous books had focused on recent history, about which she was extremely knowledgeable. Yet she abandoned that comfortable turf to devote years to exploring an era in which she would have to start from scratch, a decision that her publisher describes, justly, as "a dramatic reaffirmation of her determination to follow her own bent as an historian; to use her prodigious talents to reveal those aspects of history that stirred her and awakened her intellectual curiosity."

This is the first important point for us: Tuchman's independence. For such a decision is one that only an independent scholar is usually free to make. She earned the right to "set her own rules for playing the game of history," said David Herbert Donald, who is the Charles Warren Professor of American History at Harvard. But the kind of freedom she had as he elucidated it, is available to every independent scholar.

> Seeking no appointment, promotion, or academic honor, Mrs. Tuchman can afford to move from field to field—from European to Chinese history, from the twentieth to the fourteenth century. A professor who thus wandered over the historical map would be considered at best eccentric and almost certainly would be condemned as superficial. Looking for the approval of a broad reading public, and not that of a handful of her peers, Mrs. Tuchman can boldly undertake a book on the Middle Ages, even though she admits that she is "not fluent in Latin" and for some sources "must depend on quotations and excerpts in English by other historians." No professor could afford to make that admission. Not interested in founding a new school of historical interpretation or in having her name connected

with some novel thesis, Mrs. Tuchman is free to retell a story that may be entirely familiar to experts. The academic historian who follows well-trodden paths
is likely to be called derivative.

But with such freedom comes immense demands, as we see if we look at the
way in which Tuchman conducted the project. Entering a new field entails learning about it from a standing start and developing one's own momentum in
moving through it. Reaching for a broad reading public requires the crafting of
prose that transcends academic jargon. Treading "well-trodden paths" necessi-
tates overcoming the contempt bred by familiarity in order to make such material come to life again for new readers. One reviewer referred to Tuchman's
"inch by inch" care in constructing her narratives and building up her imaginative recreations of past times and exotic places. "I belong to the How rather
than the Why school," she explained with characteristic straight-forwardness.
"I am a seeker of the small facts not the big Explanation; a narrator not a philosopher. I find the meaning of history emerges not from what an academic practi-
tioner has recently called the 'large organizing idea' but from the discipline of
arranging one's material into narrative form."

Tracing the way she created that book, one quickly discovers that the years
of hard work started with a kind of play. "Mooching around," she called it. "I
spent about a year mooching around in the reading and not knowing what I
really wanted to do." She started just where any of us would: with the standard
histories of the period, such as Johann Huizinga's classic, *The Waning of the
Middle Ages*, published in 1924. From that book she went on to general histories (all duly acknowledged in her bibliography). "Almost every book leads you
to another," she said. "That's why I do my own research. It's ridiculous to use
researchers—you don't learn anything that way."

Roaming further afield, she tackled the wealth of primary and secondary
sources, including contemporary accounts of court chroniclers, which she read
initially in their nineteenth-century translations. She also tracked down monographs on such esoterica as the number of communion wafers sold in a particular diocese in a particular year, army payroll documents, and tax rolls. Most of
this work was done at the New York Public Library and at university libraries
at Yale and Harvard where she found things that were not listed in any of the bibliographies. But eventually, like any scholar, she had to head for the original
sources. For medievalists that means the École des Chartes in Paris. Having

climbed up four steep flights of stairs every morning to stake out a window seat (there are no lights), Tuchman pored over contemporary chronicles in the original and consulted a nineteenth-century thesis on the life of her central character. Because it was written in longhand in 1890 in old-fashioned French, she had great difficulty in making out one particular word, until another scholar in the room looked over her shoulder and said, "Mais madame, c'est un chiffre!" ("But madame, it's a *number!*")

Libraries were magical for Tuchman, as they are for many scholars. Few have expressed this magic so warmly, however!

> The single most formative experience that determined me to write history . . . was the stacks at Widener Library where as an undergraduate I was allowed to have as my own little cubicle with a table under a window, queerly called, as I have since learned, "carrels," a word I never knew when I sat in one. Mine was deep in among the 940s (British History, that is) and I could roam at liberty through the rich stacks, taking whatever I wanted. The experience was marvelous, a word I use in its exact sense meaning full of marvels. It gave me a lifelong affinity for libraries, where I find happiness, refuge, not to mention the material for making books of my own.

But books were not by any means her sole sources. Tuchman was renowned for her compulsion to traverse, absorb, and react to the actual places where the events she is describing occurred. For *A Distant Mirror* she traveled widely to soak up a sense of the way in which the countryside, the climate, and the buildings (a few still stand) affected people centuries ago. Following in the footsteps of the death march taken by the hundreds of warriors defeated at the battle of Nicopolis in 1396 (where the crusading Christians were routed by the Turks), she trekked through Bulgaria and over grueling mountains onto the great plain that approaches the Hellespont—a 350-mile route less changed since the fourteenth century than any other landscape she saw. This journey helped her imagine the barefoot, defeated warriors, her protagonist Enguerrand de Coucy among them, being led to their deaths.

Throughout all this reading, thinking, and traveling, Tuchman was distilling her findings onto "The Cards"—four-by-six cards, to be exact, cross-referenced and filed under headings "to force myself to know why I wrote it down." These cards eventually became the grist for her writing mill.

As described by *Writer's Digest* magazine: "Tuchman writes her first draft

[in] longhand, types the second, edits the second heavily, and hands over the edited manuscript to a professional typist. She is exacting. She hates sloppiness, which she claims is a characteristic of people under thirty." Nan Robertson, writing a profile of Tuchman for *The New York Times*, said, "Barbara W. Tuchman wanted to talk about excellence."

Tuchman said: "I want to call this Be Kind to the Elite Week. I think it's a scary idea that to be elite is something wicked. Some people are of more value to society than others—Mozart, for example. If you insist on the theory that everyone is equal, then you are doomed to a lowering of performance, or achievement." Need it be said that her definition of "elite" is based on talent and dedication, and not on inherited privilege? Speaking more fully on other occasions about the topic of excellence and effort, Tuchman defined "quality" in words that might serve as a credo for independent scholarship: "The investment of the best skill and effort possible to produce the finest and most admirable result possible." [2]

CHAPTER FOUR

Working with Others

Barbara Tuchman and her position in the field of history was summed up in a *New York Times* profile headline as "Loner at the Top of Her Field." Many independent scholars are "loners" who prefer to pursue their inquiries on their own. One microscopist I know finds his keenest pleasure in coming home from work on a Friday afternoon, locking the door of his apartment behind him, and spending the entire weekend in the world of wonder with his slides and specimens.

But for many of us, comradeship along the way can be heartening, delightful, and useful. Our work thrives when we link up with other researchers in ways that add to each others' strength. In fact, some of the finest enterprises in "independent" scholarship have been products of intense collaboration. Consider *Our Bodies, Our Selves*, the pioneering book on self-health produced by the Boston Women's Health Book Collective. Or the Monterey Institute for Research in Astronomy, established by seven young astronomers who realized that, if they did not hang together, they would all hang separately as far as their scientific careers were concerned. Or the many public interest studies conducted by task forces organized by Ralph Nader's organizations. Or Public History projects initiated by organizations such as the Institute for Research in History, in which teams of historians produce films, exhibits, and public presentations in their field. There are many ways you can reach out to join with others in your field, depending on your interests, style, and level.

Finding Fellow Scholars among Your Neighbors

In many communities nowadays there is a new kind of network: a *learning* network. It is simply an intellectual dating bureau that enables people to register their learning interests, find out who else in the community is interested in the same subject, and join together, if they like, on mutually agreeable terms. Thus you might list your interest as Milton, macroeconomics, or Micronesia, and you would look for similar listings by other people. As such people turned up, you would be able to find out through a phone conversation or first meeting whether their specific focus and level of knowledge matched yours and whether you found each other agreeable.

Your librarian should know whether there is such a learning network in your community. If there isn't, he or she may well be willing to ask around and find out whether other researchers in your field are known by the librarians. If so, they might be able to facilitate an introduction.

Of course you also may want to check out the experts in your field at the local college or university. Quite often scholars in academic departments lack colleagues interested in their particular line of research. Moreover, academic politics can interfere with the frankest and fullest discussions with one's departmental colleagues. Therefore, professors frequently will welcome the opportunity to discuss their field with an independent scholar.[1]

If you feel disposed to meet independent scholars *per se*, either for interdisciplinary stimulation or to improve the climate for independent scholars in general in your community, you may want to initiate an independent scholars' roundtable, as described later.

Corresponding with Colleagues

Face-to-face contacts are only the start of your network of colleagues and peers. You naturally will find yourself reaching out beyond your local community as you establish communication with authors in your field whose works you especially admire. Most scholars warmly welcome letters from readers who have really read, understood, and reacted to their works. "I live out of the way in Cuernavaca," Ivan Illich once told me. "I send a lot of letters, and I get a lot of letters back. That's my invisible university."

The natural impulse to find and nurture collegial contacts places you in contact with a wide range of people. You are no longer limited, for mental stimulation and feedback, to those who happen to be nearest you; you can reach out, selectively, to establish connections with just those individuals, wherever they may be, with whom you have the most in common.

In fast-moving fields, letters have become even more important for sharing "edge-knowledge," new developments, and frontier problems and issues. "Invisible colleges" exist in many disciplines. Persons on the cutting edge of a particular topic or issue exchange thoughts and findings through these "colleges" months, sometimes years, before their work finds its way into the published literature. It is no accident that the publications in which initial results of new experiments in science appear have names such as *Astrophysical Journal Letters*. That one contains succinct reports of fresh findings, written the very day they occur, or very soon afterward, and dispatched at once for dated publication in order, among other things, to establish the priority of one's discovery. This method is the same used for rapid communication among researchers in many other fields.

Beyond letters there are even more accelerated forms of communication coming into widespread use by researchers and scholars. The exchange of audiocassettes for oral reports on ongoing research and communication via computer or telephone are routine in some fields.

To get started in this fascinating business of reaching out to those who share your interests, let us get back to the simplest method: correspondence. How do you begin? Try a letter to one of your favorite authors in your field, and take a week to write it. Use this occasion to take a fresh look at his or her *works*, or at the particular work or topic you will be writing about. You are looking for the best link between the author's work and your own investigations, but the emphasis should be on the former. Your initial letter might have some or all of the following essential elements:

> ➤ A sincere and precise statement of your appreciation of the author's work
> ➤ A deft but convincing indication that you are conversant with that work or with the particular part of it you will discuss
> ➤ The question, issue, comment, or other point you wish to raise

> A clear and courteous statement of the kind of response you are looking for

> A crisp indication of how the topic you are raising relates to your own work

> The thrust and scope of that work, briefly, and any publication, recognition, or other testimony to its seriousness

> A polite acknowledgment of your awareness that the demands of scholarship may press heavily on the recipient, with an assurance that you will understand if this is not a suitable time to undertake an exchange of letters

> A stamped, self-addressed envelope, which is a thoughtful and compelling courtesy even for scholars who have an office and a necessity for those who do not

Your Turn for an Intern?

The use of students as research assistants has been a traditional fringe benefit for the professor. Now such help often is available to independent scholars as well. Many colleges have started to offer "nontraditional" programs for those students who prefer to learn in ways other than taking conventional courses and amassing the requisite number of credits. These programs go under such names as University Without Walls, External Degree, Learning Contract, and so forth. Students usually devote part of their time to internships, apprenticeships, or other experiences in which they learn, off campus, from people other than university faculty, working with these people rather than merely being taught by them. The students tend to be adults, ranging in age from twenty to sixty.[2]

Here is where you might obtain help for your projects. If your work might enlist the interest of students and provide them with experiences that would enrich their education, you may well be able to arrange for such internships. (This book benefited from research conducted by students from the Gallatin Division of New York University, the nontraditional unit of that institution.)

Begin by checking local newspapers for display ads recruiting students to intern programs, and check at your local library for posted announcements and for what the librarians know about such offerings. This investigation should lead you to intern programs at colleges and universities in your vicinity as well as give you the name of the person or unit to write to. You then should write a one-page letter broaching the possibility of having students work on your project, stressing the educational benefits to the students.

You need not confine yourself to students when seeking assistants. Millions of adults volunteer every year for all kinds of service, from serving hot lunches to old people to doing clerical work for nonprofit agencies. Those are worthwhile activities, but why doesn't anyone ever request volunteers for *intellectually* worthwhile work? When you do, the results are rewarding. I have just received the product of several weeks' work by my latest volunteer research associate, Marion Ausubel, who responded to a phone call to my county Voluntary Action Center. An honors graduate in English literature with a master's degree from Columbia University, she has used her background and skills to turn up a cohort of notable independent scholars whose work has been described in this book.

Organizations of Scholars

Sharing information and knowledge, learning about other resources and facilities, discovering new research methodologies—all are part of the informal networks that permeate every scholarly field. How can you become part of these vital channels of professional communication, many of which are generated by the academic community? One of the easiest ways is to join a professional organization or association in your field. Virtually every discipline has at least one and usually several such organizations. Through membership in an association in your field you may reap benefits in addition to shared information. Most associations offer some or all of the following services.

> Regular conventions, meetings, seminars, and conferences
> Books, journals, directories, and other materials
> Special libraries
> Placement and professional services
> Grants, awards, and scholarships

> ➤ Professional certification
> ➤ Affiliations with related organizations
> ➤ Divisions or committees in specialized areas of interest
> ➤ Local chapters or subgroups throughout the country
> ➤ Personal services such as insurance plans or group trips

Also, listing memberships on your vita will enhance your "professional image" (especially if your academic affiliations are limited) and will be helpful if you decide to seek work in your field or when you apply for speaking engagements, consulting positions, grants, and so forth. If you are unfamiliar with the professional associations in your field, you can find out more about them in another splendid resource: The *Encyclopedia of Associations*, edited by Denise S. Akey and published by the Gale Research Company. New additions are issued regularly. This compilation describes approximately 14,500 nonprofit American membership associations, as well as selected, for-profit, nonmembership, foreign, international, local and regional, and citizen action groups. The associations are listed under seventeen broad categories: trade, business, and commercial organizations; agricultural organizations and commodity exchanges; legal, governmental, public administration, and military organizations; scientific, engineering, and technical organizations; educational organizations; cultural organizations; social welfare organizations; health and medical organizations; public affairs organizations; fraternal, foreign interest, nationality, and ethnic organizations; religious organizations; veteran, hereditary, and patriotic organizations; hobby and avocational organizations; athletic and sports organizations; labor unions, associations and federations; chambers of commerce; Greek letter and related organizations.

When contacting an association, you should request a list of its local chapters, as the proximity of meetings obviously will affect your ability to participate in them and to meet other scholars in your field. Sometimes there is an additional fee for membership in a local chapter; sometimes you can join a local group without necessarily becoming a member of the national organization. Contact the local as well as the national group. If it is not noted in the encyclopedia, you also might want to ask whether the organization publishes a membership directory, which is a useful tool both to be listed in and to use in locating other members who live near you.

The "Amateur Wing"

Many major disciplines have well-developed "amateur wings," to use the nice phrase devised by Professor Robert Stebbins of the University of Calgary, who has made a special study of them.[3] He has identified such groups vigorously at work in such fields as astronomy, archaeology, microscopy, ornithology, mineralogy, entomology, and botany.

Independent scholars could make notable contributions in virtually every field, I believe. David Riesman suggested some years ago that the social sciences "make use of amateur and part-time observers," noting that national surveys and many other projects could not get along without such people. He spoke of the potential of "mass observation" as a resource for research, when for instance one wants to monitor TV throughout the country or observe movie audiences or parades or other nonrecurring phenomena.[4]

The potential of amateur wings hardly has been tapped. Look for opportunities in your own field for individual or collective effort in data gathering or other activities that could meet major needs of the discipline, and then consider taking the lead. That is how most of the amateur activity began in the fields studied by Stebbins.

The Hidden Conference

Among the best opportunities for making contact with peers and prospective colleagues are the major conferences held in virtually every field at least once a year. The most able theorists and researchers, at least from the academic sector of each field, present their most interesting current work at these conferences. Moreover, they are in the mood to welcome discussion of their findings and positions, which can lead to continuing communication by mail.

To get the most out of such conferences, you will need to develop the skills of decision making, coverage, networking, and synthesizing. Few conference-goers even know these skills exist. Most people who attend conferences get only about one-third of what they might out of their attendance because they fail to *plan* their participation. They don't know why they are there, what they are after, or how to get what they need. You can do better.

The general principle is to become what educator Terry Peters calls a "Self-Directed Conference Goer." Instead of just falling into the lockstep laid down in the program, "*you* become consciously responsible for deciding what you need from the conference and the best ways of meeting those needs." To implement this principle, you do some very important things well before the conference that help you decide whether or not it is really worth attending. Then you use some specific techniques while there to get what you need, avoid wasting time, and enjoy yourself. Finally, you "process" the experience and the materials afterward in order to incorporate them into your work.

Here are some steps to help you plan your participation and get the most out of your next (or first) conference.

> Be sure to have the program in hand before you leave home so that you can review it thoroughly.
> Find out which presentations will be available in printed text and consider whether they are worth sitting through. See whether tape cassettes will be available for some or all sessions so that you can consider purchasing them and using the session-time for other sessions or other purposes.
> Carry cards or information sheets on your project and yourself to give to people you encounter—speakers, other participants—with whom you want to establish contact.
> Obtain cards from those you wish to contact later or from whom you want to get papers, references, and so on.
> Set up interviews or social engagements with the most interesting participants.
> Find out who is doing the conference proceedings so that you contact him or her for any materials you need before publication.
> Think about using the occasion of the conference to organize a Special Interest Group (SIG) on your particular topic of interest: Just have twenty-five copies of a do-it-yourself flyer run off at the nearest photocopy shop or on the conference copying machine, and post them around the general meeting areas or give them out at appropriate sessions as people leave. Invite people to an organizing

session during some one-hour period that will not conflict with any other conference activity, or suggest that they join you in a particular corner of the cafeteria or dining room.

Mentors

As an independent scholar, you know how much you would value an assistant or apprentice who was knowledgeable and fascinated by your field and willing to help you in your work. So might certain senior researchers in your field, especially fellow independents who do not have the academic's ready access to graduate assistants. Why not explore the possibility of apprenticing yourself to such a person, someone who can act as your mentor? Some leading investigators need help with typing, research, and the administration of their projects. Dick Graham, a former director of the Teacher Corps, advises that the best way to get launched in your chosen field is to initiate such an arrangement. "Take anything you can get provided that you are in frequent contact. . . . Make a proposition . . . ask to be mentioned in the next thing he or she writes, as co-author if you're up to it and [he or she] is willing. Propose a study or a special project. . . ."

If undertaking to find such an arrangement on your own seems forbidding, consider the few "nontraditional" colleges that specialize in bringing about such relationships. International College in Los Angeles bases its entire program on match-ups between highly able and sophisticated independent learners (their average age is forty) and a distinguished Guild of Tutors including Ivan Illich, Judy Chicago, Vine Deloria, Jr., George B. Leonard, and Paolo Soleri. One representative student, Joseph Clinton, says he had been looking for years for a way to concentrate on studying the history and development of geodesic structures. "I never found a suitable program (among Ph.D. offerings) because all the schools had extensive requirements in subjects that had nothing to do with what I wanted to study." Through International College, Clinton was hooked up with Buckminster Fuller, and they worked out a "contract" under which the "student" traveled across the United States interviewing people who did early research in geodesics. Clinton met several times a month with Fuller to discuss his research, and talked with him by telephone between times. "The contact with Fuller has been inspiring," says Clinton, "because he is such a pioneer in his field. The association also has been useful because it has given me access to people and archives that I otherwise would not have." (The address of International College is 1019 Gayley Avenue, Los Angeles, California 90024.)

Doing a Delphi

Would you like a way to join a select group of your peers for an ongoing seminar focused on one of the key issues, problems, hypotheses, or findings in your field? You can create such a seminar and conduct it by correspondence, using the well-tested Delphi technique described below. "It's *better* than a live seminar," says one scholar who is currently involved in one. "I get more out of it, because of the time to reflect at leisure over what I really think, and the need to express it in writing—rather than being called upon to spit out my response around the seminar table. It's like the difference between the pressure on a player in a chess tournament, and the leisure you have in 'postal chess' to take your own time in making your moves."[5]

I can best illustrate the way the Delphi works by describing one in which I was involved. Naturally, the subject was central to the thesis of this book—if it had not been, I would have declined and organized my own Delphi on a relevant subject. The subject was "the unbundling of higher education," an apt phrase for what the group was to discuss. The term, *unbundling*, comes from antitrust law, where it refers to the process by which a conglomerate or monopoly firm begins to sell separately some of the products or services that it has been tying together (that is, compelling buyers to purchase) as a "bundle." An example of "bundling" might be a computer or copying machine manufacturer compelling purchasers to buy its brand of paper, service for the machines, and so on.

The person who initiated this Delphi, Professor William Wang of the Law School of the University of San Diego (he is now at Hastings College of Law in San Francisco), was interested in seeing higher education "unbundle" its package of products and services. In some respects this process has been occurring over the past fifteen years. It has become possible, for example, to pay only for taking tests showing what one knows in a subject, and, if successful, to get college credits in that subject without also having to pay tuition, take lectures, and so

forth. Wang wrote a provocative paper on this idea, but wanted to convene colleagues interested in the notion in order to refine his paper, enrich it, critique
it, and improve it. He chose a dozen or so of us from around the country.

The plan was simple and typical of any Delphi exercise: An initial paper was
distributed, and each member of the Delphi was asked to prepare a response to
it, addressing whatever issues he or she felt were most crucial. The responses were
duplicated and distributed to everyone for a second round. Then the fur began
to fly as individuals began to argue with one another's point of view, contesting
issues, modifying their own positions in light of evidence or arguments presented
by others, and developing new arguments or data on behalf of their own positions.

I found myself yielding on an issue here—because one of the other participants demolished my argument or produced a telling exception—but becoming more firmly convinced of other aspects of my position. The stimulation of
being challenged on these issues drove me to construct a tighter case and to
marshall fresh facts that, in some cases, won over my colleagues.

As each round of responses came in, Bill Wang would synthesize them, indicate where he saw us reaching a consensus, and identify outstanding questions
that we might want to address in the next round. Then out again would go the
statements from all the participants, and each of us would be at our typewriters
again. I rarely have had such an invigorating intellectual workout, nor probed
one issue so thoroughly. All scholars know that nothing sharpens one's thinking more surely than the knowledge that one is writing for one's true peers.

A Delphi exercise can be organized by anyone. The cost of photocopying
and postage may be shared, or the principal investigator may assume this modest cost as being well worth the investment. There is no question in my mind
that Bill Wang got more out of this particular Delphi than any other participant,
even though each one with whom I spoke felt well rewarded by the exercise.[6]

In this case Wang secured a small grant from a foundation interested in the
"unbundling" concept and thereby obtained subvention for his costs as well as
a small honorarium to pay the participants. Similar aid might be sought for other
such efforts, but I think this account makes clear that the process can be conducted at minimal cost without such funding. Certainly participants will be willing to forgo payment, because they should only be involved if they see benefits
to their own thought and work. The necessary photocopying and postage is the

type of in-kind contribution that often can be obtained from a local corporation with a large volume of such work, where the additional use of copying facilities hardly would be noticed.

The Intellectual Partnership

The ultimate step in working with others is the intellectual partnership. If it suits your field, your particular project, and your personal style, it can be immensely rewarding. Most of my own books have been the products of partnerships. One example will illustrate some of the advantages. Back in the early seventies all hell was breaking loose in American poetry, and a book seemed needed that would document the provocative new forms such as Concrete Poetry, Language Happenings, Found Poetry (my own specialty), and the new poetry being written by minorities and oppressed peoples. But there were three formidable problems (in addition to the perennial one of finding a publisher!).

The first problem was one endemic to independent scholars: lack of time. Having to earn my living, I did not have the time to devote to this project, time that professors for English might squeeze out of their schedule. My second problem was that I simply did not know enough, and could not learn enough, to master each one of the specialized forms of expression that such an anthology should cover. My third problem was less acute, really more of an opportunity than an obstacle. I knew and enjoyed some of the key people in the field, and felt that the project simply would be a lot more fun, as well as produce a better book, if I could work with them on it.

The solution was the creation of an intellectual partnership. I co-edited the book with George Quasha, an experienced and brilliant poet and editor in the field. We enlisted three associate editors, each one to create a major part of the book, covering the part of the field in which he or she was the leading expert. The product of this partnership was *Open Poetry*, a definitive six hundred-page anthology published in New York by Simon and Schuster. No one person could have produced this book, but an international partnership of independent scholars did it by pooling their knowledge, energy, time, and talents.

Partnerships between independent scholars and academically affiliated researchers have become common. Often they create a potent alliance of the academic perspective and the "real world," which makes for better scholarship than either party could produce alone.

Two investigators in California, one an academic, the other deeply immersed in the "real world," have yoked their expertise to create a fascinating theory about the four types of careers paths. A psychologist, Michael Driver is a specialist in organizational behavior and a faculty member at the University of Southern California's Graduate School of Business Administration. In the mid-1970s he began to notice that master's degree students heading for business careers seemed to fall into four "styles" as far as the kind of career pattern they were seeking. (Interestingly, scholars too would fall into such styles, with obvious differences in how they would pursue their studies.)

Briefly, linear careerists choose their fields early, usually develop a well-honed plan for moving up, and pretty much carry out their plan. Steady-state executives, who also frequently choose and stick with one field, do not feel compelled to have a plan of advancement, and achieve their success by becoming increasingly capable at what they do. The third style, the spiral career, is really several careers pursued one after the other, usually one career every five to seven years. Finally, transitory people are job hoppers; some just drift around, others do well as roving "trouble-shooters" who constantly seek new challenges.

Having noted this set of styles, Professor Driver teamed up with Richard A. Hoffman, an executive in the Los Angeles office of Ernst & Whinney, an international public-accounting and consulting company. He, too, had been studying career styles, and had obtained detailed data from 913 executives his firm had served. Based on survey findings, Driver and Hoffman developed a general personality profile of the people who select the four different career paths.

Obviously, the two investigators' different backgrounds made their collaboration fruitful. Not only could they draw from their separate experiences, data, and insights in developing their concepts—they could also put the findings to use in different ways in their work. Driver applies the findings to his consulting work with corporations, urging them to look at their reward system and personnel policies with respect to the kinds of people they want to attract and hold. Hoffman puts their conclusions to work on behalf of individual clients of his organization, alerting them about what to look for in a corporation to assure that its style fits well with their own personal career objectives. "We want to bring together the individual and the organization as one," Hoffman explains. "We want to make sure that if you're a steady-state person, the corporation you're applying to is a steady-state company."

Commenting on this fruitful partnership, the independent member, Richard Hoffman, said:

> The chemistry was very good between us (which helps) and we were both interested in sharing and integrating our respective perspectives, experiences, and approaches. Our skills were also complementary—he with a strong background in research design, instrument construction and statistical analysis, and I with the practical experience associated with a rather large number of completed engagements wherein executives were recruited, counseled, tracked, and developed, and with detailed files on each engagement. We designed (compromised) and proceeded on the project as a result of our individual learning interests and professional needs. Fortunately, the results were useful, supporting and expanding Mike's research interests and efforts at the University, and my own systems for conducting executive recruiting and executive counseling assignments on behalf of my clients.

Moreover, the unusual mix of research rigor and practical relevance won for this team an attention to their findings that neither of them would have obtained alone:

> Women's magazines were interested in the application of our findings to the New Woman and her career planning and management. Academic journals in the behavioral sciences were interested in the psychological and personality correlations within and between our career concept categories, the stratification of our population, and the instrument we used. Contemporary magazines were interested in the societal impact of the mismatch we found between individual needs and motives and organizational needs and objectives. Also, the relationship of the career concept categories we found to famous people. Newspapers were just interested in reporting the basic project and the findings. We have received inquiries from academicians, practitioners, businesses, executives, and a potpourri of nonprofit foundations literally from around the world. All from a project simply between Mike and me, to explore an area in which we wished to acquire hard data and knowledge which we could apply to meet our individual curiosities, needs, and professional interests.

Another such partnership reveals how these arrangements work out in practice—what problems arise, and how they can be resolved. Charles

Swann, the general manager of WRFK-FM in Richmond, Virginia, joined forces with Professor Jeffrey Hadden, a sociologist at the University of Virginia, to produce a revealing study of TV evangelists, *Prime-Time Preachers*. By using social science research methods to clarify a subject of much speculation, these authors showed that, contrary to widespread opinion, the appeal of the media evangelists was *dropping*. "Results of the study are touching off a debate about the power and influence of the television ministries," commented *The New York Times* in covering the book.

I asked Swann, the independent partner, to tell me what he had learned about such arrangements through this project. One of the first things he mentioned was the way such team efforts get started: serendipitously, in many cases. The lesson for the rest of us? Keep your eyes open for opportunities that may arise as casually and gradually as this one did.

> Although Jeff Hadden and I both lived in the state of Virginia, seventy miles apart, we had never met until we found ourselves speaking at the same conference on the electronic church at New York University. We seemed to hit it off personally. I was interested in his ideas about the electronic church because he is a sociologist and I have spent most of my time around church-related people who have their own way of thinking about things. As a result of that meeting, Jeff and I began corresponding, with the intent of getting together at some point to talk about our common work in this field. At that time, he was doing a sabbatical experience in Houston, Texas, and I got to see him briefly only once before he returned to Charlottesville, Virginia. However, our exchange of letters and our one personal encounter had pretty much convinced us that we wanted to do this book together.
>
> I suppose that the book was my idea although it became our idea immediately after the first mention. We started immediately to do and to share research with each other and correspond about ideas. By the time he returned to Charlottesville in June, we had begun to amass material and had been talking about it on the telephone and through letters for quite a while.

Do the differing viewpoints of the independent practitioner-researcher and the academically-based investigator present problems? Indeed they may, as Swann and Hadden quickly discovered.

> Jeff was concerned at the start whether I would be able to back away from the stance of teeing off on the electronic preachers and be a bit more sociological. I, of course, had checked out some of Jeffrey's work and my concern

was whether he would be so sociological that the general public would not want to read it. I think that by and large we were able to come to some kind of middle ground. This involved considerable negotiation. I think there was a lot of give and take on this point.

All scholars tend to write for their peers, I think. Jeff wrote a lot of work with his sociology peers in mind and I, of course, had written a lot of things with my mainline ecclesiastical peers in mind. But by and large, we were able, I think, to come to a middle ground of doing some important research and yet being able to popularize it so that the general public would find it interesting and understandable.

Once a pair of scholars comes to a meeting of minds about such issues, what practical problems arise? One is simply logistics:

Many of our problems revolved around the physical separation of seventy miles. He lives in Charlottesville, Virginia, and I live in Richmond. We spent a lot of time on the telephone but this was simply no substitute for being able to sit down and patiently take things apart and put them back together again over a period of hours. We got together as often as we could but it would have been a lot easier had we both lived in the same city.

Other problems stem from the difference in situations between independent and academic scholars.

Our second problem was that Jeff simply had more time than I did. He had no responsibilities at the university for the first three months that we were working on the book. He had returned to a summer of inactivity there and was able to work full time whereas I could not do that. I still had a radio station to manage and also had some minor responsibilities in communications on the seminary campus.

The fact that Jeff had more time available than I did was a problem that had to be negotiated all along during the research and writing of the book. Jeff was able to travel when I wasn't. Jeff could spend a lot more time and had access to much more secretarial service than I did at the time. In fact, we found that when the thing was over and done with that a proper recognition of the relative amounts of time invested in the book called for an adjustment of the royalty schedule.

Asked what advice he would distill out of this experience for other independent scholars contemplating such an arrangement, Swann said:

Jeff and I are good friends and I value the relationship and the experience of working with him on this book. However, I think that we both realize that, if there should ever be another collaborative project, a lot of the negotiation, the assignments and the work schedules that we had to learn about the hard way as we went along, definitely should be recognized and negotiated in advance.

I have learned from Jeff more ability to be scientific and objective and to stifle my subjective reactions, as that is required for a scholarly book. Jeff would have to speak for himself about what he learned from me, but I think he became much more willing to be a popular writer and, in fact, proved to be a very good one.

These two examples have been drawn from the social sciences, but intellectual partnership are just as appropriate in other fields. The classicist Gilbert Highet identified collaboration as one of the principles of scholarship, and urged it on his fellow humanists as one of the most potent ways to increase their productivity.

The two partners meet regularly. Each feels that he must produce something for the other to work with. A plan that frightens or discourages one man can easily be carried out by two. The drudgery, through being shared, diminishes. Each, from his experience, suggests methods that the other had not thought of. In such a case, two heads are ten times better than one.

In the sciences, dual and multiple research and authorship have become the norm rather than the exception. One need only think of perhaps the most notable instance of recent times: the work of Crick and Watson on DNA, which led to a Nobel Prize. But the phenomenon is commonplace: a random issue of *Physical Review Letters*, for example, contains only two articles by single authors out of a total of fourteen reports.

Because intellectual partnerships are always special situations, there is no handy how-to on creating one. Just be aware of the possibility and alert to specific opportunities in your own field. The excellent precedents for partnerships should strengthen your determination to seek your own version and serve you well if and when you approach a prospective partner with the idea. You may even come across the kind of extraordinary invitation made by C. W. Allen in his standard text, *Astrophysical Quantities*. Noting that a new edition would be required seven years hence, the author asked to hear from anyone interested in assuming coauthorship. "It's the only invitation I have ever known to join a best-seller in mid-flight," commented James Michener, himself a bestselling author and notable independent scholar.

Your Own Advisory Committee

When Gary Zukav first conceived the notion of popularizing contemporary physics, which was to lead to his highly successful book, *The Dancing Wu Li Masters* (New York: Morrow, 1979), he knew he needed help. "For better or worse, my first qualification was that I was not a physicist." What to do? Zukav's search for a solution to that problem led to a discovery almost as exciting for independent scholars as his revelatory insights into the new physics.

> To compensate for my lack of education in physics (and for my liberal arts mentality) I asked, and received, the assistance of an extraordinary group of physicists. I discovered that physicists, from graduate students to Nobel Laureates, are a gracious group of people; accessible, helpful, and engaging. This discovery shattered my long-held stereotype of the cold, "objective" scientific personality."

How many times have you seen the plethora of acknowledgments at the front of a book? Each of those names represents one investigator's substantial investment of time, energy, and thought to help a colleague. There is a vast fund of fellow-feeling among researchers who share a passion for a given field. You can draw from that fund.

So potent is this technique of asking the experts that, quite often, the responses constitute a valuable body of information in themselves. That is what happened in Zukav's case. Of those physicists who stepped forward to assist him so graciously,

> five of them, in particular, read the entire manuscript. As each chapter was completed, I sent a copy of it to each physicist and asked him to correct any conceptual or factual errors which he found. My original intention was to use these comments to correct the text. However, I soon discovered that my physicist friends had given more attention to the manuscript than I had dared

to hope. Not only were their comments thoughtful and penetrating, but, taken together, they formed a significant volume of information in themselves. The more I studied them, the more strongly I felt that I should share these comments with [my readers]. . . . If you read the footnotes as you read the book, you will have have a rare opportunity to see what five of the finest physicists in the world have to say about it as they, in effect, read it along with you. Their footnotes punctuate, illustrate, annotate, and jab at everything in the text. Better than it can be described, these footnotes reveal the aggressive precision with which men of science seek to remove the flaws from the work of a fellow scientist, even if he is an untrained colleague, like myself, and the work is nontechnical, like [my] book.

Ivan Illich has done much the same thing with several of his books, having leading experts comment sharply wherever they like and then publishing their comments as part of the finished book. I know of comparable instances in the fields of psychology, philosophy, marine biology, ornithology, microeconomics, and race religions.

More modest uses of an advisory committee are easier to arrange. You will be asking far less of your "committee members" than Zukav and Illich did. You might want them to react to your initial plans, to receive regular reports of your progress, to keep your interests in mind as they go about their own work (in case something of sharp interest to you comes to their attention), and perhaps to review the product of your research at the end. The development of your advisory committee may grow quite naturally out of your correspondence with other scholars, and your attendance at meetings in your field. Once you have established a correspondence or relationship with a few leading figures in your field, you will find that these people probably will be glad to become your first advisory committee members, especially as their duties will be no greater than those they are already discharging in their relationship with you. Their names should provide the leverage you need to recruit others whom you do not know personally. The more people you recruit, the easier it will be to enlist others. A roster of a dozen or so people not only will constitute the best possible network in your field, it also will be useful for collective name-dropping when you encounter such problems as admittance to exclusive research libraries or when you submit articles for publication in journals.

Your Own Institute

Consider the following organizations:

➤ Basic Choices, Inc.—a Midwest center for clarifying political and social options
➤ The Institute for Psychohistory—an association of researchers on the Freudian interpretation of history
➤ The International Research Center for the Study of Verbal Aggression—a headquarters for the investigation of abusive, scatological, blasphemous, and profane language

What do these three centers, and dozens like them throughout the country, have in common? Very little, if you consider that they consist of individual, independent scholars pursuing their inquiries in highly diverse areas. But, looked at from another perspective, they have quite a bit in common. Each was begun by one or a few independent scholars, without academic or other organizational affiliation, without any funding other than what lay at the bottom of the founder's bank account, without any staff or office or visible means of support. And each is now a thriving, productive, fascinating center of independent scholarship—often still without funding, paid staff, or endowment.

Americans always have been adept at accomplishing things through voluntary organizations, as de Tocqueville remarked early on. Benjamin Franklin and his friends organized the "Junto" to share their researches and support one another's investigative enthusiasms. Throughout the nineteenth century the lyceums and scientific societies of laymen continued the tradition. This native knack for cerebral convening seems to have atrophied or been stifled under the "academic victory" of the last fifty years. Whatever the reason, the situation is unhealthy, and it is good to see the current revival of grass-roots intellectual organizing.

Organizing your own institute is one of those ventures in which your own needs and style will so determine how you proceed that formulaic advice cannot be given. Insofar as such general advice will be helpful, you will find what you need in *Organizations, Clubs, Action Groups: How to Start*

Them, How to Run Them, Elsie E. Wolfers and Virginia B. Evansen (New York: St. Martin's Press, 1980).

William Draves:
A Scholarly Celebration of Free Universities

> Anyone can teach, anyone can learn. That means
> that anyone can create a university—a "free" university
> in which we can learn the most important subjects.
> My job, and my intellectual passion, are both the same:
> to do that, understand how it's done, help others do
> it in their communities.
>
> **William Draves**

"Create a university"? Yes, *create* a university! Not a university as great greenswards, ivy-covered towers, and football stadiums. Not a university with rank on rank of faculty, SAT tests to get in and diplomas when you get out, and departments that chop up the world of knowledge and wrap each piece in an airtight package, but a university that permeates its community, where people learn together in their apartments, workplaces, homes, churches, laboratories, studios, and stores. In Cincinnati, Jim Hatch, a record-store clerk and college dropout, teaches a class on the anthropology, history, and religion of "The Mysterious Maya." In Boulder, Colorado, a class, "How to Start a Radio Station," led to the formation of a new public radio station. In Olsburg, Kansas, twelve-year-old Sarah Nelson stunned her mother by announcing that she had just signed up for a class in blacksmithing. In Kansas City, Missouri, German-born Georg Moncki teaches "Conversational German" in a bar.

As the nation's leading expert on free universities, William Draves can give you a scholarly definition of this fresh form of adult education, but just as you are about to fall asleep, his enthusiasm breaks in to remind you that he really is interested not in new pedagogical categories but in people soaring intellectually by learning what, when, where, and how they *want.*

"Free universities are grass-roots organizations that offer noncredit classes to the general public," the definition begins. "These courses may or may not be free of cost, but they are free of academic restrictions, bureaucratic requirements, and formal class settings."

"Free U's are based on the revolutionary principle that 'Anyone can teach and anyone can learn.' The people in those classes are only there because they want to learn—not for credits or a degree or to fulfill some requirement. This movement really reflects grass-roots America's learning needs and desires. There are 200 or so around the country, serving some half million people annually."

It is unusual and exhilarating to meet someone, even among independent scholars, who has forged a lifestyle in which *doing* and *thinking* completely intertwine. Bill Draves spends his workday helping people throughout the country who are starting or running free universities.

Starting at eight o'clock each morning and working until seven or eight o'clock at night, when he still can talk to people on the West Coast where it is only five or six o'clock and classes are starting to meet for the evening, Draves helps solve problems, provides advice, links one operative with another, and dispatches resource materials. His hectic office in Manhattan, Kansas, is crammed with book shelves, phones, and cartons of literature waiting to be mailed. There is a rag-tag mixture of office and home furniture, and IBM Selectric typewriter next to a book shelf made of bricks and wood, the kind one used to throw together in college. It is a small office and certainly does not look like one's idea of a prestigious, *national* office, but the feverish pace of literature being mailed out, letters coming in and going out, and staff fighting to make the next phone call makes other offices seem like they are standing still.

Amidst the literature and flyers of the present is the rich history of the past, for the office also has six file drawers of free university catalogs dating back to the mid-sixties, when free universities first started. It is the most complete archives of the free university movement in the country. It includes the largest free university catalog, a huge poster wider than one can reach, and the smallest, an entire catalog printed on Lilliputian-sized paper smaller than an index card. There are beautiful richly colored catalogs done during the days when multicolored printing was not as expensive as it is now. These archives represent in brief, a whole social history of the United States as viewed through what Americans learned and taught over the course of two decades.

Draves credits his nuts-and-bolts experience with providing him with his expertise in the subject. His practical field work is not just a job that supports his scholarship; it is also the source and fuel for it.

> Let's make one thing clear. While I have been lucky enough to be at the nexus of the free university movement, the newsroom of all the activity out in the country, I am in no way responsible for the wondrous activities taking place in two hundred communities from rural Missouri to Brooklyn, New York. My scholarship is 98 percent borrowed upon the work of people, past and present, who have made free universities and their historical precedents possible.

Late in the evening after the phones subside (except for an emergency or two), Draves goes over what he has learned for the day. His purpose: to analyze, understand, and disseminate the best that is being done in the field. Draves has made the leap from practice to theory: He not only coordinated what amounts to a grass-roots revolution in American higher learning, he also researches, thinks, and writes about it as an independent scholar. His book *The Free University* is a manifesto for social change, a blueprint for turning every American community into a little "Learning Society."

"These new institutions tap into a real human joy in learning and satisfaction in teaching that carries on a great American tradition," Draves insists. "Before adult education became associated with colleges and universities, we had a hardy tradition of lyceums, Chautauquas, religious and political forums of all kinds. Free universities are the contemporary expression of a conservative/radical American tradition of self-reliance. That's why they have become a leading force in adult education."

Draves has been active in the free university movement for most of its history. He ran the Milwaukee Free University back in 1971, then helped to found the Learning Resources Network, which helps free universities throughout the country.

As he traveled among the free universities and went about his work coordinating the national network in the field, Draves surveyed current practice, analyzed representative free universities, noted what courses worked and why, and distilled what was known about such nuts-and-bolts matters as keeping enrollments up and expenses down. He was particularly interested in how free universities could reach new populations such as the elderly and the poor, and work in new settings such as libraries and factories.

> I am an idealist, and one of my ideals is that the university should be a university for all the people. It has been a great disappointment to me that the ideal is often not even attempted. Much of my own education has been positively furthered by the formal academic institution. I certainly would not dispose of them. But I think the mix of the community-based and the formal . . . creates a much stronger learning environment.
>
> It is quite ironic that I and others are outside of the traditional academic world, doing the research and creating the models for the future of lifelong learning—the future of those traditional institutions, in fact. As soon as we make a discovery, do pioneering research in education, the traditional institutions will adapt or adopt it, which is fine. Most of our publications are sold to the traditional institutions.
>
> But what isn't quite as fine is the lack of recognition that these traditional institutions give to those of us who are doing the research, the scholarship, the creation of what is the next step in this era of lifelong learning.
>
> What really grates is that traditional educators not only don't recognize our contributions, but they try to bury the free university movement. While the free university movement continues to grow, to hit record enrollments and increasing popularity among adults every year, traditional educators continue to say and to print that the free universities are "dead" or "declining." With absolutely no data to back up these false claims. What are they trying to do, to hide, to dismiss?

But is such pioneering work in education *scholarship*? Scholars in the field of adult education have praised *The Free University* warmly in their own journals, so by the criterion of peer review it has passed muster. "This is an important book," commented Malcom Knowles, the doyen of academics in the field of adult education. "I hope that every educational policy-maker in the country will read it." Draves himself says,

> I think the "Is this research?" question can go both ways. Some people study concepts so abstract people wonder if they will ever have a practical aspect. I guess I'm on the other end of the continuum. I am starting with the practical and mundane, but you can take that back toward the philosophical, thematic, historical, and see a lot of scholarship implicated. The history of the free university movement is a case study in change and the maturation of a spontaneous reaction to rigid institutionalization, through its own history and

eventual institutionalization. And on a practical level we debate the concepts of "quality" and freedom of speech constantly.

I would argue that Draves's book *is* scholarship in the sense that it is the production and dissemination of fresh knowledge based on the collection of data and its analysis and that it uses perspectives from philosophy, history, and psychology. It traces the history of informal adult learning from the early days of the Republic through the campus-based experiments of the sixties and seventies; it includes an entire chapter for philosophy, and the final chapters contain a sharp analysis of policy for integrating free universities into statewide and national planning for adult education.

Can something that's so *useful* really be scholarly? I hope so. But even if one accepts for the moment that it *cannot*, consider some of the products of the more practical-minded scholars. The University Seminar on Innovations in Higher Education at Columbia, which I describe on page 217, focuses on the same subject as Draves's book. This seminar is chaired by a distinguished professor of management, Alfred Oxenfeldt. He is, justly, a highly respected academic figure at the university and in his field. One of Professor Oxenfeldt's books is *Marketing Practices in the TV Set Industry* (New York: Columbia University Press). It would seem difficult to prove that Draves's book, *The Free University*, cannot hold its own in such company because it is too practical.

Draves does not downplay the problems and frustrations of operating as an independent scholar.

I haven't taken this route wholly by choice or without incurring costs. The decision to write the book was not easy. There were no university departments to give me paid leave, or lessen a teaching load. There was no financial compensation. I had to give up four times more in salary. I did try, and although I may be able to write a book, I cannot write a grant, and so my efforts at funding the book's writing fell to naught. It was only my wife and companion, herself an Independent Scholar and an independent spirit, who encouraged me to do what I wanted, regardless of financial considerations. Unfortunately, that is one of the high prices for independent scholarship. For most of us who are not superstars or able to draw an independent income of any worth, the scholarship comes at our own expense—in time, lost wages, lost leisure time.

Yet on balance Draves believes it was worthwhile:

Scholarship has to relate to practice. There are simply too many needs, too many people hurting, to play academic games for one's adult lifespan. Unfortunately, academic scholarship sometimes fails to credit the extent and impact of independent scholarship in the past. There seems to be a common historical theme of "institutionalization," in which "primitive" mechanisms for learning, teaching, and scholarship are replaced by supposedly "sophisticated" mechanisms housed in our traditional institutions.

Free universities have rediscovered that learning can be joyful, that sharing one's skills, ideas, and knowledge with others is a positive and necessary experience for all people, not just a select few.[7]

CHAPTER FIVE

Intellectual Craftsmanship

The title of this chapter is from C. Wright Mills's account, "How I Go about My Craft," which you can find in the back of his book *The Sociological Imagination* (New York: Oxford University Press, 1959). He says:

> It is best to begin by reminding [yourself] . . . that the most admirable thinkers within the scholarly community you have chosen to join do not split their work from their lives. They seem to take both too seriously to allow such dissociation, and they want to use each for the enrichment of the other. . . . Whether he knows it or not, the intellectual workman forms his own self as he works toward the perfection of his craft; to realize his own potentialities, and any opportunities that come his way, he constructs a character which has as its core the qualities of the good workman.

How do you become a "good workman"—or an ever better one? Slowly. Constantly. Unendingly. And, as Mills suggests, enjoyably, because each advance in your skills and understanding gives yet another turn to that self you are shaping through your work. As Richard Altick describes the scholar's progress: "There is satisfaction in gaining steadily greater command of the techniques of finding out what he wants to know; in proceeding with the least number of missteps to the most productive sources of information." You will need and want to stay in training, to keep your skills honed as a pianist does by practicing every day or an athlete by stretching in each workout and regularly reaching for new levels of performance. These pages only can suggest some places to start.

The first place is with models such as Mills's essay. You must find in your field such frank, personal, precise, and inspiring accounts of the best practitioners at their work. These accounts are not likely to be the standard methodological treatises. More likely you will find such passages in memoirs, biographies, notebooks, or even talks by colleagues. Mills contrasts the usefulness of such accounts with the methodological standbys:

> Serious scholars are quickly made impatient and weary by elaborate discussions of method-and-theory-in-general. . . . It is much better . . . to have one account by a working student of how he is going about his work than a dozen "codifications of procedure" by specialists who as often as not have never done much work of consequence. Only by conversations in which experienced thinkers exchange information about their actual ways of working can a useful sense of method and theory be imparted to the beginning student.

Mills proves his point by sharing his own hard-won knowledge on such practical matters as the creation and maintenance of "files" in the sense used by social scientists, the deployment of such files in intellectual production, the conduct of empirical research, the generation of ideas, and the writing up of results. You cannot do better than to find such writings in your own field and to make a fairly regular practice of re-reading them. If, like Mills's model, they combine the highest ideals of the field with useful techniques, they should serve both to refresh your morale and to suggest solutions to problems you may be facing. They should serve as touchstones of honest work.

Pitfalls in Research

It should go without saying that the independent scholar must avoid the pitfalls that threaten the unsophisticated researcher. Regrettably, it does not. Because many independent scholars often have not gone through the regimen of formal graduate study, they must master the rudiments of scientific method in their field, on their own. Therefore, I would feel remiss if this book did not point out such dangers as those in the following listing by Dorothy Welker, the Chicago-based scholar whose working regimen I've cited previously. Some readers will find this list utterly unnecessary, but for others it will alert them to skills or attitudes which they still need to nurture.

> The independent scholar may neglect to read his predecessors in his field. Hence he may waste time on a subject that has already been done. I knew of one man who spent years devising a whole system of philosophy. He didn't "waste" time reading other philosophers. The result: He unwittingly constructed a sort of midget Kantian system.

> An independent scholar may be ignorant of bibliographical methods and standards; hence he will not know how to evaluate sources. He may think any book found in a library, especially a university library, is totally reliable. He may not know the significance of the date on the title page, or be capable of testing the accuracy of a translation.

> An independent scholar may not know where to go for reliable information or service. Thus a man who needed a translation of a sixteenth-century Italian work turned, not to the Italian Department in a university, but to the Italian consulate, where he got somebody who knew only modern Italian and who filled out his inaccurate translation with guesses.

> An independent scholar may not know how to read carefully or to write precisely. I have been astonished at the incompetence in both areas demonstrated even by persons holding Ph.D.s, some of them unfortunately in print.

> An independent scholar may not have a legitimate reason for writing on his topic. It may be a nonexistent problem. Thus one writer detailed the similarities he found between Nietzsche and Mencken, without giving any reason why this was important.

> An independent scholar's background in related fields, or in general culture, may not be wide enough to provide a proper perspective on the topic. Thus a commonplace of a past era may be distorted or magnified into significant evidence. (The Baconians on Shakespeare. And one man thought he had discovered that his author "put one over on the Pope" because his work bore the imprimatur of the Holy Office even though the romance he authored was "not a true story." It is astonishing how hard it is to convince such a person that he is totally mistaken.)

> An independent scholar may naively inject modern prejudices and assumptions, or his own personal ideas about morality, into works where such matters have no relevance. At worst, he may even chide an author on his now-unacceptable views (Shylock in *The Merchant of Venice*).

> An independent scholar may lack training in logical thinking. Hence he

may present conclusions that do not follow from his evidence, or he may misinterpret that evidence.

➤ He may not know how to take accurate notes. He may fail to distinguish between making a quotation and making a paraphrase; hence he subjects himself to the charge of plagiarism. And he may not know the importance of giving credit to sources.

➤ He may be unable to resist the temptation to include colorful or amusing scenes and anecdotes that have only journalistic value.

How can you avoid succumbing to these and other pitfalls? Welker insists that

Most people need training and guidance in doing competent, let alone quality, research. All the enthusiasm and determination in the world cannot take the place of a knowledge of one's trade. I do not think we ought to encourage people to think they can simply turn themselves loose in a library and expect to come out with something publishable. Why should anyone expect to do in a library what no one would expect to do in a laboratory—perform research without knowing how?

Whatever the faults of academe, and goodness knows I have no wish to gloss them over, it does provide training in method and in developing scholarly skills and judgment. Peer groups, which have their place too, cannot take the place of expert instruction. They are valuable for inspiration and encouragement, but ignorance multiplied does not produce enlightenment; it just solidifies existing misconceptions.

Welker suggests two ways of meeting the need for instruction in technical methods.

Organize a group of independent scholars that includes retired professors. Many of these are just aching to teach again; they may be happy to help work out a plan for guiding independent scholars, either on a volunteer basis or, better, for a modest fee. Seek out an individual retired professor and ask that person to help on a one-to-one basis, preferably for a small fee. Ideally, the professor should be someone in your field of investigation. But if no specialist is available, a person in your general area of interest (science, history, literature) can be of considerable help. Perhaps your best bet is a professor of English, because scholars in this field are trained to supervise research papers even on subjects with which they are totally unfamiliar.

Beyond Traditional Methods

One way to strengthen and enlarge your skills is to look beyond scholarly sources. The world of truth seeking, discovery, understanding, invention, and creation transcends the limited ways of knowing that most of us have been taught. One of the advantages of being an independent scholar is not being constrained, by training or peer pressure, to one single mode of inquiry. Some inquiries are conducted best through solitary research and reflection; others thrive on interchange with peers. Some draw principally from books and other written materials; others require field work, interviews, surveys, widespread observation, or reflection. Some investigations are best undertaken with a sense of urgency and dispatch; others need gradual maturing over years, sometimes decades.

Consider the four quite different strategies suggested by Alden Todd, an independent scholar who regularly teaches others how to do research in ways more imaginative and resourceful than those the academy teaches its graduate students. "A first-class research worker needs techniques that combine the skills used by four kinds of professionals," he asserts in his indispensable book *Finding Facts Fast* (Berkeley, Calif.: Ten Speed Press, 1979). Those four are the reference librarian, the university scholar, the investigative reporter, and the detective. "The excellent researcher should learn certain essential skills from each, and combine them so that they support one another."

Todd proceeds to analyze the strong points and the weaknesses of these four types. He also lists the hats from which you may want to choose at various points in your inquiries.

1. The *reference librarian*, trained in library science at the university, can be a masterful source of information on printed sources—especially reference books. He is usually as strong, and as broad in his knowledge, as the reference collection with which he works. This may mean an entire library, or only one part of a library. The most helpful general reference librarian I ever met was David Cole, who spent fifty years on the staff of the Library of Congress. Many times Mr. Cole revealed to me his amazingly detailed knowledge of the open-shelf collection of some 30,000 volumes in the

alcoves around the main reading room, covering most subjects represented in that library. David Cole's breadth of knowledge was unusual. The average reference librarian, although an expert in his specialty, may know relatively little about sources outside his own collection. And he may be totally unaware of research techniques outside the reference library.

2. The *university scholar* may be one of the world's most learned men within a limited field, and may be acquainted with every important book, manuscript collection, expert and other source bearing on his specialty. From him you can learn techniques that emphasize thoroughness. His research produces new information, or he brings to light facts that previously had been buried in written accounts lost in the darkness of libraries and archives.

But too often the scholar in the humanities or social sciences works too slowly and within too narrow limits to suit the rest of us. We are operating in a world that makes fresh demands on us each day. We can admire the patience and thoroughness of the university scholar and yet remember the value of our time. This is not to express a lack of respect for the university scholar; it is only to say that our purposes are different. We can employ the best of his methods without living his life.

3. The *investigative reporter* is frequently an excellent all-around research worker, because the nature of his work has taught him to combine speed with thoroughness. His strength lies in his ability to interview the person or persons who witnesses an event, and to put an account of it in writing for the first time. A good reporter knows how to find his sources, how to ask the right questions, how to interpret responses, and where to find experts who can help him put today's event into the right context—and to do all this under pressure of a publication deadline. When a good reporter turns from daily newspaper reporting to writing a magazine article or a book, he studies background material from the library just as the scholar does, though sometimes not so voluminously.

The principal difference in method between the news reporter and the scholar is that the reporter emphasizes completing his research so that he can produce the written account, whereas the scholar emphasizes the research process itself, with thoroughness as his goal, rather than publication for payment. For researchers, the art lies in combining the strong points of both. The reporter who has learned thoroughness of inquiry from the scholar can become an outstanding journalist, and Pulitzer prizes are won by such writers. The scholar who knows when to stop digging and to start shaping what he has found for presentation, and who is a skilled communicator, can become the author of best-selling books.

4. The *detective* is frequently not far behind the investigative reporter in his all-around ability to find out what he wants to know—but he usually works within the limits of his world of law enforcement. His great asset as a researcher is his familiarity with human behavior patterns within his field. This enables him to cut through a confusion of details much more rapidly than the average person, and determine the handful of most probable places in which to search for answers. He is familiar with official documents, municipal archives, confidential indexes, credit ratings of individuals, and the like. His experience has taught him to reason out the most likely places in which to search for what he wants to know. More than anyone else, the fictional detective, Sherlock Holmes, taught the world the value of thinking a research problem through first—and then looking in the places that offer the greatest promise.

This is a fine list, but Todd is the first to admit that it is not the last word. "New techniques and resources are constantly emerging," he points out. Among those that might be added to Todd's list are:

➤ The *scientist*, who conducts experiments according to the canon of laboratory research
➤ The *clinician*, who, through practice, works toward fresh perceptions and principles, and improved performance
➤ The *philosopher*, who seeks improved understanding through reflection, logical analysis, and dialogue
➤ The *activist*, who discovers fresh ideas, perspectives, and applications for research through reflection and action

Managing Your Intellectual Projects

The use of the word "manage" may surprise or even shock you, which is just my intention. We all have been conditioned to the notion that works of the intellect are *inspired*, subject to one or another of the muses. Experienced researchers know better.

"Scholarship suffers from waste of energy, as a plant suffers from a worm at its root," declared that imperious giant of nineteenth-century scholarship, Theodor Mommsen. "The remedy is organization and concentration."

Recent findings about creative and productive people confirm his idea. The closer you look at the lives of intellectually active people, the clearer it becomes that deft management of your time, energy, and resources can greatly increase your achievements. No one has looked at them more closely than Howard Gruber, the director of the Institute for Cognitive Studies at Rutgers University.

> The people I've studied all tend to be strong, robust, energetic. They have an overall sense of purpose, a feeling of where they are and where they want to go. That goal-directedness guides the choice of a whole set of enterprises and dictates which enterprise to focus on at a given time. Creative people have a network of enterprise. They become the sort of people who can easily handle seemingly different but intimately related activities. They become highly skilled jugglers. Of course, it's not all entirely conscious, but a great deal of it is.

You can sharpen your skills of goal setting, prioritizing, juggling, and getting things done efficiently through the easily available literature on self-management. As an independent you probably have less time and fewer resources available for your studies than do academic researchers, so it is all the more important to make the most of what you have. Such skills may make the difference between enjoyable meandering in your field and "a work of achieved intention," to borrow a beautiful phrase from Robert McClintock.

How about a cram course in getting things done? *How to Get Control of Your Time and Your Life* by Alan Lakein (New York: Penguin, 1973, 1989) will help you find the time for your scholarship and to use that time well. Lakein is no "time nut"—he helps you to work smarter, not harder.

> I'm not a "time and motion" organizer, trying to get everything done in the shortest time with the fewest wasted motions. I try to put more thinking into what people do, not take the thinking out. If you follow my suggestions, you'll probably find yourself thinking more about how you really want to use your time, working less hard, doing more of the things you've always wanted to do, and enjoying your life a lot more.

Much good advice is distilled in the extract that follows, "Writing Up a Project Description" (taken from *This Way Out: A Guide to Alternatives to Traditional College Education* by John Coyne and Tom Hebert, Dutton,

1972, now out of print). You will find this worth reading over each time your inquiries reach a point where a specific unit of work needs to be planned and put down on paper.

Writing Up a Project Description

In the actual writing of the project description, (1) get your story across early, (2) be yourself, (3) be specific, (4) use simple, active language, (5) make the organization of the paper obvious.

Questions to Deal With

➤ Describe the project. List the objectives of the project in order of their importance. How did you happen to select it? What was the original impulse? Describe your search for a project.

➤ What do you anticipate will be major problems in your project? Where are the foul-ups likely to be? What will you do then?

➤ What form is the project going to take? How will you present it? Will the presentation be useful to someone besides yourself?

➤ What people are going to help you on this project? Is it a group? Who will do what? Has it been clearly agreed? How will the group make decisions?

➤ Include a budget listing transportation costs, materials, books, equipment bought or rented, lecture fees, tutorial fees, etc. Also include an estimate of your income for the period of your project.

➤ List the books you think will be helpful. What library or libraries are you going to use?

➤ When will your project be completed and presented? When will it be half-finished?

➤ What other interests, projects or jobs will you have ongoing at the same time? How much time per week or day can you give to the project?

➤ Is there a possibility of your teaching or tutoring someone in this study field after you have finished your project? Are there younger students who might like to work on the project?

➤ How will this project be valuable to you? How does it fit into your educational plans?

➤ Are you going to do the typing?

➤ Who will critique your project? (Your tutor, perhaps a newspaper editor, other students, an audience, etc.)

Betty Friedan:
The Problem That Has No Name

> I was surprised myself at what I was writing, where it was leading. After I finished each chapter, a part of me would wonder, Am I crazy? But there was also a growing feeling of calm, strong, gut-sureness as the clues fitted together, which must be the same kind of feeling a scientist has when he or she zeroes in on a discovery. . . . Only this was not just abstract and conceptual. It meant that I and every other woman I knew had been living a lie. . . .
>
> **Betty Friedan**

The power of the independent mind is best demonstrated in the genesis of movements for social change. Where do the new ideas come from, those that ignite thousands, sometimes millions, of people? Most often, the ideas come from the work of one independent, brilliant, driven thinker or investigator. Think of Rachel Carson's *Silent Spring*, which sparked the environmental movement; Ralph Nader's *Unsafe at Any Speed*, which launched public-interest research in a hundred fields; Michael Harrington's *The Other America*, which inspired the "war on poverty"; Jane Jacobs's *The Death and Life of Great American Cities*, which changed the way we think about urban life. In each of these cases, an independent mind saw something new, important, and shocking and challenged the status quo.

The Feminine Mystique was such a book. "Betty Friedan is to the worldwide sex-role revolution what Tom Paine was to the American revolution," asserts Alvin Toffler, himself an independent who discerned a truth about our time. The book's publication in 1963 propelled Friedan into national and eventual worldwide celebrity, leading her to found the National Organization for Women (NOW).

But how did it all start? What can the *origins* of Friedan's discovery of the "feminine mystique" tell us about the process, the feelings, the *experience* of making our own encounter with new truths in our lives? For Friedan started, not as an organizer, not as a lecturer, not as a spokesperson—but as an independent investigator of "a problem that had no name." "Until I started writing the book, I wasn't even conscious of the woman problem," she confesses.

So where does such an idea, such a career, start?

"Everything I know has come from my own experience," Friedan insists, looking back. That may be a truism *epistemologically*: Who can deny that all each of us knows has come into our minds through experience of one kind or another? But to realize its truth *psychologically* is something else. To really look at our own experience, at the everyday texture of our own lives and those of the people around us, to truly see it for what it is, and to be able to articulate what we see—these are vital and hard-won skills that often distinguish independent thinkers from their academic counterparts who are frequently much more bookish and abstract.

For Friedan, it was no easy matter to take a fresh, hard look at her everyday experience.

> I, like other women, thought there was something wrong with *me* because I didn't have an orgasm waxing the kitchen floor. . . . However much we enjoyed being Junior's and Janey's or Emily's mother, or B. J.'s wife, if we still had ambitions, ideas about ourselves as people in our own right—well, we were simply freaks, neurotics, and we confessed our sin or neurosis to priest or psychoanalyst, and tried hard to adjust. We didn't admit it to each other if we felt there should be more in life than peanut-butter sandwiches with the kids, if throwing powder into the washing machine didn't make us relive our wedding night, if getting the socks or shirts pure white was not exactly a peak experience, even if we did feel guilty about the tattletale gray.
>
> Gradually, without seeing it clearly for quite a while, I came to realize that something is very wrong with the way American women are trying to live their lives today. I sensed it first as a question mark in my own life, as a wife and mother of three small children, half-guiltily, and therefore half-heartedly,

almost in spite of myself, using my abilities and education in work that took me away from home. It was this personal question mark that led me, in 1957, to spend a great deal of time doing an intensive questionnaire of my college classmates, fifteen years after our graduation from Smith. The answers given by two hundred women to those intimate open-ended questions made me realize that what was wrong could not be related to education in the way it was then believed to be. The problems and satisfaction of their lives, and mine, and the way our education had contributed to them, simply did not fit the image of the modern American woman as she was written about in women's magazines, studied and analyzed in classrooms and clinics, praised and damned in a ceaseless barrage of words ever since the end of World War II. There was a strange discrepancy between the reality of our lives as women and the image to which we were trying to conform, the image that I came to call the feminine mystique. I wondered if other women faced this schizophrenic split, and what it meant.

Friedan's first attempts to pursue her project were discouraging. "Betty has gone off her rocker," an editor with whom she had worked for years told her agent. "She has always done a good job for us, but this time only the most neurotic housewife could identify with what she's saying." Friedan read that reaction on the subway, while taking her kids to the pediatrician. She got off, called the agent, and told her: "I'll have to write a book to get this into print."

Obviously, at that point she needed support in a way that every independent scholar will understand. It is one thing for an academic to undertake a major research project, with a secure salary and plenty of time off to think, investigate, and write. It is quite another for a self-employed nonfiction writer to embark on such a venture. Even modest recognition and help can be immensely supportive. Friedan recalls: "I wouldn't have even started [the book] if the New York Public Library had not, at just the right time, opened the Frederick Lewis Allen Room, where writers working on a book could get a desk, six months at a time, rent free. I got a baby-sitter three days a week and took the bus from Rockland County to the city and somehow managed to prolong the six months to two years in the Allen Room. . . ."

How did she go about her work? "My methods were simply those of a reporter on the trail of a story, except I soon discovered that this was no ordinary story. For the startling pattern that began to emerge, as one clue led me to another in far-flung fields of modern thought and life, defied not only the conventional image but the basic psychological assumptions about women."

The trail led through "the literature," of course, including the scientific studies that had been done and the speculations of the leading theorists.

> I found a few pieces of the puzzle in previous studies of women; but not many, for women in the past have been studied in terms of the feminine mystique. The Mellon study of Vassar women was provocative, Simone de Beauvoir's insights into French women, the work of Mirra Komarovsky, A. H. Maslow, Alva Myrdal. I found even more provocative the growing body of new psychological thought on the question of man's identity, whose implications for women seem not to have been realized.

These are just the sorts of sources that an academic might use in beginning such a project. But significantly, Friedan probed them in a way that revealed a truth that had eluded the experts. She early came to the conclusion that

> the experts in a great many fields [had] been holding pieces of the truth under their microscopes for a long time without realizing it. I found pieces of it in certain new research and theoretical developments in psychological, social, and biological science whose implications for women seem never to have been examined. I found many clues by talking to suburban doctors, gynecologists, obstetricians, child-guidance clinicians, pediatricians, high-school guidance counselors, college professors, marriage counselors, psychiatrists, and ministers—questioning them not on their theories, but on their actual experience in treating American women. I became aware of a growing body of evidence, much of which has not been reported publicly because it does not fit current modes of thought about women—evidence which throws into question the standards of feminine normality, feminine adjustment, feminine fulfillment, and feminine maturity by which most women are still trying to live.

Beyond seeing something in existing research that had been ignored by others, Friedan branched out in ways that most professors probably would not think or would lack the opportunity for. "I found further evidence by questioning those who treat women's ills and problems. And I traced the growth of the mystique by talking to editors of women's magazines, advertising motivational researchers, and theoretical experts on women in the fields of psychology, psychoanalysis, anthropology, sociology, and family-life education."

Finally Friedan did her own research, in order to test, refine, and confirm (or disconfirm) her hypotheses.

> The puzzle did not begin to fit together until I interviewed at some depth, from two hours to two days each, eighty women at certain crucial points in their life cycle—high school and college girls facing or evading the question of who they were; young housewives and mothers for whom, if the mystique were right, there should be no such question and who thus had no name for the problem troubling them; and women who faced a jumping-off point at forty. These women, some tortured, some serene, gave me the final clues, and the most damning indictment of the feminine mystique.

The powerful "mix of methods" that I have advocated for the independent scholar served Friedan well. She recalls how she acquired "those tools with which I ultimately was able to pierce through the Freudian mystique of femininity." Her training in psychology and its research and experimental techniques, and her work as a clinical psychologist and in applied social-science research were important. But she also affirms the value of *nonacademic* training and experiences that augmented and in some ways corrected the academic perspective.

> In my years after college as a reporter for the labor press, I learned to pierce through the fog of words and even psychology to the grubby economic underside of American reality. And as a reporter and a writer, I learned to get the story, where the answer is never known at the beginning, as earlier, as a student psychologist and social scientist . . . I'd learned to test hypotheses and to listen for the hidden clues in the patient's own words and actions.

As the project gained momentum, Friedan underwent a change that I often have noted in the progress of such inquiries. What started as an inchoate, vague impulse in a certain direction—the "messy beginnings" discussed in Chapter 1—took on shape and a distinct direction. Imperceptibly, the project became not only clearly focused, but also intensely compelling. Friedan's quest had begun like a "precarious accident," but toward the end, she recalls, "I have never experienced anything as powerful, truly mystical, as the forces that seemed to take me over. . . ." The feeling was not without its disturbing undertones. "It's frightening when you're starting on a new road that no one has been on before. You don't know how far it's going to take you until you look back and realize how far, how very far you've gone."

One could write an entire book on how far *The Feminine Mystique* has taken Betty Friedan. Fortunately, she herself has done so with her follow-up volume, *It Changed My Life*. One small incident in that fascinating and significant story is so relevant to independent scholarship that it will be told here.

> When *The Feminine Mystique* was at the printer's, and my last child was in school all day, I decided I would go back to school myself and get my Ph.D. Armed with my publisher's announcement, a copy of my summa cum laude undergraduate degree and twenty-years-back graduate record, and the New World Foundation report of the educational project I had dreamed up and run in Rockland County, I went to see the head of the social psychology department at Columbia. He was very tolerant and kind, but surely, at forty-two, after all those undisciplined years as a housewife, I must understand that I wouldn't be able to meet the rigors of full-time graduate study for a Ph.D. and the mastery of statistics that was required. "But I used statistics throughout the book," I pointed out. He looked blank. "Well, my dear," he said, "what do you want to bother your head getting a Ph.D. for, anyhow?"

The second response came from one of the nation's most distinguished social scientists, Amitai Etzioni, after the book was published. His was a handsome homage to this independent scholar and others like her, who have played such an important role in our intellectual life. "This is one of those rare books we are endowed with only once in several decades; a volume which launches a major social movement, toward a more humane and just society. Betty Friedan is a liberator of women *and* men."

When I asked Betty Friedan what overall lesson or moral she would draw for independent scholars from these experiences in conceiving, researching, and writing *The Feminine Mystique*, she said:

> It probably has something to do with becoming intellectually autonomous. From my own experience—and those of other researchers and writers I know such as Al Toffler, Caroline Bird, even you, Ron—I have the sense that the

independent investigator often has a stronger sense of self, and sense of mission, than the institutionalized academic. Maybe the reason is that she or he is pioneering on an unknown road. We free-lancers, for that's what many of us are, have to structure a growth pattern for ourselves—we can't just settle into a professorial "role" that's already there, provided by an institution. In many cases we have to innovate, to find something truly new and important, if we want to interest editors and readers, and command a following. No one pays much for rehashed, dull, or derivative writing—unlike the recognition which such stuff can command in academe.

The net result of all these pressures, if you can cope with them reasonably successfully, is a good, healthy, strong sense of taking control of your own life. That can be a powerful element in anyone's personality. It's a taste of what the women's movement did for so many of us. The most frequent—and the most gratifying—thing that readers write or say to me about my book is "It changed my life." Well, that book and the movement clearly changed *mine.* And I think that even in areas and fields that do not have this enormous import for our whole culture and society, a personal experience in following one's own mind where it leads can change your life for the better.[1]

CHAPTER SIX

Wherewithal

W e have become such an institutionalized society that most people seem to feel there is something vaguely suspicious about those who present themselves as individuals, to be judged on their personal qualities and accomplishments. What independent scholar has not been confronted with the officious secretary's query: "Who are you *with*?" Once, America was known as a nation where institutions were understood to be merely the lengthened shadows of the individuals who created and composed them. Today, the reverse is the case: Individuals derive their legitimacy, in many people's eyes, from the shadowy institutional aegis under which they operate.

"I noticed the distrust when I became independent," recalls Michael Marien, now editor of *Future Survey*, who suffered in the early 1970s from a "reduction in force" at the research institute where he was employed. "Invitations to lecture and consult seemed to decline noticeably, although I felt that I was continuing to grow wiser and more knowledgeable. It made me wonder, for the first time, how much my institutional affiliation had to do with the invitations I had gotten, and how much unjust discrimination takes place against people who are just as able have just as much to offer, but who are not connected to an institution."

More damaging than a general distrust can be the disdain directed at one's findings because one is not affiliated with the "right" sort of institution. A shocking incident of this kind made news after a story appeared on the front page of *The New York Times* (May 4, 1981) about a theory that the exodus of the Israelites from Egypt coincided with a volcanic eruption on

Thera, an island north of Crete. Professor Hans Goedicke, the chairman of the department of Near Eastern studies at Johns Hopkins University, argued that a tidal wave resulting from this eruption flooded coastal lands and thereby cut off the pursuing Egyptians.

A few days after the story appeared, the *Times* received a letter from an independent scholar, Joel Block, a science teacher at the McMahon High School in Norwalk, Connecticut. Block congratulated the professor on his "excellent idea" and enclosed an article he had written in 1974, arguing the same basic thesis, and a second one, published in 1979, called "The Exodus to Mount Sinai: A Discussion of Geological Phenomena," which further pressed the case. Block's findings had been rejected by major publishing houses and leading scholarly journals, thus depriving them of wider exposure. "I have no Hopkins title or resources," Block wrote to the *Times*, "[but am] a mere high school teacher. I've even heard it said that if my articles were any good, I would be at some college, not in a public school."

Fred Hechinger, a writer for the *Times*, sympathized with Block's chagrin. "It's not what you know, but who knows what," he remarked in a review and comment published on June 2. "At the heart of the matter is society's tendency to insist on credentials before listening seriously to a claim of new discoveries or ideas. As a place inside the establishment becomes more important, unknown scholars, authors, and researchers often find it harder to get a hearing. Only rarely . . . does the public acknowledge that an unknown and unanointed person may have noteworthy capacities."

Even more poignant than such insults to their work are the feelings of exclusion that often trouble even the most capable independent scholars. Gloria Erlich, a literary scholar in Princeton, New Jersey, talks movingly of her experience in attending the Modern Language Association's annual convention without a university affiliation to list on her name tag. "The phrase 'the bottom line' kept popping into my head, meaning the line below your name on the badge or in the program. To have nothing below your name may mean that your paper will be rejected because an unaffiliated speaker usually does not add formal prestige to a program. It can be a very naked feeling: Strangers glance at that line first, to see whether or not you're 'important' enough to merit their attention."

Obtaining a Title or Affiliation

Independent scholars can legitimately obtain a title or affiliation that will serve many of the purposes that traditional academic ones serve. Teaching part-time, an affiliation with a nontraditional institution, becoming a scholar-in-residence, joining a professional organization, or founding an institution will all provide valuable connections while not compromising independence.

Teach in a Continuing Education Program

Many institutions will provide not only an academic affiliation but also an "adjunct" title to acknowledged experts who teach on their continuing education faculties. Often these otherwise-employed professionals teach only one course, which meets one evening a week. Some of the best extension faculties in the country consist almost entirely of such people. Here are examples of such titles from a recent New York University catalog: Adjunct Associate Professor of Economics, Adjunct Assistant Professor of Film, Adjunct Associate Professor of Semitic Languages, Adjunct Assistant Professor in Anthropology, Adjunct Assistant Professor of Interior Design.

Another option is an affiliation as a research associate with a college or university or with a specialized unit within one. Columbia University, for example, appoints a wide variety of independent scholars to such positions in several of its research institutes. "It costs the university nothing, and benefits both of us," says Barbara Assiz, an anthropologist specializing in Central Asian studies, who is associated with the Southern Asia Institute.

> Library privileges are one of the "perks"—the other that the arrangement simply enables me to participate in a number of Institute activities—seminars, conferences, etc. When I publish reviews or articles, I credit the Institute, which adds some to its visibility in the field. Occasionally, on an *ad hoc* basis, I'll undertake a special project, such as chairing and programming a seminar, on a subject of special interest to me. The arrangement is ideal for me. I prefer not to take a regular teaching position, since I want to operate as a freelance researcher, free to seize opportunities which come up regularly but unpredictably, to make field trips to the Far East for further research. I've done far

more field research than many professors in my field, in large part because I've maintained a good publication record, successfully competed for field research grants, and remained active in my area of research. This was partly possible because, in turn, I have not been tied down to a teaching schedule on a campus, and I've not been overburdened preparing undergrad courses in general anthropology. I also remain active as an "informal" supervisor of four grad students in various parts of the country.

Affiliate with a Nontraditional Institution

Several nontraditional postsecondary institutions locally and nationwide use highly qualified teachers who are often unaffiliated with a traditional college or university. For example, I am currently on the faculty of Beacon College, which operates nationwide out of Boston. Beacon offers individualized collegiate and master's level education to students throughout the country by having them work with "program advisors" (faculty members) who are expert in the fields that students are studying and are also experienced at helping students plan independent programs of study. Beacon is fully accredited, and I have found my experiences with the students in its program an important part of my own intellectual life; the college also provides me, and can provide other qualified independent scholars, with an affiliation and a title.

Another kind of nontraditional institution is the "free university." These community-based, grass-roots adult education operations offer courses in quite a few communities, including cities such as Denver, Washington, Providence, Wichita, and Manhattan (Kansas, not New York). Look around for one in your community. For a report on their activities nationwide, a portrayal of how they work, and a list of them around the country, see *The Free University* by William Draves (Chicago: Follet, 1980).

Become a Scholar-in-Residence

➤ Irving Levitas is scholar-in-residence at Temple Emanuel in Yonkers, New York.

➤ Ann Gordon is scholar-in-residence at the Women's Center on the campus of the University of Wisconsin in Madison.

➤ Stephen Frick is humanist-in-residence at the Second Horizon Senior Center in Colorado Springs, Colorado.

➤ A cadre of philosophers recently served in New York City hospitals as "philosophers-in-residence."

Arrangements such as these are most often initiated by an independent scholar who has something important to offer and would enjoy an affiliation. Once offered, they are usually warmly received. Libraries appoint scholars-in-residence in history, the arts, mathematics, and computer sciences. Environmental Centers appoint independent experts, perhaps chosen from among their own most dedicated members, as independent scholars associated with the organization. Leading industrial laboratories encourage serious scientific investigations by independent researchers. Museums in the arts and sciences foster original work by qualified investigators using their facilities, resources, and prestige.

As a scholar-in-residence at Temple Emanuel in Yonkers, New York, Irving Levitas oversees a library of books in his field (Jewish thought), lectures throughout the community to colleges, voluntary organizations, and civic groups, confers with students from local schools, teaches adult education courses, and writes a weekly column on Jewish literature and history for the local paper. "There are enough scholars who talk to other scholars, but not enough to talk to the people," he asserts.

Join an Appropriate Organization

Simply being a member of a scholarly organization carries weight with certain people and institutions outside scholarly life, whose cooperation thus may be gained. Among such groups are the Academy of Independent Scholars, the American Academy of Political and Social Sciences, and specialized societies such as the New York Microscopists Society and the International Society for General Semantics.

You may find it possible to associate with one of the many think tanks throughout the country. These are policy research organizations that regularly engage experts in various fields of social research on projects. The Academy for Educational Development in New York City is one that is well established and highly regarded in its field.

Do-It-Yourself

You, too, can create an institution. The Learning Group, ECR Associates, The Learner's Forum, The Atlantic Institute, the Princeton Center for Alternative Futures are among the many organizations created over the past few years by individuals.

When he first started out as an independent scholar, Lloyd deMause, the founder of the Institute for Research in Psychohistory in New York City, had expensive stationery printed for The Atlantic Institute. It was not a deception: he was the institute and never claimed otherwise. If other people assumed that great-looking type on fancy paper meant that the Institute was a major institution, it was *their* problem—and his advantage. The Institute—or, more precisely, the letterhead—solved many pesky problems for this fledgling independent scholar. It helped him in obtaining review copies (which he diligently reviewed), securing lecture engagements (which he carried off splendidly), and meeting other interesting senior scholars (for whom he proved a rewarding correspondent).

Michael Marien, whose experience was cited at the start of this section, used this approach.

> Realizing that my problems stemmed from the lack of a suitable institutional affiliation, I concocted Information for Policy Design as a name under which to do business, and found that I was associating with others who did the same: Hazel and Carter Henderson's Princeton Center for Alternative Futures, John McClaughry's Institute for Liberty and Community, Bob Swann's International Independence Institute—and, by coincidence, my brother-in-law, an astronomer who writes textbooks and teaches an occasional course, called his activities Interstellar Media.

Grants and Awards[1]

It sounded as if a convention of independent scholars had opened a bottle and discovered a genie, who would transform their most outrageous wishes into reality. Twenty-one "exceptionally talented individuals," ranging from a twenty-one-year-old physicist to a seventy-six-year-old novelist, were each to receive awards of from $24,000 to $60,000 a year for five years from a Chicago foundation. The program, according to the front-page story in *The*

New York Times, would leave the winners "free to spend their prize money and time as they choose without obliging them to produce a scholarly paper or artistic work," in the hopes that they would make some significant discoveries or other contributions to society.

Unfortunately, most of us are unlikely ever to come across that particular genie. The story does bring to mind, however, the other, though usually smaller, sources of fiscal help. You are not likely to attract them by taking out an ad in the *Times*: "Scholar Needs Funds to Finance Project." (We wonder, though, what might happen if you took out a similar notice describing your project in a relevant professional journal?) Gaining the interest of foundations generally involves pinpointing the appropriate potential sources of assistance, and convincing the foundation that your project is worthy of its help or reward.

Basically, there are two types of funding sources to consider: those that are provided to finance the undertaking of a particular research project, study, or book (grants); and those that are given as a reward for a project, study, or book which already has been completed (awards).

Grants

Grants often are viewed as panaceas for research funding. And for many organizations and academics, they may well be that. As far as the independent scholar is concerned, however, these are fantasylands that are apt to descend into the rather muddy waters of reality very quickly.

In the first place, as the specialists at the Foundation Center Library put it: "The majority of foundations limit their giving to nonprofit organizations; they will not even consider your proposal unless you have a letter from the Internal Revenue Service indicating approved tax-exempt status. . . ." Only about two thousand of the twenty-two thousand private foundations across the country offer substantive grants to individuals. That most foundation money is now directed to nonprofits is primarily a result of the administrative and reporting requirements of the Tax Reform Act of 1969.

Your eyes may widen when a research librarian hand you the hefty tome titled *Foundation Grants to Individuals*. But you will soon discover that most of these grants are for academic study on one level or another, usually in the form of scholarships or fellowships for graduate or postgraduate research. In focusing on the grants for research rather than academic study, you will make a further discovery: Most such programs are limited to, or sharply skewed toward, people employed as academics. "You can't even compete for money from the feds unless you are ensconced in an institution," author Tom Hebert has pointed out. "It's as if the government's unspoken principle is that all good ideas come out of institutions. What an un-American idea!"

Only recently have a few of the more enlightened foundations come forward to fund important work by individuals on an equitable competitive basis, regardless of the employment status of the investigator. How can you find out if there are grants available to independent scholars in your particular field? Although there are literally scores of directories listing thousands of grants, most of these directories are geared to nonprofit organizations and students. Grants for independent individuals are to be found scattered throughout a wide variety of resource materials—from the basic directories listed below, to magazines such as the *Whole Nonprofit Catalog*, to pamphlets issued by organizations in various fields, such as the American Historical Association's "Grants and Fellowships of Interest to Historians" and the American Council of Learned Societies' "Aids to Individual Scholars" among many, many others. Using just one of these tools probably will not be very productive, especially as the number of unaffiliated grants available is so limited. Finding the right grant for you is likely to include a bit of serendipity, but there is no substitute for a comprehensive search.

Your best bet, therefore, is to find a library that specializes in these materials and has staff who are particularly adept at using them. This is where the Foundation Center, a national nonprofit service organization, comes in. The Center operates a network of over 190 reference collections, including at least one in every state. They are available for free public use.

These reference collections fall within two basic categories. The first and most useful consists of the four reference libraries operated by the Center, which offer the widest variety of services for users and the most comprehensive collections of materials. These include all of the Center's publications; books, services, and periodicals on foundations and philanthropy; and foundation annual reports, newsletters, and press clippings. The New York and Washington, D.C. libraries contain the IRS returns for all currently active private foundations in the United States. The Cleveland and San Francisco libraries contain the IRS records for those foundations in the midwestern and western states, respectively.

The second type, Foundation Center Cooperating Collections, are libraries, community foundations, and other nonprofit agencies that provide public access to a core collection of Foundation Center publications and a variety of supplemental materials and services in areas useful to grant seekers. The core collection includes *Foundation Grants to Individuals*.

A listing of the Foundation Center reference collections throughout the country can be found in Appendix 3 on page 242. Most handbooks on securing grants, including those mentioned below, also include a listing of Foundation Center collections.

If those special collections are not convenient, you are likely to find at least a few of the basic grants directories at any large public or academic library. The Foundation Center library staff recommends that individuals start with the following three; bear in mind, however, that these publications are geared primarily (although not entirely) to academic study.

> *Foundation Grants to Individuals*, compiled by the Foundation Center itself, has descriptions of grant programs for individuals offered by about two thousand foundations. Address, telephone number, contact person, officers, financial information, application periods, and other relevant data are included for each foundation. There are nine general sections: undergraduate and graduate scholarships; educational loans; fellowships; grants for foreign individuals; general welfare and medical assistant; residencies, internships and in-kind services; grants restricted to company employees or locations; and other grants whose purpose and eligibility requirements are unspecified. Also included: general information on the Foundation Center and articles on grant seeking; a bibliography of other sources of information about grants; and separate indexes of grants by subject, grants restricted by state, grants that include travel funds, company-related grants, grants for students at specific educational institutions, and foundations.

➤ The *Annual Register of Grant Support* is published by R. R. Bowker and lists similar information about approximately 2,300 grant support programs offered by government agencies, public and private foundations, corporations, community trusts, unions, educational and professional associations, and special-interest organizations. It is arranged by broad subject area: multiple special purpose, international affairs and area studies, special populations, urban and regional affairs, education, sciences—multiple disciplines, social sciences, physical sciences, life sciences, and technology and industry. It also has useful introductory information and separate subject, organization, program, geographic, and personnel indexes.

➤ *The Grants Register*, published by St. Martin's Press, provides somewhat less detailed information about each grant program than the previous directories, but it is far more international in scope. It includes information about assistance from government agencies and international, national, and private organizations in the following categories: scholarships, fellowships, and research grants; exchange opportunities, vacation study awards and travel grants; grants-in-aid—including equipment, publication, and translation grants, and funds for attending seminars, courses, conferences, and so on; grants for all kinds of artistic or scientific projects; competitions, prizes, and honoraria—including awards in recognition or support of creative work; professional and vocational awards—including opportunities for academic and administrative staff of educational institutions; and special awards—for refugees, minority groups, and so forth, and funds for students in unexpected financial difficulties. An extensive subject index as well as an index of awards and awarding bodies and a bibliography are included.

Additional sources of grant information can be found in the "Bibliography of Funding for Individuals." It has sections on grants in the fields of arts, general studies, humanities, international interests, mathematics and science, medicine and health, and minorities and women.

To use these similar grants directories most effectively, you should begin by defining your project as broadly as possible. Use the subject indexes to their best advantage, consulting as many relevant entries as possible. (If you are researching the effects of a particular drug on newborns, for example, check under the name of the drug, under "drugs" in general, under the type of drug, and under related topics such as medication, and such titles as newborns, neonatal, infancy, pregnancy, even health.) Then comes the rather tedious process of referring to each grant in the main body of the directories, reading and evaluating each on a case-by-case basis to find those that are most appropriate to your specific project. Look for foundations for which your work seems to be "a natural." If you are willing to sacrifice some of your independence, perhaps you can tie your project in more closely with the goals of a relevant foundation to increase your chances of getting its grant.

In using these directories, you should also be alert for certain kinds of data that will help you determine not only whether your project is appropriate, but also whether you are qualified for a particular grant and whether the grant is worth your time and effort in applying for it. Reprinted on the following page are sample entries from the *Annual Register of Grant Support* to illustrate some of the things you should look for. Be aware, however, that when you have requested and received more detailed information from a funding source about a particular grant program, you may find additional stipulations and qualifications.

Once you have pinpointed your potential grant sources and secured the necessary application forms, you will have to prepare a proposal. There are many resources available to help grant seekers write effective proposals, but once again the user must be cautioned that many of these resources are geared to grant seekers who are affiliated with nonprofit institutions or who are seeking funds for academic studies or research. Much of the general information these resources present will be very helpful, but a good deal of it may seem irrelevant.

Resources for help in getting grants range from courses such as those offered around the country by The Grantsmanship Center (a nonprofit organization based at 1125 West Sixth Street, fifth floor, Los Angeles, CA 90017; telephone (213) 482-9860) to workshops and seminars conducted by a wide range of colleges and professional associations.

Other resources include a plethora of books, pamphlets, and periodical articles. Among the many standard books on the subject, available at most libraries, are Robert Lefferts's *Getting a Grant: How to Write Successful Grant*

What to Look for When You Are Looking for Grants

NATIONAL ASSOCIATION FOR
RETARDED CITIZENS, INC. [2362]
2709 Avenue E. East
Arlington, Texas 76011
(817) 261-4961
Founded: 1950

AREAS OF INTEREST:
Mentally retarded persons of all ages; education; agencies; medical care and rehabilitation.

TYPE:
Research grants to support promising projects in the mental retardation field. Assistance is available for programmatic and preventive research that promises to affect the daily lives of mentally retarded citizens and their families.

YEAR PROGRAM STARTED:
1952.

PURPOSE:
To promote the welfare of the mentally retarded citizens of all ages by fostering the advancement of research, treatment, services and facilities, and by developing broader public understanding of the problem of mental retardation.

LEGAL BASIS:
Nonprofit (Tennessee) corporation.

ELIGIBILITY:
Individuals with demonstrated competence to do the research that they propose are eligible.

FINANCIAL DATA:
Grants vary in amount, depending upon the needs and nature of the request. Funds may be awarded for personnel, equipment, expendable supplies and travel. *Amount of support per award:* Varies. Requests under $5,000 preferred. Total amount of support: $11,000 for the year 1979.

NUMBER OF APPLICANTS MOST
RECENT YEAR: 7

NUMBER OF AWARDS:
2 for the year ending December 1979. Matching fund requirements: Preferred, but not required.

COOPERATIVE FUNDING PROGRAMS:
Association is willing to engage in cooperative funding; however, it has done so only on a limited basis in previous years.

APPLICATION INFORMATION:
Official application materials are available upon request to the Research Department at the address above.
Duration: Usually 1 to 2 years, nonrenewable.
Deadline: None.

TRUSTEE:
Jack May, Chairman, Research Advisory Committee

OFFICERS:
Philip Roos, Executive Director
Ronald Neman, Research Director

ADDRESS INQUIRIES TO:
Director of Research

SPECIAL STIPULATIONS:
Applications must be made in four priority areas established by the Board.

Hints

Eligibility

Find programs that stress "individuals." Look for indications that requirements are flexible and open, such as "demonstrated competence" or "qualified investigators."

Avoid programs that require nonprofit or academic affiliations or special degree requirements that you may not have.

Financing

Look for specific limitations in the amount awarded per grant. If information is not specific, compare the total amount given in a year to the number of awards.

Chances of Award

Compare the number of awards given annually to the number of applicants to find an appropriate ratio (for example, two out of seven).

NATIONAL CENTER FOR THE
PREVENTION AND CONTROL
OF RAPE [2363]
5600 Fishers Lane, Room 15-99
Rockville, Maryland 20857
(301) 443-1910
Founded: 1976

AREAS OF INTEREST:
The National Center for the Prevention and Control of Rape, established within the National Institute of Mental Health, is the Institute's focal point for activities related to the social problem of sexual assault. The Center supports studies of the causes of rape, laws dealing with rape, the treatment of victims, and the effectiveness of existing programs to prevent and control rape.

TYPE:
The Center supports research and research-demonstration projects dealing with rape prevention and treatment. Applications for clinical/services training grants are also being accepted.

YEAR PROGRAM STARTED:
April 1976.

PURPOSE:
To support research and research-demonstration projects; to disseminate information; to develop and distribute training materials; to provide technical assistance. To develop, implement, and evaluate promising models of mental health and related services for rape victims, their families, and offenders.

LEGAL BASE:
Public Law 94-63, Title III, Part D authorized the establishment of the NCPCR within the National Institute of Mental Health.

ELIGIBILITY:
Investigators affiliated with public or nonprofit private agencies including state, local, or regional government agencies, universities, academic or research institutions, and other nonprofit organizations and groups may apply for Basic and Applied Research Studies and Research-Demonstration Projects. Community Mental Health Centers may apply for Research-Demonstration Projects on Consultation and Education.

FINANCIAL DATA:
Grants vary in amount depending on the nature of the project. Recent awards range from approximately $40,000 to $150,000 per year.
Total amount of support: $2.7 million for the year ending September 30, 1980.

NUMBER OF APPLICANTS MOST RECENT YEAR: 52 applications received in fiscal year 1980.

NUMBER OF AWARDS: 7 research grants funded in fiscal year 1980.

APPLICATION INFORMATION:
Information concerning application procedures will be supplied on request.
Deadline: March 1, July 1, November 1, with announcement in December, April, and July. Earliest starting date is nine months after submission.

ADDRESS INQUIRIES TO:
Chief, National Center for the Prevention and Control of Rape.

NOTE: These excerpts have been taken from the *Annual Register of Grant Support* (Bowker), and are reprinted with permission of the publisher.

Proposals (Englewood Cliffs, N.J.: Prentice-Hall, 1978), Virginia P. White's *Grants: How to Find Out About Them and What to Do Next* (Plenum, 1975), and *Foundation Fundamentals: A Guide for Grantseekers* (The Foundation Center, 1981). These as well as others like them will in turn refer you to additional handbooks, articles, and brochures, as well as to many other sources for locating grant information.

Alternatives to Grants

The process of grants hunting may become somewhat demoralizing for the independent scholar who spends hours researching potential sources only to find that the best ones are reserved for nonprofit organizations, academics, and the like. If you find the perfect grant—and win it—it will probably seem worth the effort. But what if you don't?

Fortunately, there are some other places out there in the waters of financing scholarship. These may not be fantasylands either, but they may be in far more productive seas as far as the individual is concerned. There are several alternatives, all of which are worthy of consideration.

One is to seek funding from corporations. Your project might, for example, appeal to a particular corporation because it could help the users of a product manufactured by that corporation. Finding such a corporation can be much more difficult than traditional grant seeking is, particularly because corporate giving is often done on a much more informal basis. It can be like groping in the dark because there are fewer sources of information available than there are for foundation giving.

To make things even more difficult, corporations are like foundations in focusing their giving on nonprofit organizations rather than individuals. It's not that an individual could not convince some companies to provide support for an appropriate project—especially if the area of interest relates to the nature of their business or if there is a clear public relations value in such support—but it's only fair to point out the severe limitations.

In selecting an appropriate corporation, one should characterize the interests of that corporation—using such resources as the Foundation Center's extensive *National Directory of Corporate Giving*—and appeal to those interests in the funding request. Again, it may prove beneficial, if you are willing to sacrifice some control, to shape your project toward those interests.

Your request should be for a specified project rather than for a commitment for continued support.

You might also consider approaching local companies or institutions for funding on the same kind of basis. Research into a particular aspect of a community's history might serve the interests of a local historical society or public library; a socially beneficial project of another nature might appeal to a local bank or corporation in the interest of public relations.

Independent scholars might seek "sponsoring" organizations to receive a grant on their behalf. Because existing nonprofit organizations are eligible for so many more grants than are individuals, such an organization could serve as a conduit for those grants for you. If the local historical society were interested in your research project but did not have the funds itself to finance it, perhaps it could serve as the recipient of a grant that would. In that case, we suggest that *you* do the legwork in locating the appropriate grant sources, and offer to do the paperwork as well. If you appeal to the organization's own goals and interests, and save it the time and labor that it might not be adequately staffed to handle, you will be eliminating a possible reason for refusal.

A similar and particularly interesting possibility is to approach one of the numerous magazines that have turned nonprofit because of postal rate increases to serve as a sponsoring organization for you.

One of the disadvantages of seeking corporate funds or receiving a grant under the auspices of an organization is, of course, that you may be losing some of your control, your independence. A partial solution to this problem is to form your own nonprofit organization! After all, if nonprofits are the folks who are getting most of the grant money, why can't you have part of that action?

Incorporating is not nearly as difficult a process as it sounds, but the energy required to get started can create a big drain on one's creativity. It *is* time consuming; things such as program plans and budgets must be submitted to the Internal Revenue Service for approval. The trick is to get it right the first time, using resources such as those available at the Foundation Center Library, and obtaining legal assistance if necessary.

Awards

If you are willing to postpone your rewards until after you have completed your research, there's yet another land out in those financing waters. Thousands of organizations, societies, associations, and corporations offer a wide variety of awards, honors, and prizes for achievements in particular fields. These may be particularly productive waters as far as the independent scholar is concerned, because, unlike most grants, these awards are made mainly to individuals. Moreover, the vast majority of these awards are not tied to academic study or affiliations.

> The American Physical Society International Prize for New Materials, a $5,000 prize established by the IBM Corporation, is awarded annually to a scientist of any nationality "to recognize and encourage outstanding achievement in the science and application of new materials, including theoretical and experimental work contributing significantly to the understanding of such materials."

> The Society for Italian Historical Studies offers the Helen and Howard K. Marrao Prize of $250 annually "for recognition of a distinguished and scholarly work of book or essay length dealing with Italian cultural history or the cultural relations between the United States and Italy." It also awards a $200 prize to a "young scholar" for the best unpublished manuscript in Italian history submitted during the year.

> The Society for Computer Simulation has awarded $500 annually to individuals "for outstanding contributions to the art and science of simulation," including a single contribution of theory, design, or application; an accumulation of worthwhile contributions over an extended time; or contributions to the field of simulation education in teaching and writing.

> The American Philosophical Society recognizes "the best essay of real merit on the science and philosophy of jurisprudence" with a diploma and the $2,000 Henry M. Philips Prize for its author.

Although these examples and thousands of others like them tend to be less bountiful than grants—several hundreds of dollars instead of several thousands, for example—they do offer benefits that may have a long-range significance for your scholarly endeavors. They restrict your work as might financing through a grant, whether corporate or institutional; and they are often preferred for a general series of "achievements" over a period of time rather than for a specific project. Even an award that carries no financial re-muneration (some are in the form of certificates, medals, and the like) of-fers short- and long-term advantages. The credibility established by an award on your vita can open doors to other awards, grants, professional positions, consultant work, publication opportunities, and so forth.

The easiest way to find out which awards are available in your field and whether you are eligible to get them is to consult a directory called *Awards, Honors, & Prizes*, which is available in most large libraries. It is edited by Gita Seligman and published by Gale Research, Inc. The directory lists more than sixteen thousand awards and prizes for achievements in such areas as adver-tising and public relations, art, business, government, finance, science, edu-cation, engineering, literature, technology, sports, religion, public affairs, radio and television, politics, librarianship, fashion, medicine, law, publish-ing, international affairs, transportation, architecture, journalism, motion pictures, music, photography, theatre, and the performing arts. The bulk of the volume is made up of "awards for service, achievement, etc. which are incidental results of personal or professional endeavors." Also included are some of the better-known competitions and events in which winning is the sole objective. Scholarships, fellowships, and study awards to students are not included.

The main section of the book is arranged alphabetically by the name of the organization making or sponsoring the award. Each entry includes the organization's address, the exact title or name of the award, its purpose and terms of eligibility, its exact form (for example, a medal, citation, scroll, sum of money, and so on), and, if it is different from the sponsor, the name of the person or organization that established the award. In addition to a list of subjects and a cross-referencing system through which one seeking information about awards is directed to appropriate subjects, the directory has an extensive subject index in which the awards granted in each field are listed along with the sponsoring body and the page numbers for the main section of the volume where the listings appear. A complete alphabetical index to the specific name of each award is also included.

One last easy, useful, but oft-forgotten source of information about awards and grants in particular fields: the thousands of professional jour-nals that sit on the shelves of individuals and libraries around the country.

Many of us read only those articles and columns in our periodicals that deal with particular topics that interest us, bypassing completely the other sections. Frequently, those other sections contain announcements of awards and grants in our fields.

Other Sources of Financial Support

Until the grant folks have informed you that your check is in the mail, there are several other ways you might consider funding your research:

> ➤ writing on your subject for pay—for journals, magazines, newspapers, or under a book publisher's advance
> ➤ teaching or lecturing
> ➤ consulting
> ➤ creating an income-producing organization in your field
> ➤ finding employment congruent with your interests
> ➤ finding a patron

To begin thinking creatively about such possibilities, apply this basic principle: Consider your field in a fresh way—from the *outside*. Instead of focusing on what is important to you, or to your peers in the field, brainstorm about what might be of interest to others. What kinds of people and what sorts of organizations might find your expertise useful or necessary or enjoyable? What topics or aspects might be presented, and in what new ways, to engage their attention, interest, and support?

Does this sound like an unlikely approach for your field? That is what many historians thought ten years ago, before some of the more enterprising among them began asking such questions of themselves, one another, and the great world outside academic history. The answers have led to the burgeoning of "public history"—a congeries of activities through which historians are being paid to "do history" outside academe, for organizations ranging from government agencies to private corporations to nonprofit groups. Historians have plied their scholarly craft on behalf of sponsors and employers such as Dataproducts Corporation and the Los Angeles International Airport, as well as for conventional patrons such as the State of California Office of Planning and Research, the Historical American Engineering Record, and the United States Forest Service. Some have organized their own public history consulting and research firms; others have written and edited for a wide public; still others have designed and created exhibitions, films, conferences, and other products and events for a variety of sponsors. Many have taken jobs as research associates, staff associates in appropriate organizations, policy advisers, and contract project managers. So pervasive have such opportunities and accomplishments become for historians, that the field has generated its own journal, *The Public Historian*, devoted to "the professional application of history and the historical method of research outside of the academic environment for the benefit of the community, government, and business sectors." [2]

Perhaps your field seems less susceptible to practical application or widespread dissemination than history is. Let us say you are a philosopher. Certainly *philosophers* cannot hang out shingles, offering to serve clients and organizations for a fee. Or can they?

For four years philosophers worked, as philosophers, within several major hospitals in the New York area under a program sponsored by the Society for Philosophy and Public Affairs (itself an organization devoted to encouraging socially relevant uses of philosophy). [3] The codirector of the project, Victor Marrow, raised just that question.

> The prospect of hanging out the Philosophical Consultant shingle may seem bizarre to most philosophers. But the question remains: If philosophers help medical workers, why don't they help others? In fact, one medical resident came close to recommending just such a philosopher-client relation, by proposing that philosophers make themselves available for consultations with residents who are preparing to discuss troubling ethical issues with a patient or family members. The more squeamish of our profession should recognize that psychologists, physicians, and the clergy already take it upon themselves to advise patients and families at such trying times. Wouldn't a philosopher be more appropriate and more helpful?
>
> At the risk of shocking, I see no objection to philosophers offering their services even to a wider public. Philosophers certainly have much to say about individual rights, personal and social imperatives, and moral principles with respect to topics ranging from marriage and the family to the military draft and suicide. Now that some philosophers have moved beyond the ivy walls of the university, should other philosophers deinstitutionalize themselves altogether?

Writing

Writing for publication in your field is obviously the most common way of extending your activities and sometimes getting paid for them. In the fields of history and philosophy, for example, the possibilities of using skills to earn a livelihood are exemplified by the notable cases of, respectively, Barbara Tuchman and Mortimer Adler. But thousands of independent scholars in other fields write for people outside their fields in ways that produce income.

Such opportunities naturally will vary greatly from field to field. A Chaucer scholar has fewer options than someone studying youth unemployment, but in general, with the burgeoning of specialized magazines, journals, and book publishers in this country, there never has been more possibilities. So common has it become for experts in virtually every field to write for a wider public that sessions on this subject are now standard fare at major writers' conferences throughout the country. If you attend the largest such gathering, the annual Non-Fiction Writing Conference of the American Society of Journalists and Authors, for example, you will find sessions, workshops, and major presentations on topics such as "Writing Out of Your Specialty," "Turning Your Expertise Into Articles," and "From Specialist to Author: How to Do It."

There are many good books on nonfiction writing for publication; seek out the newer ones that reflect the current trend for an introduction to the craft. For book publishing opportunities, see pages 158–61.

The possibility of publication may prove to be more valuable than merely suggesting wider audiences for your findings. It should be an essential exercise and discipline for any scholar in any scholarly field. Scholarship that does not find way to communicate its product beyond its own inner circle will fail to command sustained support from the society and may lapse into pedantry or obscurantism. "If you cannot—in the long run—tell everyone what you have been doing," said Erwin Schrodinger, a physicist, in his book *Science and Humanism*, "your doing has been worthless."

Fees

Fees for teaching, lecturing, or consulting provide a different way of getting paid for applying and advancing your knowledge. The opportunities for teaching have been discussed earlier. To develop lecture opportunities you will need to engage a little self-promotion by mailing inexpensive brochures to potentially interested organizations.

Becoming a consultant is a process even more mysterious, to most people, than becoming an author in one's field. "There is no curriculum in any college or university which leads to a consultancy," notes Hubert Bermont, a leading consultant and author on consulting. "Nor is there any degree which authenticates proficiency as a consultant." To remedy this deficiency, Bermont has created The Consultant's Library, a series of books, newsletters, and other materials designed to share his and others' knowledge of the field. His catalog, actually an information-packed booklet that includes the tables of contents and the complete introductions of publications such as "How to Become a Successful Consultant in Your Own Field," "The Successful Consultant's Guide to Winning Government Contracts," and "The Successful Consultant's Guide to Fee Setting," is available from The Consultant's Library, 815 Fifteenth Street, N.W., Washington, D.C. 20005.

Now we come to the more radical alternatives.

Your Own Institution

Creating an income-producing organization in your field is a bold enterprise, and it probably represents a long haul, but it can be immensely rewarding. You will be aligning your work with your intellectual vocation, associating continually with your fellow investigators, and spending your work-time at tasks directly related to your primary interests.

Several people have created such organizations: Reinhold Aman created the International Maledicta Society, Lloyd deMause, the Institute for Psychohistory, William Irwin Thompson, Lindisfarne, Ralph Nader, the Center for Responsive Law. One common factor, however, was that the viability of each institution depended on a mix of income-producing sources, often including membership fees, lecture fees, publications, and occasional grants.

Salaried Research

Finding paid employment congruent with your research is an option that is available and attractive to some independent scholars, though others prefer to keep their work-life and their intellectual pursuits quite separate. We already have discussed how this kind of thing has burgeoned in the field of history and how it is not inconceivable even in philosophy. *Individual* solutions often can be devised or discovered by enterprising independent scholars. Richard Grossman, whose field is humanistic psychology and holistic medicine, is employed by a New York hospital to help doctors increase their awareness of human factors in disease.

Patronage

Finally there is the now-quaint but once vigorous and noble tradition of private patronage. While it seems anomalous in this age of institutions, there is no reason that the tradition of patronage of one individual by another might not be revived. Persons of wealth with an enthusiasm for a certain subject can share in the intellectual adventure of those who want to pursue that subject in depth. For example, in the introduction to *You Are Extraordinary*, which Aldous Huxley hailed as a "marvelous" exploration of human individuality, the author, Rogers Williams, acknowledges benefiting from such patronage.

> When I first became interested in the basic idea that lies behind this book, Benjamin Clayton . . . on his own initiative without asking any expert advice sent a contribution of $5,000 to further my efforts. That was twenty years ago. The initial contribution was itself helpful, but the encouragement and help that has come during the intervening years has been tremendous. It is remarkable that with a total of about five years of schooling, he could project the usefulness of my unconventional ideas when other much larger foundations and granting agencies with access to expert committees discouraged my efforts.

Gilbert Seldes says in the front of his monumental compilation, *The Great Quotations*: ". . . many outstanding works were produced through the intervention and support of patrons of the arts. In a sense, this gracious custom has been revived in order to publish *The Great Quotations*. To these twentieth century patrons of the arts who saw the worth and need for an anthology of the truly great quotations, this book is dedicated." There follows a list of well over fifty patrons of the book.

John Snyder:
Mapping the Earth

> I wasn't seeking any compensation, even though I knew that the government was letting contracts to solve the problem. I've just always loved maps, and I'd run out of *simple* things to do.
>
> John Snyder

"You have solved a problem that has eluded the combined governmental, industrial, and academic community for three full years," read the letter that arrived in John Snyder's mailbox on March 6, 1976. "Though this undertaking was pursued as a hobby and done for enjoyment, you have made a significant contribution to the achievement of the Geological Survey's mission. It is a pleasure to inform you that you have been selected to receive the Survey's John Wesley Powell Award, given for beneficial contributions to the Survey's work by private citizens."

What had this devoted amateur done that had defied academics and professionals in the field? In nontechnical terms, he had sharpened the images of the Earth as photographed from space satellites by creating a set of equations through which such pictures could be converted into accurate maps.

The problem was twofold: first, the satellite is moving while it takes pictures of 120-mile swaths of the rotating Earth at a shot; second, because the earth is not really round, the spacecraft orbits in an ellipse and not in a perfect circle.

The importance of solving the problem was pointed out by Dr. Alden P. Colvocoresses, Cartography Coordinator with the Geological Survey:

> You have provided the sought-after link by which Earth surface data obtained from orbiting spacecraft can now be transformed to any one of the common map projections. This is an essential step in automated mapping systems which we see developing. Because of your efforts, the Survey can now deliver to NASA, and all others concerned with Earth-sensing space systems, a set of documented equations and accompanying computer programs which

will greatly simplify the problem of mapping and monitoring the Earth's surface features.

How did it come about that John Snyder had succeeded where full-time, well-funded professionals had failed? Several attempts both by government scientists and by outside contractors already had foundered when Snyder first heard about the problem. "Typically, I was taking part of my vacation time to attend a geodetic symposium at Ohio State," Snyder recalls, "where I heard Dr. Colvocoresses describe the problems of making maps from images acquired by the Landsat survey satellites which orbit the Earth." The speaker had engagingly confessed that none of the Survey's experts had been able to devise equations by which cartographers could transfer a particular point on an image to its accurate longitude and latitude on a map. Dr. Colvocoresses concluded: "Here is a real challenge to the cartographic community."

"I figured I was the last person who would be able to solve the problem," Snyder confesses. "He was appealing to members of the academic community; how could I, an amateur with absolutely no formal training in mapping technology, tackle it. But I felt I was kind of running dry in the mid-seventies as far as my mapping interests went. I'd run out of simple things to do, and the pocket calculators had just come out in an economical form. So the problem nagged at me."

He had been intrigued by maps since childhood, and they had been an intense avocation since he was a high school student in Indianapolis. Snyder taught himself the trigonometric methods of making map projections, from the classical ones by Gerhardus Mercator, the sixteenth-century Flemish cartographer, to the stereographic projections used in contemporary polar mapping. This love affair with maps has lasted for thirty years: Each evening after his day's work as a chemical engineer (before his retirement), Snyder would retreat to his small den to read, write, and think about cartography. His fascination with maps already had yielded some impressive products. Lying on the tiny coffee table in Snyder's den in Reston, Virginia, is his book *New Jersey's Civil Boundaries, 1606–1968*, and tucked in a shadowy corner behind his desk is an award of merit from the American Association for State and Local History—the book has become something of a classic in the literature, and Snyder is highly regarded among map experts. Most recently, he received an award from the New Jersey Historical Commission for "outstanding service to public knowledge and preservation of the history of New Jersey."

After hearing Dr. Colvocoresses's challenge, Snyder took a first shot at the problem, dispatched the resulting formulas to Washington, and sparked a lively correspondence between the two men. "By July, Colvocoresses had taken to calling me at Ciba-Geigy during working hours," Snyder recalls. "It suddenly dawned on me that he was seriously interested in the work I was doing. From that point on, I got so absorbed in it that I never stopped again to consider whether I had the ability and the background needed to work out the solution. I loved the subject and Colvocoresses's constant encouragement and guidance kept me going."

Still, he could not figure out how to determine the curve that the ground track should follow on the map and then how to convert the images to appropriate map coordinates. The inspiration finally came to him during a lunch break. It was a "straightforward calculus-trigonometry-algebra arrangement." The first set of equations he generated, however, could solve the problem only if the world were a perfect sphere. No one else had gotten that far, but it was not good enough: The earth is an ellipsoid, flattened at its poles and bulging at the equator. It took another month to produce the equations based on an ellipsoid earth. "That was dog work," Snyder said, "taking equations for a sphere and applying the geometry of the ellipsoid."

Within four months, Snyder presented his solution, more than a hundred pages of tiny calculations meticulously penciled onto looseleaf paper, together with hand-calculator programs ("a poor-man's printout," he calls it) and an IBM computer program. Snyder estimates that the work took fifteen hours a week over a period of forty weeks, for a total of six hundred hours. He mailed the results to Dr. Colvocoresses, who had them tested in the Geological Survey's computers. The problem had, indeed, been solved.

A grateful government, in the person of Dr. Colvocoresses, who had issued the challenge, handsomely acknowledged the amateur's achievement: "By applying your unique mathematical capabilities and thorough understanding of geodesy and map projections, you have accomplished a scientific feat of high value to mapmakers throughout the world. You derived the transformation equations between the Space Oblique Mercator projection and the surface of the Earth in a few months time, and at only token cost to the government. Future generations who will use maps produced from satellite data will owe you no small debt for this truly remarkable accomplishment."

The reaction of Snyder's friends and colleagues at work to the award was typical of what one often wants to say to independent scholars working in an arcane field. He explains: "The study of satellite map projections, like many other highly technical areas of science, is so technical that it is difficult to explain to the lay person, and even to other scientists unfamiliar with one's field. So people tended to say things like: 'Congratulations! I don't know exactly what you did—but it must be great!' "

Snyder's achievement turned his lifelong avocation into a second career. After receiving the Powell award, he cut his workload as a chemical engineer in half so that he could serve as a paid consultant to the Geological Survey, applying his eighty-two equations to the production of maps based on the first satellite projections. Subsequently, he retired from Ciba-Geigy, moved with his wife to Reston, and started working full-time at the Geological Survey on map projections, including some for the space shuttle "Columbia." "So I'm no longer an independent scholar in the mapping field," he confesses. "Here, I'm paid at roughly the same rate I would have received at C-G. There's a difference, though, I almost never took home work from C-G. Since coming here to work on map projections, I spend many hours working on concepts at home. Sometimes it's directly work-related, sometimes it's more theoretical and for fun—though in scientific work you never know what may come in handy down the pike. So, now, it's really impossible for me to separate my job from my labors of love."[4]

Interlude: Encounters along the Way

This book began with some recollections of conversations that awakened me to independent scholarship. Once I began to search out independent scholars a few encounters occurred that seemed to say much about the field.

The button on his lapel read, I'M NOT JUST A BUM—I'M AN INDEPENDENT SCHOLAR. Vince Kavaloski had thought of the slogan when a group of fellow independent scholars in Madison, Wisconsin, had asked him to talk at one of their early "roundtables" about his struggle to do his own research, which happens to focus on the history of the Great Books movement. Knowing that the slogan might be taken amiss by the participants, he explained what it meant to him.

> The idea of being an independent scholar is quite an ambivalent one, at least for me. We spent much of our last session talking about the *disadvantages*: you don't have access to research money, to assistance, to resources. But we all know there are also *positive* points to being an independent scholar.
>
> So I've tried to capture this ambivalence in my slogan, which others liked so much that we had these buttons made up for anyone who wants one. The sentence just sprang out of my mouth while we were discussing what I might talk about at this session. But the more I thought about it, the more I realized that it was a message from my own unconscious.

I was trying to say, to myself and anyone else who wanted to listen: "I'm not lost in the world just because I don't have an institutional affiliation. I'm not just another unemployed Ph.D." There's a small defiant voice inside of me asserting that I was never that comfortable within academe. I wasn't just pushed out, I was also drawn out. There was something that "called" me to do work that didn't fit into academia, into departmental or specialized areas.

Both these sides are embodied in this little button. The side of it which expresses some sense of failure, regret, frustration, negative self-image. But also the side of it which is trying to find the positive assertion. I'm searching for models of independent scholarship to buoy myself up with.

That search goes on—in Madison, in Wichita, in Boston, in New York, in Washington, in other cities and towns where independent scholars have joined together to encourage, support, and help one another. That early session in Madison, and the energy and dedication of Chris Wagner and her cohorts who started the "roundtable" there, taught me that the best source of support for independent scholars lay within their own ranks. Although I have worked as hard as I can to obtain the other kinds of support that independent scholars need and deserve, *self*-help remains the most reliable strategy.

It was a setting out of an Expressionist movie. Picture a federal bureaucrat's office, secretary-level and therefore quite vast, but with nothing in it except a desk, two chairs, and a wooden hatrack standing in the corner. That was the scene as I talked with John Gardner, who recently had been appointed Secretary of Health, Education, and Welfare, our voices echoing disquietingly in the high-ceilinged and uncarpeted office. To add to the surrealistic effect, the conversation really was not meant to be between *us*. (Why, after all, would a newly appointed high governmental official take the time to sit around talking to me?) The conversation was meant to be between Gardner and an invisible constituency, for I was there under assignment from *The New York Times* to profile him for their Sunday *Magazine*.

What startled me right off the bat, therefore, was that Gardner *did* talk to me. Rather than coming on as a politician with canned rhetoric, he began quite simply, person to person, to reflect on what this job as head of the federal government's programs for *people* meant to him.

> As a boy in California I spent a good deal of time in the Mother Lode country, and like every boy I listened raptly to the tales told by the old-time prospectors in that area, some of them veterans of the Klondike gold rush. Every one of them had at least one good campfire story of a lost gold mine. The details varied: The original discoverer had died in the mine, or had gone crazy, or had been killed in a shooting scrape, or had just walked off thinking the mine worthless. But the central theme was constant: riches left untapped. I've come to believe that those tales offer a paradigm of education as most of us experience it. The mind is worked for a little while and then abandoned.

Gardner leaned forward intently to his point. "It's a sad but unarguable fact that most human beings go through their lives only partially aware of the full range of their abilities. No one knows why some individuals seem capable of self-renewal while others don't. But we've got some important clues to what the self-renewing person is like and what we might do to foster renewal."

As we talked and the office grew darker with the gathering dusk, Gardner's craggy face and lanky frame grew more and more animated. I realized I was hearing the personal credo of an independent thinker and activist.

> Exploration of the full range of one's own potentialities is not something that the self-renewing person leaves to the chances of life. It is something we must pursue systematically, or at least avidly, to the end of our days. We must look forward to an endless and unpredictable dialogue between our potentialities and the claims of life—not only the claims we encounter but the claims we invent.
>
> The society could do much to encourage our self-development. But up to now the conception of individual fulfillment and lifelong learning finds no adequate reflection in our social institutions. For too long we have paid pious lip service to the idea and trifled with it in practice.

Gardner discovered, as so many of his predecessors have, that governmental bureaucracies are notoriously resistant to change. What impressed me tremendously, however, was how in the years that followed the man himself lived up to his own principles, going on to found Common Cause, the citizen's lobby, and Independent Sector, dedicated to sustaining the nongovernmental, nonprofit organizations that add so much to the health of American society.

Here was a fresh insight into independent scholarship. The *institutions*

of our society need to be changed if each of us is to be permitted, and enabled, to add our unique discoveries to the common culture. Society must
find ways to welcome, sustain, nurture, reward, and use the basic human impulse to understand the world.

The landscape suggested somnolence: cows grazing near fields planted with
corn and beans, row on row of the Great Smoky Mountains fading into the
distance, bloated clouds sailing through the sky. Myles Horton gestured
out from the porch of his home at Highlander, the "research and education" center in New Market, Tennessee, which he had founded (at another
location) in 1932. At the bottom of the hill, a group of coalminers, union
members, just breaking up their morning seminar on social change, were
making their way to the dining hall for lunch. As their husky chatter wafted
up the hill, there was suddenly, despite the sleepy setting, a sense of awakening.

"People—ordinary *working* people—are *creative*," Horton declared, obviously excited himself by the excitement in those workers' voices.

> Working together, learning together, they can create the knowledge they need
> to improve their lives, and the whole society. The more you get to know
> them, the less "ordinary" they turn out to be. It's to them that we have to
> look for knowledge about how our society works, and for wisdom about the
> best way to change it.
>
> Education is supposed to prepare people to fit into the system and sup-
> port the system, and really it's to turn people into nuts and bolts to keep the
> system together. How can you get truly independent thinking, independent re-
> search and inquiry, in a system like that. Highlander says no, you can't use peo-
> ple like that. You've got to allow them to do a lot of things that don't fit any
> kind of system, you've got to have a lot of deviation. There's a lot of dynamic
> in that, a lot of power that scares people.

The people it scares have harassed Highlander throughout its history, with
red-baiting, police raids, burn-outs, evictions, and close-downs. Horton
was once arrested during a rash of coal strikes and officially charged with
"coming here, getting information, and going back and teaching it." Highlander
was a center of union training in the thirties and grass-roots civil rights training
in the sixties. Today it is still unique as the one place in the region where work-

ing people—coalminers, millworkers, farmers—can gather to study their problems, learn the facts, and come to their own conclusions about what to do.

At the end of our conversation, I confessed to Horton that the kind of collective learning I had seen occurring at Highlander was very different from the largely individualistic truth-seeking of many independent researchers. He responded:

> Individualism is enhanced by being part of a group. Instead of telling people they should go it alone, they should be competitive, they should compete, we say here: Work together and you'll be a better person. We're going to try to build on what you know and your experiences, and help you understand that your neighbors have some experiences, and other people in another place, maybe even in another country, have some experiences that relate to this problem. All these are related, tied in with your experience. I remember one fellow that came here from the mountains up near the North Carolina line. He said, "When I came here I had one little piece of pie that had all the answers. And Joe here, he had a little slice. And Myles told us about somebody else who had a little slice. Now we've got the whole pie, now I know everything. I'm going to take the whole pie back home with me instead of my little slice." But he was proud of the fact that he contributed a little slice. . . . .

I remembered my telephone conversation with Hazel Henderson several years before and her offhand comment that contemporary problems called for cooperative intellectual efforts. Here at Highlander, I realized, I had found such an enterprise. Perhaps there could be yet other ways for individuals to share their strengths in the quest for knowledge and understanding.

PART THREE

Independent Scholars in Action

Independent scholars are often impelled by social purpose. Their pursuit of knowledge and understanding frequently focuses on some issue or problem that affects people's lives. Their books may present new, vital facts about ourselves or our society, or they may promote understanding of hidden or suppressed realities. They may report original research as well as synthesizing prior studies of an important, interdisciplinary problem. The practical thrust of such researchers and writers is reflected in every aspect of their work. You can see it in the reasons they start, the motivations that keep them going, the methods they use, the problems they encounter, and the reception their works receive.

Alvin Toffler:
A Journey Past Time

> Independent thinkers and writers do not simply translate other people's ideas into acceptable English. They often generate new paradigms, new (often researchable) hypotheses, new syntheses—in short, they raise significant questions that academic scholars or scientists (frequently limited by institutional or disciplinary blinders) overlook or deliberately ignore.
>
> **Alvin Toffler**

Alvin Toffler might not use himself to exemplify this conviction, but I will. For his career shows how an independent researcher, writer, and thinker can win a major role in the world of ideas.

Future Shock was an international bestseller, published in twenty-five languages, with ten million copies in print in over one hundred countries. The book's basic concepts have been quoted, cited, and discussed by world leaders in every political camp from Indira Gandhi to Juan Peron, from the president of the United States to the prime ministers of Japan, Canada, and other nations. The book garnered prizes and honorary degrees for its author, and the title now appears in many dictionaries and as a basic entry in *The Dictionary of Modern Thought.* Toffler's works are taught in universities from Paris to Beijing. They are read avidly by business executives, government officials, housewives, and students.

Summing up the impact of *Future Shock* in academe, the editors of the *Chronicle of Higher Education* wrote: "Although clearly intended for a general audience, even among academic futurists, it [is considered] 'enormously influential' and a 'landmark book'." Clearly, Toffler is the world's best known and one of its most distinguished social analysts and futurists.

All of which may seem to place him in some celebrity stratosphere making his experience useless to the rest of us. But the opposite is the case. Toffler's success certainly makes his present lifestyle unique, but his struggle in winning that place could not be more applicable. In fact, there are thousands of serious researchers and writers who, without having achieved Toffler's renown, have shaped their lives and their work along the same lines—and benefited substantially.

Toffler asserts:

> Freelance writers like myself and the hundreds of serious nonfiction authors in this country usually have different purposes, different methods, and different styles from academicians. A great many academics tend to look down on them as mere popularizers. But these non-institutionalized investigators often make striking, creative contributions to our understanding of the world around us. And those contributions often occur *because* of, rather than in spite of, their independent status. It is the freedom from disciplinary and departmental blinders that often leads to fresh concepts. It is a myth that the university has a monopoly on the production of knowledge in our world.

Toffler's own career illustrates this thesis. At each stage, from its beginning and his apprenticeships, through the way in which *Future Shock* came to be written, to his present activities, it illustrates the distinctive outlook of many who make their living as independent intellectuals.

> When I got out of college, I'd been taught that there was a clear-cut pecking order in the world of writing. Literature and fiction were better than nonfiction; nonfiction better than journalism. But when I stepped back and thought about it, I didn't see how I could write meaningfully about life, or communi-

cate with anyone but Ph.D.s unless I got out and touched people, sharing the way they worked. So together with my wife Heidi, I got work in the Ohio steel foundries and auto plants: welder, millwright, truck driver, car assembler. I learned to use my hands and talk with Americans who got up at five in the morning and carried lunch buckets to work. I got a realistic picture of how things really are made—the energy, love, and rage that are poured into ordinary things we take for granted. Even today I can't pass a welder at work without feeling a twinge of nostalgia for the brilliant blue beauty he sees through his mask.

That early experience seems to have established one strong strain in Toffler's intellectual style: the impulse to "touch people," to learn at first hand what they are thinking and feeling. His approach to hypotheses formation and research stands in contrast to that of most university-based researchers.

Too many academic social scientists insist that data must be impersonal, quantified, previously printed in "the literature." Of course, I want to know what's in the scholarly journals—even though they lag behind state-of-the-art knowledge in most fields by at least two years. I read the journals and technical papers and the computer printouts. But I also use my other senses, other ways of learning, to understand the world. I get out. I travel. I interview. I nose around. I talk to everyone from working people to businessmen to statesmen. It helps me to synthesize theory and practice. I think of my methodology as an enriched blend of scholarship and journalism.

From the factories, Toffler worked his way into the trade union press, and eventually to Washington—drawn there because it looked to him and Heidi as if that's where the action was, circa 1957. He started at the bottom, "stringing" for a rum bunch of newspapers and magazines. He became the accredited Washington correspondent of a Pennsylvania daily and covered Capitol Hill and the White House.

He also sought out freelance work.

I went to the National Press Club building, which consists of what seems like hundreds of offices—many of them little one-room cubicles—in which the Washington bureaus of newspapers and magazines from all over the country are located.

I took the elevator from the top floor and worked my way down along all the corridors, stopping in at every office and saying, "I'm a writer. Can you use me?" Few could. But the magazines were hungry for copy, and soon I was completing a magazine piece every week or ten days. I'd get up in the mornings and go to Capitol Hill, cover some hearings, and interview a bunch of people, taking copious, almost verbatim notes. In the afternoon I'd dash across town to the Department of Commerce, the Department of Health, Education, and Welfare, the Federal Trade Commission, or the White House. Then I staggered home and wrote until late at night. My bedtime reading consisted of congressional committee reports.

I would do colorful personality profiles of politicians—Johnson, Kennedy, Goldwater, Humphrey—for *Coronet* or some other popular magazine, and then I'd do a long piece of political analysis, based on information from the same interviews, for one of the intellectual magazines.

All the legwork, the constant interviewing and research, provided the equivalent of a graduate school education—more, in fact, and better, because it wasn't specialized. One day I would cover hearings on disarmament. The next day it might be agriculture, and another day some labor problem. I wrote stories about chemical additives in food, stories about water pollution, stories about [the] military-industrial complex—about many topics that became "hot issues" a decade later.

By covering all these different topics, I became keenly aware that government was increasingly out of touch with what really was happening in the country. All sorts of trends were under way that were going unobserved— changes in the culture, in family structure and organizational structure, changes in technology. Our government seemed to have no detection mechanisms for scanning the horizon for change.

An odd kind of ambition—*intellectual* ambition—seems to have driven Toffler from one job to the next during this period. Obviously he was learning fast—but many young people do that. What distinguished the young Toffler was restlessness, an impulse to find the next challenge. "When I had been with *Labor's Daily* for two years, I felt I had learned just about everything I could and that it was time to move on again. That has been consistently true in my career: leave when you've learned."

One thing that made it easy for Toffler was the moral and intellectual support he got from his wife, Heidi. Many spouses hate the freelance existence, with its money problems, its ride-the-roller-coaster ups and downs. Heidi Toffler thrived on them. Even in those early days, Heidi worked closely with Toffler, discussing research, ideas, data with him, debating with him. "At times, she helped do leg-work on stories," Toffler recalls. "On other occasions, she tore up my manuscripts, and helped me reoutline them." Over the years, she became a superb editor. Today, they still work together. She often travels with him, conducts interviews, and lectures on her own.

The way in which the idea for *Future Shock* came to Toffler is nicely symbolic of his style. He was deeply interested in social and cultural change and was writing about it in one form or another. But his ideas had not yet jelled. One day he was on the phone, in direct, "real-time" contact with another investigator, pursuing some questions about what anthropologists call "culture shock." Characteristically, he was talking across "disciplinary lines" to a psychologist, Dr. Rachel Gittelman-Klein, rather than an anthropologist. "During the conversation . . ." Toffler can still remember, "an analogy occurred to me: If a person could be dislocated geographically in space, a person also could, in effect, be dislocated in time. If one could have 'culture shock,' one also could have 'future shock.' That analogy changed my life."

Between that flash of insight and the publication of *Future Shock* came the most rugged regimen of intellectual labor in Toffler's life. "I worked my tail off," he candidly confesses. "This book was not subsidized. I got it done by writing a magazine piece one month and then crawling off and writing a little bit of the book for the next few weeks and then scurrying and writing another magazine article. I was deep in debt, and it took five years to finish the book."

What must be realized is that Toffler didn't get the opportunity to write *Future Shock* because he was an acknowledged authority. He *became* an acknowledged authority because *Future Shock* was so widely recognized as presenting a fresh theory of human and social adaptation. His present authority was earned by the quality of his work, not conferred by an institution. Before he became Alvin Toffler, he was merely Al Toffler, a not-so-young-anymore writer working harder than he should on an idea nobody else quite understood.

> When I wrote *Future Shock*, I had no expert status, and couldn't really speak in my own voice. I had to use selected quotes from others, including certified experts, to make my points—as journalists always do. After *Future Shock* came out, people could judge my work and my ideas for themselves. That resulted in whatever status or legitimacy I now possess. To me, that's the nat-

ural and healthy process by which status should emerge—as a judgment based on a person's quality of thought, not on his or her diploma, or the length of one's academic bibliography.

Nor did Toffler set out with commercial success uppermost in mind. "Bestsellerdom does not seem to be Toffler's primary reason for seeking a popular audience," said *Business Week*, a periodical not likely to overlook pecuniary motivation, after the publication of his book *The Third Wave*.

> My work isn't just a commercial product. It matters to me that I'm heard, that changes take place in our society. So though my writings draw upon, synthesize, and present extensive data from a wide range of social sciences, I take great pains to write—and *rewrite* it to a degree that can drive me crazy— to assure that I *communicate*. For me, just to develop the knowledge and convey it to others in the field, isn't enough. That's just what we mean by "academic" writing. I want to make a *difference* in people's lives.

Toffler has certainly made a difference. Has that made a difference in him? What stance does he take today, to his work? The answer is that he finds himself exactly where he started, in one significant respect. "Most serious writers and intellectuals would agree, I think, that this kind of work gets harder instead of easier. We tend to bite off ever bigger mouthfuls. The challenges we set for ourselves become more complex. As my understanding deepens, the problems of explanation become even more difficult. So I work to learn, and learn to work."

CHAPTER SEVEN

Sharing Your Work

Teaching—as Socrates Taught

Teaching your subject will increase your command over it, impel you to brush up on aspects you may have neglected, and force you to look at your subject in a new way as you devise ways to present it to others. Moreover, your students are likely to stimulate your thinking if your teaching is good enough to provoke intelligent questions; they may have information and insights that will add to your understanding of the subject. Finally, there is much satisfaction in seeing others gain knowledge or skills in a field that you care about deeply. There are other rewards as well. Depending on your field, your teaching may lead to lecture engagements, writing or consulting assignments, or other opportunities. And, of course, you actually can get paid for doing it.

Teaching opportunities for independent scholars are burgeoning today as adult education courses proliferate in virtually every community. At most colleges, universities, and community colleges you will find teaching opportunities in the continuing education, adult education, or "lifelong learning" programs. These programs usually welcome competent people from the community who want to offer worthwhile courses that adult students—and often younger ones too—will find attractive enough to take even though they do not have to. Just write to the dean of the program in your locale, explaining what course you would like to offer, what you would cover, your expertise, and, of course, any successful teaching experience you have had: Generally, no teaching certificate is required.

For guidance on how to conceive, plan, promote, and teach these kinds of courses for adults, see *Teaching Free: An Introduction to Adult Learning for Volunteer and Part-time Teachers,* by William Draves, available for $5.00 from the Free University Network. If you want to see how far-ranging and imaginative such courses can be, send for a copy of the latest catalog of the New School for Social Research, 66 West Twelfth Street, New York, NY 10011, or of the School of Continuing Education, New York University, Washington Square, NY 10003. Both of these catalogs are book-length listings of courses developed by experts, most of whom are not professors.

As you become more accomplished and noted in your field, continuing but nicely irregular arrangements often can be made with a college or university that is interested in your strengths, unusual though they may be. The superb mime Bill Irwin describes a long-term relationship he had with Oberlin College in a "quasi-, quasi-, quasi-teaching assistantship. . . . I taught physical comedy. Or, as the catalogue put it, 'arena slapstick for the actor.' That made the chairman of the department happy."

Less unusual, and an appealing model for independent scholars to aspire to, is the arrangement that William Manchester, the author of *The Death of a President,* had with Wesleyan University.

> I don't teach a regular course but I do lecture and I advise students who are candidates for honors, and I dine with students every Wednesday evening. But nothing that can't be cancelled, because I don't know when I'm going to have to leave on a research trip or simply be inaccessible. I might say that I accept no salary from Wesleyan. It's the other way around; I contribute to Wesleyan. The office I work in is provided by Wesleyan, but I supply my own equipment and secretary.

If you are not yet expert enough in your field to undertake a complete course yourself, but you are knowledgeable enough to plan and conduct one "with a little help from your friends," then why not coordinate a course that consists largely of guest appearances by local leaders and experts in your field? Here you conceive, design, and write up the offering for the catalog, and invite five or six outstanding figures, who usually are glad to give an evening to meeting with a group of students keen on their subject. As coordinator, you introduce the guest speakers, start the questions after their presentations, and suggest connections between one speaker and another. Incidentally, you usually get a chance to have dinner with them either before or after the class. Result: You, in effect, get to design and conduct the class *you* would most want to take at this point, composing it of some of the experts you most want to hear from and talk with. And you get paid for it.

You may go even further than teaching a single course by developing a group of courses constituting a program. This idea is not as far-fetched as it might sound at first. For example, Harold Jaffe, an architect and designer interested in teaching the theory and practice of solar power for domestic use, developed a program offered through C. W. Post College. It started with a free orientation lecture (with slides) on solar energy to draw people to the campus and interest them in the program (the lecture was followed by a question and answer session and refreshments). Three course were offered: Solar Homes; Wind Power: Making Your Own Electricity; and Wood Power: Heating the Entire House with Wood. Each course was five or six sessions. To advise on the development of these courses, each of which was taught by a local expert, Jaffe assembled an advisory board of other knowledgeable local people, including some from energy companies, the public schools, the local science museum, a merchant academy, and the regional Builders Institute. Another offering was a two-part series of workshops on the use of solar energy, with the first ten sessions taught at the local science museum's Appropriate Technology Demonstration Center and the second ten held on the campus. All of these courses were displayed on one newspaper-sized page in the College's Continuing Education catalog, under the rubric Solar Energy Resources Institute, Harold Jaffe, Director.

Other kinds of organizations that regularly provide courses for adults, and might welcome your proposal to teach a course in your field, include YMCAs, public school systems, churches, and, perhaps most interesting of all, the "free universities" that have grown up in many communities over the past twenty years. Free universities can be started by anyone with the energy, and commitment to gather some teachers of interesting subjects, put up a bulletin, promote a program, and administer a small operation.[1]

An alternative to teaching a class through a free university is one-to-one sharing of your knowledge through a "learning network." These are "intellectual dating bureaus" through which pairs of people link up—either peers in a given subject or a teacher and learner. Such one-to-one teaching sounds odd to most of us on first hearing, but of course it has a noble tradition in Western education. "A tutorial education has always been an elite one," noted John Coyne and Tom Hebert. "The essentials of a tutorial education [are]: one, sometimes two students meeting regularly [once a week or at least every two weeks] for an hour or more with a person deeply informed about an area of knowledge or field of experience."

Although teaching through a college, school, YMCA, or free university will appeal to many, you may prefer to do your teaching, as your scholarship, completely independently. "I prefer to teach for free, rather than being an 'adjunct' connected tenuously with some college or university," says one researcher.

> The $800 or so that I might get paid to teach a noncredit course isn't essential to my livelihood, so I'd rather be free to offer my services when and where I like—such as teaching in prisons, which appeals to me—and not having to deal with academic bureaucracy. Not only that, but I feel that when working as an adjunct, I'm in a way supporting the academic "system"—and I feel more comfortable and autonomous finding my own way outside it. In that system, I always feel that, as an independent, I'm going to be a second-class citizen. When I teach on my own terms, I'm respected as a person making an important contribution.

Even in the realm of private teaching there are far more opportunities than you might think at first. Norm Livergood, a independent scholar, reported that "since resigning from a tenured position in academia in 1970, I have been privately teaching a wide range of students, from graduate 'scholars' (who have to learn how to learn) to those who have rarely made it through high school (but who still have the seeds of desire to learn)." Livergood views private teaching as part of a great tradition, parallel to that of independent scholarship itself—a tradition beginning with Socrates and Aristotle and particularly strong in the American grain, carried on by figures such as Emerson and private teachers such as Thomas Martin and James Marye, who tutored the founders of our nation. "The likes of Bronson Alcott would have looked with suspicion on any teacher who needed the 'authority' of an external institution to feel secure," he remarked. But he insisted that private teaching is challenging:

> If it's to be genuine and successful, it cannot be a mere importing of academic jargon and gimmicks into the private marketplace. It should force us to ask, as

genuine teachers should have been asking all along, what is the essence of education and what are the foundations of the particular disciplines? For example, we ought to have known that the tradition termed *philosophia* by certain Greeks and named *tasawwuf* by Central Asian sages could not be rigidly systematized into academic "philosophy."

As a private teacher, you'll have to do your own promotion and deal directly with such elements as payment of student fees. In my experience with promotion, I've gone from using a small newspaper ad announcing a class on a particular philosopher to a fully illustrated flyer announcing a comprehensive study program, mailed to ten thousand persons at a time.

The reward comes from the students, of course. Livergood has found that the students attracted to private teaching by independent scholars have qualities that should enrich your own studies.

Fortunately, if you can learn how to teach, certain students find it exciting to engage in genuine—as opposed to academic—learning. Private students are much more motivated by understanding, by liberating themselves from delusions, than they ever were by grades, credits, or degrees. You can require much more commitment to learning from your private students than you could ever hope to in an academic class that meets one to three times a week. You can limit your private students to those few who genuinely want to engage in real learning.

You can find opportunities for freelance teaching in virtually any community, but you have to use imagination and resourcefulness in cultivating those opportunities. John Michael, an independent scholar of holistic health and nutrition, has offered his workshops in Chicago and Houston. "Anyone can easily learn to grow fresh foods by using the Indoor Farming Techniques," his brochure declares. "This is the most economical way to obtain living, organic produce. . . . With these living foods a rainbow variety of culinary dishes can be prepared to satisfy the most discriminating tastes."

In even less propitious circumstances, Hal Lenke found ways to share his expertise in his rural West Virginia county. "I have been a teacher-at-large— at large in the sense that criminals or wounded or rogue animals are spoken of as being at large. For the two years before that, I was a teacher positioned, located, a classroom teacher, a teacher-at-small." Lenke's vision of his role as a "teacher-at-large" is capacious, but its elements will suggest specific roles that many independent scholars might choose to play.

The teacher-at-large that I am groping for is a teacher of and to his community. His motto is to rise to the occasion. Specifically, such a teacher would do research for people and bodies of the community, from town government to a bank to the Chamber of Commerce to the school board to a farmer to a woman on welfare. He would obtain information or show others how to find what they want to know. As a financial proposition, he might either open up shop the way a doctor or lawyer does, advertise for clients, and charge them, or work in exchange for services or goods. Or, he might be paid from a community fund.

Publishing Your Work

The title of this section has been carefully phrased: My message is that publishing your work must be an *active* undertaking. That is why I did not say "Getting Your Work Published," implying a passive process.

You should consider a wide range of options, including the do-it-yourself route, which can take the form of a newsletter in your field, a magazine or journal, or a self-published or small-press book.

Starting a newsletter is a favorite strategy of mine, as I have mentioned earlier. It takes relatively little of your time, it puts you at the center of news and ideas in the field, and the cost is minimal. You can start with a quick-and-dirty one-pager run off by the local instant printer or even photocopied at the office of someone who works in an organization that would like to make a small, unconscious contribution to culture.

There is no question that the traditional, mainline outlets for the products of scholarship are often closed (or at best clogged) to the unaffiliated. The general "trade" publishers, whose names we all know best from the numbers of books they publish and the advertising they do, have become even less receptive over the last several years to worthwhile but commercially unpromising books. "Everything that has happened in publishing during the last [few] decades," comments one of the nation's leading book critics, Christopher Lehmann-Haupt of *The New York Times*, "has conspired to focus greater and greater emphasis on the few big moneymakers the industry produces every season, and consequently to exclude from publication those minimally commercial but artistically venturesome books that are, or ought to be, the lifeblood of the business."

Even among the university presses, the independent scholar faces special obstacles. I asked the director of one of the nation's leading presses to tell me frankly how he reacts to a submission from someone who is not connected with a college or university, or lacks a Ph.D. The man's wife is an independent scholar; I thought that he might well lean toward sympathy for such work. He did, but not very far.

> I have to admit that absence of credentials does worry me a bit as we look at curriculum vitae that does not include them, and assuming that the project described is of average interest but not remarkable. In deciding what to pursue further, it is not necessarily easy to say (given the constraints on our time), that we should regularly look at work by people without, say, Ph.D.s. Ideally, we would; in practice, because of the pressures of time we sometimes do if the project is very promising, but *might not* if it were not. As for the absence of an institutional affiliation currently, on the part of scholars, I would hope that publishers would realize that many good people are outside of institutions—and yet, to be realistic, it is possible that some *hesitate* over submissions from unaffiliated authors. I feel we should try not to hesitate.

I do not want to imply that trade publishers and university presses are not worth trying, but I do not think you should depend on their providing the solution to the problem of publishing your work.

The how-to of conceiving, researching, writing, and publishing articles in journals in your field is not within the scope of this book, and there are good guides readily available. One serviceable and easy-to-read guide, useful even if your field is not education, is *Writing for Education Journals*, by Laurel Beedon and Joseph Heinmiller (published by the Phi Delta Kappa Educational Foundation, Eighth and Union, Box 789, Bloomington, IN 47402). Most libraries have a copy. It covers such useful topics as Beginning to Write, Searching the Literature, Getting Ideas, Structuring a Thesis and an Argument, Going Through Drafts, Querying Publications, and the Technical Requirements for Manuscripts.

You will need to find, or to assemble yourself, an inventory of publications that might be suitable for your material. Do not assume that you are aware of all the possibilities without taking a fresh and vigorous look. I am constantly astonished at how many outlets can be found by looking more closely and resourcefully at the options. If your field permits, you might also have the opportunity to write about it for a popular audience of nonspecialists.

Book Publishers

All right, here it is: How to go about getting your major work out between hard covers. By now you realize that my advice is not to wait too long to report your findings and insights, to begin building your audience, and not to depend on a publisher to ride up, sweep you into the saddle, and bound off into the pages of *The New York Times Review of Books*. With these cautions in mind, how can you find those publishers who are most likely to be interested in your book, and what are your alternatives if they are not interested?

To get started, use those resources that are most accessible to you. Take a close look at the books in your field that are on the shelves of your own personal collection or of your local bookstore or library. You are likely to discover that many of them are issued by the same publishers. Browse through your subject area in the library's card catalog or in the *Subject Guide to Books in Print*, an extensive listing of books currently in publication arranged under some sixty thousand different subject headings. Published annually by the R. R. Bowker Company, it is readily available even in the smallest library or bookstore.

Once you have identified the names of publishers who may be interested in works in your area, you will want to find out more about them in order to narrow your scope. There are several basic sources of information about book publishers. Perhaps the most widely used is *Literary Market Place (LMP)*, published annually by Bowker. An extensive alphabetical listing of the most active book publishers in the United States includes each publisher's name, address, telephone number, key personnel, subject specialties, founding date, number of books published annually, advertising agency used, and the like. There is a separate listing of the same publishers classified by subject matter, which is particularly useful when beginning your search. Bowker also publishes the *International Literary Market Place (ILMP)*, which contains similar information about foreign book publishers.

A source of information about publishers that is popular among authors is *Writer's Market*, published annually by Writer's Digest Books. Its alphabetical listing of publishers contains information similar to that found in *LMP*, as well as information on royalty payments, advances, queries, manuscript requirements, and response times, sample titles of recently published books, and other information of special interest to writers. It does not have a subject index to the book publishers.

A particularly interesting approach to selecting potential publishers for your book is to find out exactly what books each one is publishing. This will help you to determine more precisely which publishers handle books like yours and perhaps will help you to eliminate those whose titles are too popular, too restrictive—or even too similar! A unique source of this information is Bowker's *Publishers' Trade List Annual (PTLA)*, an annual compilation of publishers' catalogs arranged alphabetically by publisher in six volumes. *PTLA* also has a useful subject index to the major fields of activity the publishers specialize in. Like the other sources mentioned, it is available in most libraries.

Small and Specialized Presses

Literary Market Place, Writer's Market, and *The Publishers' Trade List Annual* often do not include many of the smaller, more specialized presses that may better suit your needs. To find such publishers in your specific field, there is a resource that is well worth your attention: *The International Directory of Little Magazines and Small Presses,* which has the additional advantage of subject indexes that permit you to determine at a glance the publishers that specialize in your field.

A guide to the world of independent publishing, *The International Directory of Little Magazines and Small Presses* is published annually by Dustbooks. The most popular and long-lived of the small press directories, it contains invaluable subject and regional indexes as well as a separate listing of distributors. The main section includes each press's name, editors, address, telephone number, type of material used, founding year, printing and production data, reporting time, payment or royalty and rights arrangements, and similar information for potential authors. Although it tends to emphasize "alternative" publications, as that is the scope of many small presses, this directory is a unique and invaluable source.

Alternatives

The scholar-in-search-of-a-market has several alternatives to the traditional but time-consuming and often unproductive ways of finding a publisher. One alternative is to use an agent; another is to publish the book yourself. These are many advantages—and disadvantages—to both approaches. These are outlined in *Writer's Market* and other books like it, and it is wise to heed their advice as well as to consult others who have taken those routes.

Listing of agents' names, addresses, telephone numbers, and areas of specialization can be found in the *Literary Market Place, Writer's Market,* and *The International Directory of Little Magazines and Small Presses*. Among the spate of other books that deal with publishing approaches and alternatives is a particularly good one called *How to Get Happily Published,* by Judith Applebaum and Nancy Evans (New York: HarperCollins).

If you are willing to combine a "no frills" method with a do-it-yourself approach to publishing your book, you will be interested in University Press of America (UPA). UPA has been operating successfully for many years, issuing scholarly monographs and textbooks in the arts, sciences, social sciences, and humanities. Its scheme is innovative: UPA issues your book in an attractive, dignified, but uniform format, and *you* take on the full responsibility for preparing camera-ready copy, editing, proofreading, and so forth. Finished books are off the "press" in two months.

From that point on you get the full services of a scholarly publisher: UPA markets and promotes the book, does mailings to every appropriate college professor and academic librarian, sends review copies to academic journals, asks authorities for comments, presents the book at conventions in your discipline, advertises appropriately, provides examination copies for prospective textbook adoptions, and services wholesalers.

An advisory board of well-established academics oversees the program and stands behind the standards for acceptance of manuscripts. UPA also works with a number of scholarly societies and associations in issuing their proceedings, monographs, and other products.

To make this innovative publishing program financially feasible, UPA has a variety of requirements for publishing. To find out more, contact them at 4710 Auth Place, S.E., Washington, D.C. 20023.

Finally, consider self-publishing—not as a last resort, but as an exhilarating exercise in talking full responsibility for the dissemination of your own work. "The rewards are great—and it is a lot simpler than it may seem," according to the authors of the authoritative *Encyclopedia of Self-Publishing*. "Not necessarily easy, mind you, but simple." You would be following in noble footsteps: Anaïs Nin, Walt Whitman, Gertrude Stein, Mary Baker Eddy, James Joyce. Nowadays, the proliferation of quick-printers has put the technology for self-publication on virtually every streetcorner—at competitive prices. Moreover, self-publication and publication by an established publisher are not mutually exclusive. It is more and more commonplace for an author to publish something independently, and then have the same work bought by a publisher for reissue when it has proved successful. So, if you have important findings or viewpoints that are ready for release, do look into this avenue: You could have your work in print and beginning to have impact ninety days from today.

Nontraditional Products of Scholarship

How important is it for you to produce something from your inquiries? And what forms might that product take? I will admit at the start that there is a hardy tradition in virtually every discipline of brilliant, widely admired figures who did not "produce" in the conventional sense. One thinks of Christian Gauss, the legendary professor of literature at Princeton in Edmund Wilson's day; Adelbert Ames, who was incapable of presenting in written form his revolutionary hypotheses about the nature of perception; or Bernard Muller-Thym, the revered management consultant renowned for his reticence. Nonetheless, I believe that a focus on a product is frequently beneficial, and often necessary.

First of all, it is useful for yourself. It spurs you to turn inchoate impulses into communicable forms. You must make distinctions, judgments, decisions: write this word or that, pick up the subject from this angle or another, aim the camera in one direction or elsewhere. Only in these ways do one's thoughts take shape, become clearer. "One never knows what he knows until it is written," insists Ronald Berman, a former chairman of the National Endowment for the Humanities.

But there's a second, external reason for aiming to produce something tangible. If you seek recognition in your field, you will have to be judged by your works. No matter how committed, dedicated, and sincere you may be, no matter with what diligence and depth you pursue your quest, it is by your public product that peers must judge you.

"Results which do not reach other scholars have no value," insists a director of one of the nation's leading university presses, stating the point perhaps too strongly, but effectively.

> They cannot be criticized, they have no influence, they cannot be improved upon or applied. A product and its dissemination strike me as being particularly important for the independent scholar, because publication forces one to do one's best work. Moreover, it can help hone that work by involving the criticism of an editor and their advisors, and it leads to even more responses in the form of reviews and other commentary.

Such scrutiny by one's peers is the accepted means for validating one's work in academe. The procedures include book reviews, footnotes, barbed or complimentary, correspondence, shoptalk, invitations to presentations at conventions and other gatherings, speaking engagements, and, of course, promotions. But independent scholars are excluded, by their lack of affiliation, from having their work judged in a fair manner in this system. Often the academic journals are closed to them. They frequently do not have contacts going back to graduate school days, and then nurtured through academic careers at several institutions. They do not have their way paid to the scholarly conclaves. They lack the daily support and stimulation of colleagues in their departments.

Moreover, many independent researchers are working in nontraditional fields. The products of their inquiries *are* vital, but they are and should be *varied*, as should the ways in which they are judged. An "applied historian" who makes a policy recommendation based on her research is judged first and foremost on whether the recommended policy proves efficacious. An artist-scholar such as Judy Chicago, the creator of "The Dinner Party," is judged by art critics as well as historians, and by thousands of viewers of the work. A scholarly or scientific collector of, say, mineral specimens, wildlife samples, or historically important microscopes will be judged by his or her peers, and by the curators of the major museums that would welcome the collections as invaluable additions to their holdings.

Consider these representative products, each a worthwhile if unconventional embodiment of serious research and significant thinking:

> ➤ *A set of photographs.* The task of mapping and documenting all the European Paleolithic cave paintings has been undertaken by Luc

Jean-François Debecker. This major enterprise, which he has pursued since 1950, required visits to more than 150 caves where such paintings are known to exist. In awarding him one of the Rolex Awards for Enterprise, the prize committee said: "The results of his project will lead to new and important understandings of our past."

➤ *A work of art.* Judy Chicago's "The Dinner Party," described by the director of the Brooklyn Museum, Michael Botwinick, as embodying "enormous research, energy, and persuasion," is based on encyclopedic data on the lives of the 1,038 women honored in the work.

➤ *A film.* Scholarship reported through the medium of film has become almost commonplace: two examples are *Shoptalk: Modern Times Come to a New York Printing Plant,* an oral history film produced by the Institute for Research in History with support from the New York Council on the Humanities; and *Trials of Alger Hiss,* a 166-minute award-winning presentation of evidence obtained under the Freedom of Information Act, as well as historical footage, exploring this crucial incident in American history.

➤ *An exhibit.* Like film, an exhibit is a distinctly contemporary addition to the genres of scholarship. But one need only recall the profound effect of such major exhibits based on broad research as Ruth Benedict's "The Races of Mankind" in the 1940s, or Margaret Mead's later "The Family of Man," to realize that some outstanding researchers and theoreticians have made a deep impact through this medium. Adelbert Ames's famed visual demonstrations, originally constructed at Princeton, and Buckminster Fuller's World Game suggest the further reaches of such nonverbal or transverbal sharing of knowledge and understanding.

➤ *A park.* Central Park in New York City is the embodiment of the learning and thought of Frederick Law Olmstead.

➤ *A space shuttle.* Robert Truax, an ex-NASA scientist, built his own space shuttle in the driveway next to his house. Experts in the field generally agreed that it was likely to work. He did it to show that NASA's monopoly on such operations is conducive to inefficiency and failure to exploit fresh ideas.

➤ *A murder mystery. The Daughter of Time* by Josephine Tey is a detective story based on substantial scholarship devoted to determining whether or not Richard III did indeed murder the princes in the Tower.

➤ *A Native American village.* In Virginia, Everett Callahan has reconstructed an authentic Stone-Age American Indian village—a community using only primitive tools, weapons, and pots. His goal was to recreate a sixteenth-century community of the Powhatan Indian Confederacy, a highly organized nation that had an important influence on white American history. Callahan worked on the construction primarily by himself, though an archaeological assistant and students from Catholic University helped him occasionally.

➤ *An A-bomb.* John Aristotle Phillips chose the assignment "How to Build Your Own Atomic Bomb" for a junior-year term paper at Princeton in the 1970s. The rest of the class insisted that it was "impossible," but Phillips wanted to demonstrate the danger that terrorists could indeed create such a weapon with publicly available knowledge and materials. "You got one of the only As in the department," he was told after he handed in his paper, "but the question has been raised by the department whether your paper should be classified by the U.S. government."

Intellectual Activism

Independent scholars are pioneering in a new area that I call "intellectual activism." By that I mean they are undertaking activities that are not in themselves scholarship or science. These activities do not create new knowledge, but they make *existing* knowledge more accessible, understandable, useful, or enjoyable to others; they create the conditions for fresh discoveries or stimulate others to discover; they do something that benefits scholars, scholarship, or the general culture. They constitute an attractive diversity of options from which you can choose the one, or several, that suits your own style and strengths:

➤ speaking to wider audiences than one's peers

➤ stimulating media coverage of intellectual work or findings

> applying knowledge through consulting
> creating and conducting conferences for broad audiences
> working with educators on informing the school and college curriculum with new knowledge
> politically advocating public recognition and support for the life of the mind
> bringing scholarly work to a wider public through exhibitions, films, radio programs, and so forth
> applying scholarly knowledge and skills in other institutions, such as hospitals or business corporations
> preparing materials for, and leading, Study Circles
> organizing conferences and exhibits

Intellectual activism has been cultivated most extensively in the humanities, where such activities have burgeoned in recent years with support from state Councils on the Humanities. "Traditionally, humanistic reflection has been confined to the academic community," asserted Jay Kaplan, as acting director of the New York Council on the Humanities. "What we call 'public programming' seeks ways to bring these insights to wider audiences." Just what is a public program in the humanities? The question is best answered by noting some of the projects supported by the Council:

> an exhibition on the "History of the Black Community in Syracuse," drawn from photographs, documents, and oral histories provided by people in the community and accompanied by a symposium linking this particular experience to broader historical themes
> "The Vikings," a series of lectures in New York City and several upstate towns timed to coincide with a major exhibition at the Metropolitan Museum of Art
> a conference on hazardous waste disposal in the Buffalo region, bringing together scholars, government representatives, and concerned citizens to explore economic and political aspects of social regulation
> a series of walking tours led by a historian, discussing changing work experiences in the financial, the garment, and the diamond-cutting districts in Manhattan

Kaplan has good advice for independent humanists—and, by extension, researchers in other fields—who want to devise such programs. "The format for any program should be determined by the particular concepts you're working with, and the intended audience. Certain complex ideas may truly require such traditional presentations as lectures, seminars, conferences, or symposia." Some Council-funded projects exemplify this:

> ➤ In Greenburgh, a series of illustrated lectures, "Introduction to the World of Islam," was presented by Muslim, Jewish, and Christian scholars.
> ➤ "Broadcasting in the Public Interest," a symposium on the policy implications of new telecommunications technologies was held at Hunter College.

"Other ideas may require other forms," Kaplan suggests. "Photographic exhibitions, media (film, radio, video) presentations, panel discussions, and workshops are a few of the other formats that may be used. Formats may also be mixed, in order to attract diverse audiences or to express ideas in a variety of ways." Among such projects he cites:

> ➤ "Still Beat Noble Hearts," a dramatic presentation about the nineteenth-century writer Margaret Fuller, emphasizing the relevance of her experience to women today; it was accompanied by a lecture and discussion period
> ➤ The Bedford Stuyvesant Restoration Corporation, which celebrated the contribution of blacks to the cultural life of New York City by presenting a festival of art exhibitions, cabaret, dance performances, bus tours, and lectures

"Outreach is a vital aspect of humanities programming," says Kaplan. "This can include bringing humanities scholars to new settings in order to reach new audiences." He goes on to give some examples of the ways in which scholars have worked in the community.

> ➤ In the mid-Hudson Valley, scholars in literature and philosophy, under the sponsorship of Bard College, offered seminars in nursing homes, churches, senior citizen centers, and the county jail.

➤ A performance/lecture series, "Music by Women," has been presented in community centers, firehouses, and at noontime concerts for office workers.

➤ In a Long Island hospital, philosophers-in-residence presented seminars on medical ethics to physicians, staff, and members of the public.

Kaplan notes that new audiences may be reached in other ways.

➤ The THREADS program brought humanities seminars to people working in the textile trades. Sessions were geared to the working hours and workplaces of the participants. Materials were prepared in English and Spanish.

➤ The Mass Transit Street Theatre performs in factories, in schools, and at street fairs. Discussions follow performances, which treat such themes as worker safety and health, working women, and the urban fiscal crisis.

➤ "Brooklyn Borough Hall: A Mirror for Change" was an exhibition, installed at the Borough Hall, that explored the way in which architecture reveals transformations in a neighborhood.

"Active public participation in the planning and creation of programs increases their impact," he says. Two such community-oriented groups are:

➤ The Educational Film Library Association, which involved citizen committees in libraries and around the state in screening and evaluating films for a series of public showings on the subject of work and worklessness

➤ The Monroe County Photo-History Project, in which area residents were invited to bring photographs predating World War I to a workshop; specialists discussed the historical circumstances in which the photographs were taken, as well as how to identify and preserve photographs

"Libraries, historical societies, and museums are familiar gathering places and excellent locations for representing programs," Kaplan proposes. "There are many other possibilities, including shopping centers, banks, newspapers, county fairs, and the department store windows." For example:

> An exhibition of paintings, "Images of Labor," was shown in union halls and labor education centers.
> Turn-of-the-century community photographs were displayed in factory lunchrooms in Queens.
> "Places of Origin," a photographic exhibition depicting areas of emigration in the late nineteenth and early twentieth century, was shown at the Statue of Liberty.

"In fact, that most public of places—the street—is not to be overlooked," Kaplan concludes, noting two more imaginative projects:

> The Cooper-Hewitt Museum incorporated plazas and parks, monuments and buildings into its exhibit, "Immovable Objects," which drew attention to the nature of the urban environment.
> An Urban Folklore Festival focused on the many types of performances found in city streets, including mime, juggling, jump rope, hopscotch, and hawkers' cries. In addition to street performances and videotapes, there were panel discussions by anthropologists, musicologists, and social historians.

Two other kinds of programs that particularly appeal to me are Scholars in the Schools, which has been tried in only a few communities, and Study Circles.

Independent scholars who thrive on contact with youngsters might make a substantial contribution to school programs. I have served as a poet in schools under programs funded by the U.S. Office of Education and the National Endowment for the Arts. Why not historians, inventors, or birdwatchers in the schools, or experts on Emily Dickinson, chess, Arabic culture, or local ecology? Some schools have moved in this direction, assembling People Banks, lists of experts in the community who are willing to participate in school programs.

Independent scholars can devise curriculum materials that present their fields to thousands of students in hundreds of schools. For example, Patrick Millder, a mathematician in Albuquerque, New Mexico, whose research focus is on the flight dynamics of model rockets, has devised a program in which high school students conduct computer studies of the ballistics of model rockets and predict flight paths. As president of the National Association of Model Rocketry, he has worked on the National Model Rocket Program for Schools, for teachers of grades seven to twelve.

Still another alternative for intellectual activism is provided by the growth of Study Circles, a lovely idea borrowed from the Scandinavian countries and introduced in this country by Norman Kurland of the New York State Department of Education. A Study Circle is a method of informal education for adults. Between five and twenty people with a common interest study a particular topic together. They learn from one another, from prepared materials, and from other sources. A trained facilitator helps the group to set and meet its goals, makes sure everyone in the group participates, and assists in securing additional resources when needed. Facilitators help the group by providing assistance and suggestions; they do not themselves teach or direct the group.

Most circles follow a study guide designed specifically for their use. The guides provide a framework for discussion and include some information about the topic. However, there is no previously set body of knowledge to cover, there are no examinations to pass, and no marks. The participants identify their own concerns, needs, and objectives. The study guides are designed to foster and support group decisions about how the circle is to operate and what the topic, process, and outcome of the Study Circle are to be. Schedules and meeting places are determined by the participants. Groups usually meet once a week, in places available at no charge, such as community centers, libraries, classrooms, churches, workplaces, and homes.

There are many ways in which independent scholars can link up with these burgeoning Study Circles, according to Karen Osborne, who worked with Norman Kurland out of the New York State Education Department to promote the movement.

> Study Circle participants need the scholars and the scholars can gain tremendously from being involved in the Study Circle movement. Study Circle participants need information since groups are not led by a teacher or an expert in the field of study. Initially, this information comes from each "Independent Scholar" within the circle. Additional information can be in the form of study guides, issue papers, books, guest speakers, panel discussions, film presentations, and field trips. Independent scholars have information to share and

can use the Study Circle format as a forum for their works and ideas while helping Study Circle participants gain information they need for a rich Study Circle experience. Just as the Circles need the scholars so the scholars need the Circles. Through Study Circles, an informal dissemination network of the scholars' works can be established as additional circles form and use the materials and presentations developed by the scholars.[2]

Hazel Henderson:
Alternative Futures

> It really energizes you to know that it is possible to find your way without some academic giving you a map and a diploma. If someone had put me in Economics 1, I might never have fought my way out. I'm not only relatively unschooled but also unchurched, in fact not institutionalized at all. I operate as an individual in an institutionalized society. This gives me a view of society unmediated by many of the organizational filtering devices that color the perceptions of most of my fellow Americans.
>
> **Hazel Henderson**

"From Park Bench to Podium" might be the headline for an article on Hazel Henderson's progress as an independent futurist. No story better illustrates how one can move from "messy beginnings"—she literally started in a fog— to making an important contribution to social thought.

Twenty-five years ago Hazel Henderson was a self-confessed "absolutely ordinary corporate wife and mother, dividing her time between sitting on a New York bench in the park with the baby carriage, shopping at Bloomingdale's, and entertaining with her husband, an IBM executive complete with gray flannel suit." Fifteen years later, a typical week on her calendar included:

➤ jetting to Washington from her home in Gainesville, Florida, for a seminar with top-level administrators and visits on Capitol Hill with members of Congress

➢ doing her week's grocery shopping at the Hogtown Granary Food Co-op where she is a life member

➢ proofreading an article on solar energy for the British journal of appropriate technology, *Resurgence*

➢ biking twenty miles to meet her weekly quota of "noncognitive exercise"

➢ speaking at the University of California at Santa Barbara, as Visiting Regents Lecturer

How did Hazel Henderson go from being a predictable product of corporate bureaucracy to being an independent but listened-to-voice on major public issues? She did it largely through her struggle to awaken the rest of us to the necessity for just such a transformation in our own lives. This woman's odyssey shows how uninstitutionalized intellect can probe to the roots of some basic problems facing each and all of us, come up with its own conclusions, and thereby make an important contribution.

Henderson came to this country from England in 1956 and married an American journalist and corporate speechwriter, from whom she is now divorced. Out of this unlikely background has come a complex person "made up of a good chunk of small-is-beautiful advocate E. F. Schumacher, plus bits of environmentalist Barry Commoner, consumerist Ralph Nader, and visionary Buckminster Fuller," in the words of Brad Knickerbocker of the *Christian Science Monitor*. Yet the mix is distinctly her own, and to it she added unique capacities. "She has no difficulty working within the system," commented *Science* magazine, the prestigious journal of the American Association for the Advancement of Science, in profiling her. "She simply grabs the available handles and turns them into levers."

She first learned how to do that when she noticed, sitting on her park bench with her baby one day in 1961, that the air she was breathing stank. It reminded her of the London smog that regularly killed hundreds of people. But her perception was not much heeded by anyone else. A letter to the mayor brought an official response that what she was smelling was just "mist from the sea."

She got the notion that the city's television stations should help raise the public's awareness of air pollution, so she researched the Communication

Law relating to stations' obligations to serve the public interest. She also found out there was something called the air pollution index—this back when the term itself was unfamiliar.

"Most of the things I've done I've done because I didn't know that you couldn't do that," she recalls. Not knowing that Americans cannot take the initiative in using the mass media for their own purposes, instead of just sitting passively in front of the tube, Henderson began a one-person campaign, writing to the Federal Communications Commission (FCC) and the heads of the three major television networks, modestly suggesting that the public's "convenience and necessity" would be served if the local stations broadcast the air pollution index for each day as part of the weather report. She peppered every public official she could think of with photocopies of this correspondence, and soon an encouraging reply came from an FCC official—which was immediately photocopied and dispatched to the network presidents. Within five weeks all three local network stations were broadcasting the air pollution index. "Wow! This is a cinch," Henderson remembers thinking.

Significantly, she achieved this first breakthrough as an individual. It showed her the potential power of the independent person, acting on her perceptions but bolstered with facts and an understanding of how the systems works.

> I did it alone. There was no group at that point. I just followed my impulse to do something about a situation that troubled me, did the research, typed the flurry of letters, got the response. Subsequently, I've learned the power of joining with others, of course. But I've never forgotten how important it is to trust your own perceptions, and if you feel impelled, to act on them. People have a lot of insights, feelings, convictions, which they think are peculiar to them, and not worth inquiring into, sharing, or acting on. So we really need validation of these impulses—the assurance that it's not *we* who are crazy, but the system.

Henderson's next campaign, through Citizens for Clean Air, further harnessed the media by mounting an advertising campaign to raise public awareness of the problem. She pestered Madison Avenue ad people until she found a young agency, Carl Ally, Inc., willing to do free commercials. Then she enlisted William Bernbach, of the giant Doyle Dane Bernbach firm, to back her effort to get the stations to air the public service announcements. Result: $350,000 worth of free broadcast time for the campaign. For that endeavor Henderson was named Citizen of the Year by the New York Medical Society.

At this point, however, she was beginning to realize that a deeper analysis of problems and issues was needed. So many of the things that bothered her about American society seemed to point in the same direction: toward the deeper structure of the system. Giant corporations, bloated governmental bureaucracies, centralized systems of all kinds, overuse and misuse of technology—these underlying causes needed to be probed.

Henderson undertook a do-it-yourself advanced education in the interrelated subjects that bore on these issues. She studied economics, but rather quickly came out on the other side. "Economic policies are too important to be left to the economists," she concluded. "I came to the conviction that economic thinking as practiced by academic economists is a form of brain damage, and that the economic theories prevalent today are just so much intellectual snake oil. The economists have to be exposed as charlatans." This was well before our current disenchantment with the ways in which the nation's best economic brains have coped with the American economy. Henderson has a way of smelling something bad in the air, well ahead of others, whether she is sitting in Central Park or listening to the President's Economic Message to Congress.

So Henderson pursued her personal inquiries in field after field, mastering much of many, but being entrapped by none. "The learning jag that I went on was one that everybody is capable of," she insists. "If somebody is telling you something that sounds like a crock and doesn't look as if it fits what's happening to you, check it out. Tell yourself, 'I'm going to learn about that because I want to know where the bodies are buried.' I taught myself economics with that frame of mind. I felt somebody was pulling the wool over my eyes."

What is her "field," than? That question has badgered many broad-based scholars, particularly those whose studies are interdisciplinary or innovative. "The disciplines have become straitjackets for people who want to think creatively about our major problems," she asserts. "As I traveled around looking for my authentic colleagues in the kind of research, thinking, and writing that I wanted to do, I found that most of the people I found most congenial were calling themselves 'futurists.' They've transcended some discipline, or several of them. And they're seeking, as I am, more complete ways of describing the reality in which we live." So at the top of Henderson's résumé it says "Independent Futurist."

Such freedom has its costs, as all independent scholars know—and Henderson has paid them. She has had to cultivate resourcefulness and tenacity in overcoming the kinds of resistance with which the system confronts all nonaffiliated researchers. Getting published, for instance, loomed as a hurdle for her as it does for so many. She overcame it with characteristic panache. "I sent this paper to the only woman on the masthead of the *Harvard Business Review*," she recalls. "With it I sent a belligerent letter which said: 'I'm not a writer, not an academician, not an economist, not a scientist. I'm a *citizen* trying to define what a good society is. This is where I've come out.'" The article was accepted, and Henderson still savors the moment when she got the news. With that credit, subsequent publishing came easier.

To summarize Henderson's thought is not easy: She has entered so many fields, has tackled so many subjects. But basically she advocates the "devolution" of our present gigantic institutions. She seeks a shift toward a less centralized, more self-sufficient society that would rely on renewable or solar energy, local self-help rather than centralized bureaucracies, cooperativeness rather than competition, and emphasis on health and well-being rather than on material consumption and military preparation.

Henderson never sought the academic validation of a degree. Her touchstone has remained: Is this knowledge useful to fellow citizens in creating a better society? "My validation was, could you organize a bake sale around it?"

Her writings were brought together in her first book, *Creating Alternative Futures: The End of Economics*. Names of international experts commended the book so much that their quotes hardly could be fitted on the cover. Jacques Cousteau said: "In this book are most of the ideas we are fighting for. Anybody longing for a better life must read it." Alvin Toffler, whose *Future Shock* first won a vast audience for futurist literature, called her an "econo-clast": one of "a handful of thinkers forging imaginative alternatives at a time when conventional economics is tottering into senility." From overseas, Barbara Ward hailed Henderson's "clearsighted exposition of the dangers of overcentralization and the advantages of operations conducted on a smaller and more 'human scale.' "

Particularly interesting from the point of view of independent scholarship were some remarks by E. F. Schumacher, the doyen of the appropriate technology movement, in his foreword to the book. Of course, Schumacher was impressed: "Mrs. Henderson's essays, every one of them, have more 'reality' than almost any other writings on societal problems I know." Schumacher went on to note that her status as a independent scholar may have been an advantage rather than a handicap. "What are her credentials?" Schumacher asked rhetorically. "There aren't any. She has never attended college. Maybe this accounts for the amazing *freedom* of her thinking, a freedom matched by courage and power."

Henderson herself attributes much of her productivity to her freedom—freedom from routine and freedom from institutional typecasting. When she was offered an honorary M.S., she declined, and recalls thinking: "What I would do is pick up a peer group and they would be telling me what to say, wouldn't they? Society at this point needs a few wild cards." Like many other independent scholars, Henderson has found her true peer group, her authentic colleagues (as opposed to those one happens to share a departmental office with on a campus), outside the usual academic pigeonholes. "We're teaching each other about agribusiness, ecology, world armaments, and the links with multinational corporations. It's all happening outside academe."[3]

CHAPTER EIGHT

"Play for Mortal Stakes": The Intellectual Pleasures of Your Work

But yield who will to their separation,
My object in living is to unite
My avocation and my vocation
As my two eyes make one in sight.
Only where love and need are one,
And the work is play for mortal stakes,
Is the deed ever really done
For Heaven and the future's sakes.

Robert Frost
"Two Tramps in Mud Time"

There is one subject on which you are already an expert, one on which you already spend the better part of your waking hours. I mean, of course, your work. Why not seize upon and cultivate the intellectual dimension of your occupation or profession? You can take what you already know so well, view it in a fresh light, use it to develop wider knowledge or deeper understanding, and come up with a product of value. If your work is important to you, it might be the place from which to launch your research.

Most jobs in the American economy today offer the potential to exercise what Charles Kettering calls "the research state of mind." Our whole economy has been shifting gradually but inexorably toward an information society in which the work of more and more people involves, not the direct production of goods, nor even the provision of services, but the processing of information. In such a work world, it is possible to make two conjectures about anyone who has been employed for any extended period in an occupation, job, or profession that engages the mind. If you fall into that category, these statements should apply to you.

➤ You have learned more than you may realize from the work you have been doing.

➤ You are better positioned than you think to discover significant new knowledge, to share some important insights, or to attain a deeper understanding—if you take the time and set your mind to it.

To begin, simply ask yourself these two questions about your daily work.

1. What do I know?
2. What would be worth discovering?

Savoring the Meaning of Your Work

Solving specific problems is the first level at which your mind can function productively regarding your work. The second level is discovering and savoring some of your occupation's subtler facts, connections, meanings, and significance.

Does that seem far-fetched, given your field? Perhaps it is, if your job is doing ironwork on an office building under construction. I know *I* would have seen little potential for the play of intellect in such a job. But that was before I read *On High Steel: The Education of an Ironworker* (Quadrangle Books, 1974). The author, Mike Cherry, is one of those men you see clambering up the columns and walking along the beams that form the skeletons of office buildings under construction. To explore some of the subtler dimensions of his everyday work, Cherry kept a journal during his work on one undistinguished building which he helped "top out." "It's no taller than its neighbors," he comments dryly. "It has no visible architectural peculiarities, it is not an odd color, and though a good friend of mine fell from its forty-fourth floor to the street, there is no plaque to mark the spot."

Cherry's intent was to "make something of the work, lifestyles, attitudes, and aims of one trade." His book also serves to illuminate a significant part of contemporary American worklife and economic life, hitherto invisible to outsiders. Social scientists would call it "naturalistic observation" by an especially perceptive and articulate observer. Humanist scholars might label it "high-level reportage, unconventional memoir-writing, occupational autobiography, or genre painting in words."

Cherry took the time to look closely at his daily work; he teased out its significance and put it down on paper. Studs Terkel called the resulting book "a rare work and an important one."

Any field, then—not only those usually thought of as intellectual—can yield material for reflection, analysis, or mere delight in detecting hidden meanings. Exploring your daily work in this fashion will not only improve your competence, but also humanize your job. You will find that the closer you look, the more interesting and rewarding your work will become. "Job enrichment," to use the jargon, takes may forms, but primary among them should be the understanding of one's work in its fascinating historical, social, economic, scientific, and cultural context.

By becoming more aware of the larger resonances of your occupation, you will become both more capable and more interested in your job. You will see more options, more ways to accomplish your own goals. You may find yourself starting a journal of your own experiences, as well as of case studies of situations you participate in or learn about. Such perceptions and analyses lead quite naturally to more formalized writing for newsletters, journals, or magazines. Your discoveries will enhance your time on the job, probably increase your motivation, and possibly improve your performance. And if you *do not* find *some* aspect of your work that engages your mind this way, it may well be time to ask yourself whether you are in the right line of work.

Five Who Played "for Mortal Stakes"

"My researches are my greatest adventures," says Frank Braynard. He might well add that they usually have been related to his daily work. For most of his career, this independent scholar of America's maritime history has contrived to work in jobs that feed into, and in turn are informed by, his chosen subject.

Braynard has written a large "biography" of the S.S. *Leviathan*, considered by many to be the grandest of all the great passenger liners to cross the Atlantic. In addition, he has written several other well-received books about ocean liners, six books of sketches, and one about the port town (Sea Cliff, Long Island) in which he lives. "My volumes on the *Leviathan* are more than the history or the biography of a ship," he asserted. "They are social history. They cover some of the realities of prohibition, tell of the early exploits of aviators, relate some of the views of the poor about the rich (which were full of envy, but an envy tempered by a dream among the poor immigrants that they would one day be rich too)."

At the same time, Braynard has earned his living at a series of related jobs: editor at the American Merchant Marine Institute, assistant marine editor of the *New York Herald Tribune*, lobbyist trying to boost government subsidies to ocean liners, manager of public relations for a towing company. Through *pro bono publico* activities, too, he has expressed his enthusiasm for old ships. He helped create the South Street Seaport Museum, a highly successful venture in popularizing New York City's maritime tradition, and he conceived and managed Operation Sail, the bicentennial event that brought an armada of "tall ships" into New York's harbor and which has become a Fourth of July tradition. Braynard has also served as chair of Operation Ship, Ltd. and curator of the maritime museum at the U.S. Merchant Marine Academy at Kings Point, on Long Island.

Braynard's library includes over forty file cabinets jammed with all kinds of things about passenger liners—menus, schedules, programs, pictures, deck plans, news clippings. It is a vast collection, kept shipshape. Most of the files are in the basement of his house, but there are books and pictures and memorabilia on the two main stories of his house. In a room in which he writes on the second floor, there is a dazzling collection of paintings, photographs, and sketches. This scholar has surrounded himself, both at leisure and at work, with the stuff of his quest.

David Dugan (a pseudonym) has leapt from his work into an entirely different life of the mind; until his retirement he was a letter artist and typeface designer for metal types.

> My interest in letter forms led me to the study of calligraphy and to intriguing Italian texts. I have long been able "to get the gist" of much of the masters'

writings. I am now learning more precisely about what they wrote by trans-
lating three sixteenth-century Italian masterworks on how to write in various
calligraphic styles. One is by Arrighi, another by Tagliente, and the third by
Palatino. Of the 272 pages about 60 percent is in the Italian of the times, about
15 percent is in Latin, and the rest is in various other languages.

    I am a Latin taster, having survived five years of Jesuit-taught Latin and
three years of their Attic Greek. I have kept both fairly alive. The Greek is
the more faded. I have since informally dabbled in Spanish, with a little French
and less German. My focus is upon etymology, rather than translation. I see
the old Italian I now encounter as having great similarities to Classic Latin and
contemporary Spanish, which is comforting.

His daily work on the project brings him into constant and intimate
contact with texts that mean much to him. "Knowing that I am making a
unique contribution to the field gives a focus to my life," he reports. "Seeing the work grow toward fruition page by page is gratifying."

While the project may seem narrow in scope to outsiders, it has broader
significance to students and scholars of the field and of the languages involved. "In a broad way, it appears to me that the Italian language was evolv-
ing rapidly in the time span of these three works. So far I have gotten no
closer to the time period than a dictionary (Barretti) dated 1728, which
leaves a language-time gap of about 250 years. Compare American English
of today with our own Colonial period!"

In some respects, Dugan's scholarly activities attract even more attention
than he would like. Requesting anonymity when interviewed (hence the
pseudonym), he explained, "He who can translate Latin and lets it be known
is often beset with requests—you can easily guess the usual subject matter!"

While working for the National Aeronautic and Space Administration
(NASA) some years ago, Volta Torrey was assigned the task of looking into
windmills as an alternative energy system. "I began doing research in the
Library of Congress and the Smithsonian, and enlisted the help of friends
across the country to track down old windmills for me," he recalls. Soon he
was traveling around the country, getting more and more interested in the
operation and history of these structures that had been all around him, but
never much noticed, during his boyhood in Nebraska.

Torrey's growing preoccupation with windmills resulted in a book, *Wind*

Catcher, and a continuing interest that has fueled further research and made him one of the nation's leading experts on this subject of "molinology." He believes that the mills, perhaps together with a revival of the steam engine, offer some attractive possibilities for America's energy future. "The wind can be a very valuable supplementary source of energy," he says.

Torrey's interest has broadened to include other aspects of the origins of American technology. He is intensely interested in the life of Oliver Evans, a friend of Washington and Jefferson, whom Torrey believes deserves the credit for bringing the Industrial Revolution to America. "I've dug up enough information to write a biography of Evans," he says.

Another scholar who gradually transformed her job until it became coterminus with a long-dreamed-of research project is Ella Merkel DiCarlo, who worked as a newspaperwoman for a Massachusetts daily.

DiCarlo worked her way up from general reporter to the wire desk to become assistant to the publisher, and was placed in charge of, among other things, the editorial page. She wrote most of the editorials, handled the letters to the editor, and selected columns and cartoons to run on that page. But she also regularly indulged her penchant for local history by researching and writing pieces on the history of the community. An initial product of this research, done on her own time, was *The Black Community in Holyoke, 1770s–1970s*, published by the Oral History Center of nearby American International College. The Center's director calls it "an important historical document. DiCarlo has done us all a service by revealing the power of oral history to augment the written record and thus add to our historical understanding of this area. . . . Holyoke is the richer because Ella DiCarlo brought to her project years of historical concern, a newswoman's eye and ear for revealing data, the skill to ask worthy questions, and the ability to communicate her findings clearly. I hope her effort may serve as a model and as a stimulus to other local historians to do as well."

DiCarlo's independent scholarship, carried out both as part of her writing job on the newspaper and in great depth on her own, gradually transformed her job into a full-time, paid exercise in full-scale scholarship.

Because of the historical pieces, I am being relieved of all editorial duties except two columns, in order to prepare a book on the history of the area covered by the paper, which it wants to issue to celebrate its 100th anniversary as a daily.

I'll do the research and write the book, having already become sort of the unofficial local historian in the absence of anybody else (both the library and the museum now regularly send people out to see me for information). I'm quite excited about all this as I'd planned to do the very same thing when I retired. In fact, I'd begun to make files and cards as I ran into interesting bits of information which hadn't been dealt with in anything written about the area so far. This project will enable me to retire feeling I've achieved something.

David Forrest, a New York psychiatrist, has parlayed a life-long enthusiasm for the poet e. e. cummings into both a deepening of his professional insights *and* part-time literary scholarship. "cummings deals with some of the most powerful questions in psychoanalysis," Forrest says. "His power as a rhetorician is such that he goes to the limits of expression—the thoughts that lie too deep for tears." Forrest believes that psychiatrists can learn as much from poets such as cummings as they can from the more familiar technique of reading the most perceptive novelists. In cummings's poetry he finds instructive examples of the way we all use defense mechanisms to deal with pain, love, death, loneliness, and aggression. Over and above the clinical applications of insights he gains from cummings's poetry, Forrest is entranced with the poet's work in its own right and has written many scholarly papers on the poems.

The Further Reaches

Some independent scholars have used their occupational experiences and knowledge to investigate broad issues in our society and culture. "The 'doers' in our society really have a lot of terribly important things to say to the rest of us," insists Samuel Florman, an engineer. "But they rarely take the time, or cultivate the skills, to say it." His successful use of his engineering and construction background demonstrates how occupational expertise can provide the launching pad for far-ranging reflection.

Florman has been in the construction business in the Northeast for almost all of his working life. Periodically he stepped back from his daily work and reflected on some of the larger social issues and problems produced by our engineering triumphs. His reflections have been warmly received, at first by others in the profession and then by a wider reading public. "A useful 'read' for engineers given to self-scrutiny," said *Time* magazine in a review of his book *The Existential Pleasures of Engineering*, "and a stimulating one for the layman interested in the ancient schism between machines and men's souls."

How does a man whose working hours are devoted to running a successful construction company nurture the inclination to do such thinking and writing? "It's not easy—but it's marvelously worthwhile and satisfying," says Florman. He started modestly. It took time to position himself to speak to a broad national audience on the subjects that meant most to him. "I began by writing articles on construction matters for industry publications twenty years ago. Then I branched out to other topics, generally tackling the relationship of my own profession to the general culture. I found that professional engineering journals are anxious to have materials of broader interest and concern, and I'm sure this is true in most fields. Writing such articles is an excellent way for people in practically any field to embark on serious thinking, writing, and publishing."

After a few years, Florman had enough pieces on the relationship of engineering to literature, history, philosophy, art, and music, to make a book. But it took several years of approaching different publishers with the articles, and with the basic idea of a book built around them, before the appearance of *Engineering and the Liberal Arts* in 1968.

"I started with McGraw-Hill, and was turned down. I returned to them after a two-year period and the idea was accepted, since they were then embarking on a continuing education series for engineers in mid-career, and thought that my book would fit nicely into this series. In publishing, as in much of life, serendipitous timing is everything."

Perhaps the most important benefit of publishing that book was that it led to a number of speaking engagements that accelerated Florman's thinking and eventually led to the germ of his *Existential Pleasures*. Such benefits are commonplace in intellectual and creative work. Most authors can recall how much their first publication meant to them in confirming their identity as writers.

Existential Pleasures started as a speech to a professional society and elicited request for reprints from engineers all over the world after its publication.

"I could sense a craving for philosophical introspection behind the requests and reactions," Florman recalls. "It fed my own enthusiasm—I was spurred to much more productive work, as I realized that the case for engineering had never been articulated adequately. My field had been taking a beating from the antitechnologists for decades, and something needed to be done about it—not just for engineers, but so that anyone who cared to could come to a more intelligent appreciation of the good and bad in the field.

However, it was no easy matter to find a publisher—even with a well-received book under his belt. Only half a dozen of the forty publishers to which Florman wrote even answered his letter. Most said that they would be willing to look at the manuscript after it was finished. But after his experience in placing his first book, Florman had no appetite for writing another one and *then* trying to sell it.

Finally St. Martin's Press accepted the idea as presented and offered a contract and a modest advance. "Before I read your pieces I felt almost certain I would have to decline your project," wrote the editor, Thomas Dunne. "As a rule we publish for the general trade audience. But you have succeeded in addressing both the professional engineers and nonengineers, and I am delighted to say we would like to publish the book. I have just come from an editorial meeting where I compared your style and tone to *Lives of a Cell*."

The book received the kind of reviews every author dreams about. *The New York Times* called it "gracefully written . . . imaginatively engineered"; *The Wall Street Journal* hailed it as an "urbane, witty, intellectually far-ranging, large-spirited hymn to *homo faber*"; and *The New Yorker*, considered the arbiter of high style, called it "enchanting."

Once again, recognition revved up Florman's juices and the opportunities for them to flow. The book caught the eye of editors at *Harper's* magazine, who asked him to write several articles looking at contemporary affairs from his unique perspective. The most important of these writings have been issued as *Blaming Technology: The Irrational Search for Scapegoats* (St. Martin's Press).

> My basic motivation for doing all this goes beyond my enthusiasm for engineering. My main impulse is to look at my life, look at the world around me,

and consider the ideas that have been expressed by great thinkers of the past and present—then to speculate, argue, enter into "the great debate." That's something which I would think a great many people would like to do, and can do. And doing it from a point of view of your occupation or profession can be great asset, rather than a limitation. I believe it helps to speak from a particular place, rather than attempting to address humankind from an amorphous, all embracing, nonspecific philosopher's tower.[1]

Sabbaticals for "Practical Scholarship"

We need a new kind of scholarship: practical scholarship. Growing out of practice, it would feed back into practice by providing new knowledge or sharper understanding of some vital sector of our culture or society. One powerful means to encourage such inquiry would be to offer sabbaticals, which academics long have enjoyed and benefited from, to everyone who is interested and qualified. Although the idea may seem utopian at first hearing, two successful models already exist. Combined, they would constitute just such a program. One comes from academe, the other from the world of business.

The academic recognition of the need for sabbaticals for *practical* scholarship that will directly benefit society emerged from the experience of a professor who produced a piece of scholarship of an unusually practical kind— and who thereby inspired a grants program to encourage others to follow her example. This successful program points toward a promising form of support that should be made available to people in every field where it is appropriate. It offers the hope that as a society we might tap the knowledge and wisdom that each of us acquires in our particular professional field.

The late Mina Shaughnessy was for many years director of writing programs at City College in New York. Toward the end of her life she had learned some important principles from her work with students who had difficulty expressing themselves in written form. Using her classroom as a learning laboratory, she had uncovered the hidden patterns of logical thought that, paradoxically, produce errors in student writing. What she had learned could help others throughout the country to teach underprepared or handicapped students the skills they would need to succeed in college. But her job responsibilities prevented her from undertaking a book explaining what she had discovered.

With a timely, modest grant from a foundation, Mina Shaughnessy wrote that book. *Errors and Expectations* has since become an inspiration and a handbook for hundreds of directors of writing programs and teachers of writing throughout the country. Its contribution in helping a generation of very different college students is widely recognized.

This was a new kind of scholarship—or at least, a kind not readily recognized in Mina Shaughnessy's field. Her findings would not have qualified for publication in the major journal in the field. Mina Shaughnessy's scholarship was *practical.* It grew out of practice and addressed a problem in the real world, but it used the skills and powers of scholarship to discern some new truths about the problem. Shaughnessy used just those abilities that are developed in advanced literary study: close and sensitive reading of texts and sharp reflection on an author's motivations, background, and verbal behavior.

Could Mina Shaughnessy's practical scholarship be a model for others? Some leaders in academe think so, and they have launched the Mina Shaughnessy Learning From Practice awards program. Under the auspices of the Fund for the Improvement of Postsecondary Education (FIPSE, a federal grants program that is widely regarded as the most successful ever conducted to foster change in higher education), this program provides to others support that enabled Mina Shaughnessy to write her book. "We are convinced that there are others like Mina Shaughnessy," says the prospectus inviting applications for the awards, "who, if given additional support to relieve them from the demands of other commitments or to obtain needed services, can make a lasting and profound contribution to postsecondary education improvement."

I was privileged to help judge the applications for the first round of these awards, and it was an exhilarating experience. Unlike applications for more conventional scholarly stipends, these came not just from professors seeking to do arcane research that would advance them professionally, but from a wide variety of people with important practical knowledge: counselors, union officials, museum directors, librarians, CETA and industry trainers, and members of community-based organizations. Here was an array of intelligence, commitment, knowledge, and energy not confined to one occupational sector nor to one limited set of subject matter disciplines. Each application was based on actual practice, and proposed a product that would be of tangible benefit to others. These products share with scholarly papers the basic characteristics of extending or refining our knowledge and of codifying or reflecting on some important data. But they transcend the usual image of what a product of scholarship might be. Among their purposes are: to synthesize new knowledge emerging from actual practice or program evaluation; to reconceptualize curriculum, particular disciplines, or ways people learn; to formulate changes in federal, state, and institutional policies that promise to enhance learning opportunities and improve education quality; to identify needed directions for future improvement based upon the experiences of the past.

I believe the principles inherent in FIPSE's Learning from Practice program could and should be extended more widely. Sabbaticals for the purpose of practical scholarship should become commonplace. I would hope that more and more corporations, nonprofit organizations, government agencies, and other employers would provide subventions for that purpose. Even without such support individuals with a strong inclination toward study and reflection could elect to finance such leaves-of-absence themselves—sometimes with the expectation that the self-renewal that they achieve would make them even more valuable in their occupation and thus enable them to recoup some of the costs.

Would American business and industry be willing to support such sabbaticals—and could they afford to? For the past twenty years the Xerox Corporation has allowed twenty or more of its employees to have a year off with full pay and benefits in order to pursue social-service projects in their communities. Those employees have worked in such fields as literacy, civil rights, drug education, and penal reform. They have done work as varied as the needs of our society: William Wellstead worked with his wife to design and implement a marriage enrichment program in Monroe County, New York; Patrick Lynch established two centers to monitor Sudden Infant Death; Frayda Cooper organized a multitown program providing services for the aged.

On the occasion of the tenth anniversary of the program, the vice president, Robert Schneider, said, "It's clear to us after ten years that the employee we get back is without question a much broader-gauged individual."

What would you get if you crossed FIPSE's Learning from Practice awards for practical scholarship with Xerox's Social Service Leave for worthwhile projects? Answer: Sabbaticals to produce new knowledge or understanding, growing out of practical problems and feeding back into practice. A program of such sabbaticals would go beyond the FIPSE awards by involving people in *all* fields. It would go beyond the Xerox program by focusing on *intellectual* projects as well as on service work.

Such research sabbaticals, sponsored by major companies, could enlist the mental capabilities of American workers at every level, from the factory floor to the executive suite. A factory foreman might take a year to develop and create a plan for raising the quality of work life and productivity in his industry. An advertising executive could be supported while she probed the impact of televised commercials for political candidates and the profession's responsibility in this area. A paper company executive might devote his sabbatical to documenting the impact of his industry on the nation's forests. Incidentally, each of these projects actually has been conducted by an individual in the field, at great personal sacrifice, often with destructive delays due to the press of making a living or to conducting it as a retirement project. Each project would have been done sooner and better if research sabbaticals had been available. Even more important, thousands of other similar projects that would otherwise never be conducted at all would and could be done.

A society based on brainpower, on good new ideas, no longer can rely on one sector (academe) or on a specialized subunit (the research and development divisions of companies) to produce its new knowledge. It can and must harness the intellectual capacities of a far wider section of its highly educated, mentally adventurous work force. What could be more exemplary of the great American tradition of Benjamin Franklin, Thomas Edison, and Buckminster Fuller?

Buckminster Fuller:
Exploring the Universe

Every time man uses his *know-how*
His experience increases
And his intellectual advantage
Automatically increases.

Know-how can only increase.
It is therefore scientifically clear
That:—wealth which combines
Energy and intellect
Can *only increase*, and that wealth can
Increase *only with use*
And that wealth increases
As fast as it is used.
The faster—the more!

Buckminster Fuller
"How Little I Know"

"The mind at work" is nowhere better exemplified than in the mind and work of Buckminster Fuller. Most Americans have a distorted picture of "Bucky," a natural consequence of his having been on the cover of *Time* magazine, of speaking whenever he was asked, and of constantly coming up with concepts and inventions, such as the geodesic dome, that caught our imagination and changed the very landscapes in which we lived. Few people realize that Bucky-in-the-making was very different from the cerebral, abstract, almost mythical figure he had become by the time he died, at the age of eighty-seven, in 1983. For the better part of his life, Fuller looked like a failure—to others, certainly, and at crucial moments, to himself.

Early on, he occasionally tried to turn his ideas into a way of making a living—and usually failed before he discovered that, if you follow your inner vision and seek ways to realize it, the "making a living" will take care of itself. More than once he rejected all thoughts of *ever* making a living, planning to devote himself completely to his intellectual quest—and regularly found that his pure research led right back to a potentially profitable product or service!

Fuller exemplified "the problem-solving mind." He even interpreted tragedies in his own life, such as the death of his father and of his infant child, as "failures of design"—problems that he saw himself having been born to solve. He constantly tried new fields, roles, and assignments, and each time figured out how to turn his work tasks into grist for his personal research.

He was the first person to point out to the physicist himself that Einstein's theories could be put to practical use, and he is best known throughout the world for the geodesic dome. He took the ultimate step of creating for himself, not only his job, but also an entire industry within the field of shelter construction. Few individuals in our time have enjoyed the intellectual pleasures of their work as keenly as this man.

The best way to understand the real Fuller is to start with the lowest point of his life. Living in Chicago with his wife and baby in 1927, Fuller had just been fired from his job. Outsiders had taken over the Stockade Building Company, which he had founded with his father-in-law in order to manufacture a new kind of building system they had developed; the new owners dismissed Fuller summarily without severance pay.

"All these things happening when there was a new child and we were stranded almost penniless in Chicago. . . ." he has recalled. "I said to myself, 'I've done the best I know how and it hasn't worked. I guess I'm just no good; people seem to think so; even my mother has always been afraid that I was worthless. I guess she was right.'"

At this "critical detonation point," he walked out of his apartment down to the shore of Lake Michigan, intent on not coming back. The harsh winds swept in over the lake from Canada, waves lapped at his feet, the black waters stretched almost invitingly beyond where the eye could see. But as he stood there at midnight, the *answer* he thought he had found—to dispose of himself so that his wife and daughter could fall back on her family's capacity to care for them—suddenly gave rise to fresh *questions*.

The theme of Fuller's meditation was the absolute necessity for *independence* of thought—the mandate to make his own personal investigation of the most basic questions: "Now you must think for yourself. You have gotten into this mess by taking other people's word for things—your family and your father's friends who told you that your ideals were impracticable, that this was a tough, hard world with not enough goods to go around, therefore you must get yours first and then perhaps you can afford the luxury of ideals. But, if I am to believe in myself and the validity of my own ideas, I must stop thinking as other people told me to and rely on my own experience."

Fuller came to the conclusion that night that "you do not have the *right* to eliminate yourself, you do not belong to you. You belong to Universe. . . . You and all men are here for the sake of other men." Years later he put it this way: "I did have many more types of experience than most . . . just by the good luck of being fired out of *this* and forced into *that* pattern. . . . I had to do something about looking my experience over. . . . And, if these experiences are put in order, they might be of use to others. . . . Whether I like it or not, I am the caretaker of a vital resource: me!"

Thus Fuller started out afresh with a set of questions much like those suggested at the beginnings of this chapter: "What do I know? What would be worth discovering? From then on, Fuller excelled at extracting from all of his work experiences, both past and future, the maximum intellectual grist for his mental mill. "I am not a genius," he often insisted, "but I am a terrific package of experience." One of the conclusions he came to that night on the shore of Lake Michigan was: "My experiences are on inventory and of value to others."

The key to his approach was that new sense of independence—independence from what he had been taught, from what other people were thinking, even from the unexamined assumptions embodied in the words we use. Eventually he came to call himself "the most unlearned man in the world" because of all that he had *unlearned* in order to think his own thoughts. "Bucky realized that if he were to follow his resolution to believe only those things that he could verify from his own experience," writes his lifelong friend, Alden Hatch, "he must clear his mind of everything he had been told."

His first and most dramatic step was to stop talking. He decided that he simply would not speak to anyone nor allow anyone to speak to him until he felt that he knew what words he wanted to use and what they meant. Thus, he would be forced really to understand what he was thinking, to think thoughts that were based solely on his experience, and to avoid parroting untruths learned from others. His silence lasted for almost two years. "Out of this intense period of silent thought emerged in embryo most of the great philosophical and mathematical innovations that have made his fame and moved the world forward a little," concludes Hatch, who summarized Fuller's mental independence:

> Bucky's determination not to accept anything but his own experiences as a basis for his philosophy did not apply to books, provided they were about facts—facts of history, facts of mathematics, facts of physics—but he reserved the right to reevaluate them in the light of his own experience, and mostly he did so drastically. He did a great deal of research in the public libraries—presumably he had to speak to the librarians—very briefly. This disposes of the canard which one of his relations put out that "The only books Bucky ever reads are his own." However, one could definitely say from that time forward that the only thoughts Bucky has thought have been his own.

Fuller continued to cultivate his independence throughout his life. He awarded *himself* the kind of sabbatical I have proposed, to put his thoughts in order, distill what he learned from his experience, and create a communicable result from his experimentation, investigations, reading, and thought.

I have focused on these crucial psychological aspects of Fuller because it is from them that all his ideas, inventions, and insights sprang. The record of Fuller's accomplishments is familiar from other sources: the geodesic domes that we have all seen everywhere, from children's playgrounds to world fairs; the Dymaxion house suspended from a pole with floors hung from it as from a Christmas tree; the three-wheeled Dymaxion car, which outperformed other automobiles in its time and for the many years to follow; the Dymaxion map, which first depicted the earth's land masses without distortion; the World Game, which enables students to join in planning our global future. What is important to us as aspiring independent thinkers and researchers are not Fuller's particular products, which may not even lie within our field of interest, but rather the frame of mind from which such inventiveness and insight emerged.

As Fuller's career developed after 1927, the relation between his thought and his work continued to be ambivalent and paradoxical. For example, he first chose to enter the field of housing because of its practicality: Shelter is a basic human requirement. Because innovations in the field generally were accepted so slowly (he estimated fifty years), it was "safe," by which he meant: "If I aim to be fifty years ahead of my time I shall be safe. No one will interfere with me because I'll be so far ahead that I will pose no threat to all the people who have a vested interest in opposing progress. They'll just call me a nut."

Sure enough, in 1972 a business executive told Fuller, "We've got a new industry coming to East St. Louis. I suppose you've heard about it."

"What is it?"

"Mass production of bathrooms."

"They are right on time. I designed the first one forty-five years ago."

Despite playing it safe by being fifty years ahead, Fuller was plagued by all the ills and frustrations that routinely afflict the independent thinker and researcher. When he produced his first distillation of his findings and ideas, *Nine Chains to the Moon*, in 1938, a friend, the popular author Christopher Morley, commended the book to his publisher, Lippincott. But when the editor came to a chapter in which Fuller explicated Albert Einstein's then-little-appreciated theory of relativity and outlined possible applications to everyday life, the editor balked. It was well known that there were only about ten men in the world capable of understanding Einstein's ideas. When the editor reviewed the list of those men, and other lists of distinguished academics of the day, he failed to find Fuller's name anywhere. Therefore, Lippincott wrote Fuller, the house would feel guilty of "charlatanry" if it published his book.

How did it feel to this outsider to be rejected because he was not duly enrolled in the scientific establishment of his day? One of his biographers describes the impact: "Like all new authors, he had fantastically high hopes for this book into which he had poured so much thought and, yes, emotion. In his fervid imagination he had pictured it sweeping the world with a new revelation of truth. Now to be accused of charlatanry was like the lye on his brain."

Fuller sent the manuscript to Einstein in Princeton. Several months later, at Einstein's request, he was summoned to a soirée at the Riverside Drive home of Dr. Morris Fishbein in New York City. When Fuller arrived, as he recounts the incident, the famous physicist rose immediately from a crowd of admirers and said, "We must talk together," and led Fuller to Fishbein's study where they could be alone. On the table was the manuscript. They sat down on either side of the table, and Einstein said at once, "Young man, I've been over your book and am notifying your publisher that I am pleased and satisfied with your explanation." Then he added, "You amaze me. I cannot conceive anything I have ever done as having the slightest practical application. I evolved all this in the hope that it might be of use to cosmogonists and to astrophysicists in gaining a better understanding of the universe, but you appear to have found practical applications for it."

From then on, even during brief periods of affiliation with one or another university, Fuller has been essentially an independent. (One biographer describes his longest-standing affiliation, with Southern Illinois University at Carbondale, as a "home base where he touched down briefly. . . . Fuller traveled constantly, teaching students all across the country.") At his eighty-sixth birthday party, it was the theme of his independence, both as advantage and disadvantage, that was struck most touchingly. The actress Ellen Burstyn, a long-time friend and fan, said on that occasion, "It's criminal that he doesn't have a a position now. At Princeton, for example. Or Harvard, for God's sake. It's unthinkable that a mind of that magnitude should not have a home, you know. He's in top form."

But Bucky himself seemed utterly unconcerned about his lack of affiliation.

At the age of thirty-two, I decided I was either going to commit suicide or discover what a penniless human could do on behalf of humanity. I decided on the latter and realized that human beings were introduced into Universe for an important reason. They're like bees, you see, bees who go out and get honey without realizing they're also performing cross-pollinization. I realized that we are only throwaway, that we've never designed anything, that Universe exhibits a mathematical orderliness which naturally implies a greater intellect at work, and that we are part of that design. Then I made a commitment never to use this knowledge for personal gain or political power. My life has been, as a result, one miracle after another.[2]

CHAPTER NINE

Scholarship as Your Joy, if Not Your Job

Take a job as a professor? No way! I love my life: I've got my job at Merill Lynch which already pays twice what I'd make starting out as a prof, my social life in a cosmopolitan city rather than a string of teas with the dean—and my *research* is going *great*!

An independent scholar

Yᴏu do not have to be a professor to be a scholar. That is the lesson I have learned from former would-be academics who are successfully pursuing their research outside academe—and loving both the research and the rewards of working and living in the real world. I don't want to be beamish about this: It is not easy. You will have to devise your own regimen of research and thinking and writing, which will be quite different from the academic model. You may find academe sniffish until you become established and possibly unwelcoming even then. But success will bring immense satisfaction and possibly even extrinsic rewards beyond the ken of most academics.

First, let's put things in historical perspective.

"Scholarship has always flourished quite well outside the university, and it flourishes still," insists Professor Robert Everhart of the University of California in Santa Barbara. "Very few of the world's seminal thinkers have made a career of the professorship. Most have only occasionally been residents of academe, and many have never associated with universities, preferring to focus on their scholarship wherever they are."

Everhart cites some stellar exemplars of what might be called "unattached scholarship," including Thorstein Veblen, Karl Marx, John Stuart Mill, and Charles Darwin. "Had Darwin worked for a publish-or-perish institution, he certainly would have perished," Everhart notes dryly.

Everhart challenges our unexamined assumption that "the site of scholarship [is] associated with some mythical path to nirvana called the university career," causing us to "look condescendingly at everything else as bad karma. Knowing no other model, many of us continue to believe that all significant work, at least in the social sciences and the humanities, has been nursed at the breast of mother university."

People with a vocation for scholarship or scientific inquiry, Everhart urges, should "de-emphasize the false criteria we have used as career beacons and begin practicing our true craft—a craft that calls for the ability to critically analyze literary, social, political, historical, economic, and cultural phenomena. Opportunities exist where we are." [1]

Nowadays many young scholars have no other choice. In fields such as English literature, history, philosophy, art history, foreign languages and literatures—in fact, in the whole area of the humanities—more Ph.D.s are being produced each year than can possibly be absorbed by the academic community. Fewer than a third can find college jobs.

The dearth of new faculty posts in many academic disciplines already has aroused fears of a "lost generation" of scholars in major humanistic and scientific fields. Perhaps, without discounting the gravity of the situation, we might rephrase that as a "lost generation" of *professors*. That would be a blow to academe and a diminution of our educational system—but seeing it as the demise of *scholarship* is to equate serious research with the professoriate, a historical and philosophical mistake.

The *Chronicle of Higher Education* reported that "Independent Scholars Find There Is Life Beyond the University."

They are men and women with graduate degrees, who, in the economic crunch of the past five years, have lost academic jobs or discovered that the jobs they once expected have not materialized and may never do so. For some, what started as a crisis in their professional careers has now become an opportunity to work independently, beyond the "hegemony" of the university. Many of [them] said they wouldn't go back to an academic job even if they were offered one.

The first rock-hard question faced by many would-be-academics these days is: "Should I get a Ph.D. at all—given the bleak prospects of obtaining a faculty position in my field?"

When I meet people with that problem, my first impulse is to take them up to talk with Richard (Buz) Gummere at Columbia, a veteran counselor of students and the author of *How to Survive Education*. He has thought deeply about it.

> Frankly, I'm worried about people who decide not to go on to the doctor's degree. I admit that if your motive toward scholarship is *professional*, it might make sense to back off. That is, if you're fixated on becoming a teacher and full-time scholar, or on enjoying the detachment and independence of the professoriate, or if your finances are sparse, then the decision makes sense.
>
> But it's different if your motive is a need to become a deeper connoisseur of Tacitus or Beaudelaire or a disciple of Von Ranke, or to reevaluate Pitt's hand in the Balance of Power or the influence of pseudoVanvitelli stairways in Calabria, or to work with colloids or quarks or almost periodic functions.

But what about employment?, most students counter. "Look, the job market is much harder to predict far ahead than many think," Gummere argues. "Nobody really knows what will be the need for scholars, let alone teachers, in the late 1990s. So I encourage humanists, scientists, and others of philosophical bent, who can afford it, not to turn away lightly from scholarship."

Moreover, Gummere points out, advanced academic training is becoming much more "marketable."

> Suppose when you get your doctor's degree the academic job market were just as bearish as today and the new fields for scholars outside it had not burgeoned much either. Suppose, for example, the movement of Public History hadn't kept on growing and the Wells Fargo Bank in San Francisco, with a history department staffed by three full-time Ph.D.s, had not been much imitated.
>
> Nevertheless, I expect that scholars would have continued to become more attractive to employers, as they are becoming today in the corporate as well

as the rest of the employment scene. Recently, just out of this university, from various arts and sciences graduate departments, stranded academics have found good jobs in government, public affairs, finance, manufacturing, and consulting. The enthusiasts keep up their scholarly work in their spare time, continue professional memberships and even do some part-time teaching.

Whether you stay on for the doctorate or not, the moment will come when you must leave the university. How does it feel? Kathleen Spaltro saw it coming:

> Early in my graduate program I realized the enormous personal risk, the exorbitant cost of planning to stay in academe. I made a decision then about which I see no reason to waver—the decision to finish my career as an academic by finishing my doctorate and then to change careers. Investing in an academic future seemed and seems a bad investment.
>
> Since I had no desire to leave unfinished part of my life, I resolved to stay until my dissertation was finished. Since I also desired, rather strongly, to have a successful future, I also resolved to finish that dissertation and my graduate education in as little time as possible. Before I got to dissertation writing, however, I learned as much as possible about opportunities outside academic life for people like me, for people with my skills and personal qualities.

Spaltro solved her practical problem of finding employment—she got a job in the public relations department of a major Chicago hospital—but more important is how she felt and thought about her situation.

> I am a scholar, and am not less so because I leave the university. The need to learn, the fascination with a special subject, do not leave. I already have the beginnings of another book flashing in my mind.
>
> I am only the more certain that my scholarly urges will not let me alone because for me, as for many other people, scholarship serves as a way of formulating and resolving personal questions. I am not primarily a fact-grubber, though my curiosity ranges over several fields of interest. My idea of a scholar—and it is not everyone's—consists of the notion that a man or woman might care so much about a question that he or she would burrow endlessly among old books and documents to find the answer. And then that the scholar would expend enormous energy thinking issues through and writing his thoughts out, for his own enlightenment and that of others. So my idea embraces, not the notion of the accumulation of facts for their own sake, but the pursuit of facts because they matter so much in one's everyday existence.

If ideas have no compelling influence upon our lives, if they exist in dry catalogues of facts, why should we care about them at all?

So I have hope that my scholarly writing may perhaps continue, and, knowing myself, I am fairly certain that my scholarly interests will persist. They have always expressed my needs as a human being intent upon "right action."

Spaltro sees a world of opportunities opening up as a result of, and concomitant with, her scholarly interests:

The need for educated people with excellent communication skills and/or language ability abounds in that forsaken, "nonhumanistic" world. Moreover, by concentrating on teaching as *the* profession (that is, as the source of income supporting scholarship), humanists condemn the world outside to the untender mercies of those without their humanistic understanding, and to the control of those contemptuous of that knowledge. Have we not abdicated our position of responsibility, withdrawn to a posture of "splendid isolation," betrayed our trust? The current—and continuing—job crisis in academe devastates many. But it also presents us with a rare opportunity to face this issue, to define our fundamental concerns as more than self-concern.

Young scholars from diverse fields share Spaltro's conviction—even in fields where there is no job crisis. Garrett De Bell, for example, dropped out of a doctoral program in zoology at the University of California at Berkeley because he felt that the detachment of most academic scientists is an important cause of the environmental crisis. De Bell left academe to devote full time to population problems at the first Washington lobbyist for Zero Population Growth. He edited and contributed to *The Environmental Handbook* and *The Voter's Guide to Environmental Politics.*

"Scientists should practice their calling with full concern for its relevance to the problems and needs of our time," says De Bell. "This will require radically new ways of training, research, and even lifestyles to make their work relevant."

The turning point in De Bell's academic career came when he realized that success in academe would probably divert him from more important concerns:

I finally settled on a thesis on the population dynamics and bioenergetics of a species of wolf spider. At the time I started on my project I really liked the spiders I was working on; but as I became increasingly aware of what man was doing to the world's ecosystems and the irrelevance of my going through the motions of getting a Ph.D., I figured I would wind up hating the spiders by the time I got my doctorate. One day I just walked off the campus and never came back as a student. For a few months after that I taught ecology at the Berkeley Ecology Center, which seemed a lot more important than academic games.

Science in academe suffers grievously, De Bell concluded, from its isolation from the real world—the same kind of isolation that troubles Kathleen Spaltro.

The trouble with the academic approach is that it rarely is directed toward solving the problems. It is not enough to understand that mercury concentrates in food chains, and that that is an interesting example of the cycling of materials in nature. Why is the mercury there? Its sources have to be found, and its discharge into the system has to be stopped. This will involve studying the industries that use mercury (as a fungicide in paper manufacturing, as an electrode in chlorine productions, in the manufacture of many plastics). It will be necessary to find out what can be done to eliminate mercury loss into the environment of all of these processes, and furthermore, to look for ways of doing without materials whose production releases mercury into the environment.

Independent scholars in other fields testify that they find their real-world situations preferable to being ensconced in academe.

"I spent fourteen years within the ivy walls," says Richard Haight of Network Research in Denver.

I remember having the suspicion that the "outside world" had no place for such as I, like a planet that would not support life. I am embarrassed to recall that I used to say, "If you're not an ape, the only sensible place to be is on campus." Wrong. True. I had some of the most gratifying and important experiences of my life within the university system.

But when I finally found, and created, my own style and place, I felt much better, and I think I have become more effective and productive. I had to accept that I have a particular way of working that is out of phase with academic life, and that I have legitimate scholarly interests that happen to question some of the basic assumptions and practices of the university system. Though I earned a Ph.D. in English literature, my interests are quite a bit broader than that, and I prefer to work expansively rather than as a specialist. None of the foregoing means that I am particularly wonderful. But I *am* willing to say that others might do well to question whether their unique combination of personal style, scholarly interests, aptitudes, and so forth really suggests an academic career or an independent career.

Prior to joining Network Research, Haight spent two years as associate director of the Colorado Humanities Program, a funding agency. In that capacity he visited most of the campuses in Colorado and spoke to dozens of "faculty folk."

I discovered a truth that most of us are too polite to utter—many campuses are nearer the intellectual atmosphere of Mickey Gilley's Bar in Pasadena, Texas, than of Harvard Yard. At one rural, two-year college, I found the well-educated Dr. So-and-So teaching *seven* sections, with five preparations. He said that there were only one or two English or art majors on campus, and the biggest event on campus the previous semester had been a concert in the gym by the Marine Corps Band.

The point is, not only are there three new Ph.D.s for every available job, but there are five or ten new Ph.D.s who are overtrained and overspecialized for each job available. The situation is a sorry replay of those nineteenth-century English novels in which young theologians took poor parishes in bleak backwater areas and grew more and more bitter and crabbed as the years went by.

Haight works with many would-be or ex-academics at Network Research:

To make a composite story of it, the scholar comes in rather hesitantly and tells his story apologetically—not finding an academic job, or being denied tenure does that to people. What can you do? "Teach at the university." What would you like to do? "Teach at the university." Would you consider doing anything else? "I guess I'll have to."

It's often pathetic. But we steer them to a career counselor, one we know and trust, and that sometimes is very useful to get them to clarify their own skills and interests and stop feeling so useless. Then they might need a business card; I really believe in business cards. I think that if I were ever a panhandler I'd save up to have business cards printed. Even an unemployed ex-academic can become somebody through a business card—consultant, communications expert, researcher, speaker, tutor, archivist, writer, historian, gentleman companion, literary secretary, whatever. Stationery is useful, too. Most jobs are gotten through contacts, so if an independent scholar wants to find work that uses the knowledge and skills gained in graduate school, it is very useful for him or her to get out into the community and be active, involved, meeting people. The magic of this process is that pretty soon the ex-academic becomes very positive and confident. One unemployed oral historian I know spent months looking for a suitable job, but kept turning job offers down. She finally realized that she wanted to go into business for herself, creating family or company histories.

I associate independence with creativity. A scholar, like an artist, needs to surround himself with people and an environment that will support his or her creativity. Many find what I have called "academic squalor" poisonous to their creativity and they would do better elsewhere. Furthermore, the academic schedule—classes, office hours, committee meetings, semi-obligatory public events, etc.—can be very distracting. Academic life is not usually as leisurely as most people think. A scholar can end up preparing classes and grading papers evenings and weekends to the point where the job takes up all of his or her time. In my own case, I have a long, slow warm-up to research or writing, and then, when I am thoroughly involved, I become very perseverative—I work long and hard until the job is finished. I have been much more productive since I left the university system and could set my own schedule and align with my own internal rhythms.

We now have a small class of people in this country whom I would call "starving scholars." They can learn from starving artists that it doesn't take much money to live a rich life. The operating principle is to do *directly* what you desire to do rather than teaching or selling cars as a *means* to the end you desire. This may entail living cheaply near a large university or in a stimulating neighborhood, teaching an occasional course in a continuing education program, buying used books, using the university library—always dress like faculty folk—and networking to meet people you can talk to or to take care of other needs.

Independent scholars need to get for themselves what a university system supplies. Some may need students, while others will be relieved not to have deal with them. Some may need stimulating colleagues, while others need solitude. Some may need research facilities and materials, while others need typing or photocopy services. I am sure that some kinds of research call for equipment that can only be found at universities, and I can only sympathize with those who have been denied use of such equipment. On the other hand, I regret it if such scholars don't go on to a manageable research design, or find some other way to use their skills.

Anyway, my work at Network Research has shown me that independent scholars can find other ways to meet their own needs besides getting an academic appointment. There is indeed life beyond the university.

Leo Miller:
The Scholar Outside

> Every edition of Milton's early poetry hereafter, and
> every biographical account of his youthful development,
> will have to be based on these two contributions, which
> make all previous publications obsolete. Most of my
> contributions have this character: supplying factual,
> verified data, replacing guesses or hypotheses.
>
> Leo Miller

In these words, Leo Miller expresses the justifiable self-confidence of the
scholar who has contributed to that basic work of fact finding and meaning
making which underlies all humanistic learning. Without this unremitting
attention to the factual basis of our knowledge of the past, we would be cut
off from the roots of our culture, of our very humanity. Such study is not
narrowing. Properly pursued, it can be—indeed, *must* be—broadening.
For Miller, it is the focus of a life infused with

> a hunger for knowing, for scientific inquiry and verifiable data, a knack for rec-
> ognizing unspoken assumptions, for distinguishing hearsay from valid evi-
> dence, for finding jigsaw puzzle pieces which were not even known to be
> missing. One *studies* incessantly in business, in politics, in "freedom-riding"
> civil rights struggles; asking people questions; traveling over Europe, Asia
> and Africa as an individual, not in a group tour; in books and museums, by-
> passing the secondary popularizations and going directly to the source. A
> Freud centennial year? A time to go through everything published by Freud,
> Jung, Adler, and then decide which one made sense. Another year, Sotheby
> Parke Bernet held a sale of Rembrandt etchings, during which it was possible
> to hold in the hand and examine closely at least one original example of every
> etching he made: then one can have an idea about Rembrandt.

Milton, then, was only one of the many avenues Miller pursued. What
drew Miller to this poet? One hardly has to ask, given the poet's status as
one of the two greatest in the English language, a master of humanistic learning and a pillar of our literary and artistic heritage. But for Miller, there

also is Milton's complexity—a quality that speaks to this scholar's own broad interests.

> To understand his treatise on theology, one delves into Calvin, Ochino, Spinoza, deeply. To understand his epic style, one must absorb Homer, Virgil, Dante. To feel his essays on the right to marry for love safeguarded by the right to divorce for incompatibility, one must grasp the evolution of the family through the ages. To do a footnote on Milton's peculiar opinion favoring plural marriage under certain circumstances required the research which led to the book on *The Polygamophiles*. Milton attacks Adrian Vlacq, a man whom mathematicians praise: a mystery, which led to a monograph on the history of logarithms to solve a great robbery. Following Milton's steps as undersecretary for foreign affairs in Cromwell's government leads to an exciting manuscript diary of a German diplomat that begs for publication.

Such scholarly inquiries contribute demonstrably to the community—first to the particular community of peers working in the same field and then to the other and later scholars for whom one's work will provide the basis for further advances. Miller's researches have added substantially to such scholars' and readers' understanding, supplying answers to questions that have baffled critics, filling in gaps, and clarifying events.

> My book, on Mylius and Milton, is an exploration into the early history of international diplomacy in the formative stages of the modern state system. *Milton and Vlacq* is actually a treatise in the history of mathematics and logarithms, which elicited responses from mathematicians at MIT and in Holland. *Milton's Portraits* was a study in art history which called forth a long discussion article by the curator of the Ashmolean Museum in England.

A scholar is judged first by his peers, and Leo Miller's achievement after many years has been so recognized. He serves on the Board of Advisors of the *Milton Quarterly* (published at Ohio University and endorsed by the Milton Society of America), reviewing each issue before its appearance to help maintain a high standard of scholarship. His colleagues credit him not only for his substantive findings but also for his methodological contributions, such as new bibliographical research techniques for investigating books published under the imprimatur of the Roman Catholic Church; polasographic techniques for interpreting manuscript material; and approaches to determining the correct meaning of texts in Neo-Latin and archaic German.

But Leo Miller is more than a witness to the intense satisfactions of doing true humanistic scholarship outside the academy. He is also a witness to its heart-rending frustrations. From what Leo Miller has achieved is the result of unremitting struggle, not only to meet the *intellectual* challenges that all researchers face, but also against obstacles placed in his way merely because he pursued his inquiries outside of academe.

"The first problem is simply access to the materials," Miller notes.

> The libraries which house the rare books, archives, and manuscripts I need are closed on weekends, evenings, and holidays—just the times when a scholar who is employed full-time to make his living must do his work. The persons in charge are usually young employees, acting under strict instructions to keep "the public" out, and admit only those with faculty or graduate student identification cards.

Overcoming that obstacle—not just once, of course, but constantly, over and over again—one nevertheless does one's work, finds one's sources, gets one's hands on the materials one needs. The next problem is getting one's work considered by the journals. There is a strong old boys' network among the academics in this field, as in most others. Editors favor colleagues whom they know from graduate school days, from mutual friends, and from conferences, and those who can reciprocate with acceptance in *their* journals.

Miller's way around these obstacles was to find his first publication opportunities not in the United States but in England and Canada. "Some of those papers had been rejected in this country by editors who said quite plainly: 'This subject belongs to Professor So-and-So.' "

Eventually, one has a book to offer. Has acceptance in the journals won enough recognition to get a reading at a university press? Not for the independent scholar. "A stone wall," says Miller. "They will not even consider or look at a manuscript by an independent—while they print tons of trash by tenured mediocrities."

Nevertheless, one gets one's book out somehow. *Will* people in the field now have the courtesy to give it a critical review and judge one's work on its merits? Miller recalls a speaker at the Modern Language Association annual convention who summed up one's prospects. "This man said, seemingly as a matter of *pride*: 'Professor X always reviewed my books, and I always reviewed his.' "

The most serious problem is lack of funding. Each independent scholar feels this in a different way. For Miller it hurts when he desperately needs funds for photocopying sources, travel to archives, and secretarial help. In July 1981 a Milton symposium was held in England, an international affair. Miller was among those invited to speak; he reported on his work in Westminster Abbey. Before the symposium, the arrangements committee sent out a form letter that those planning to attend merely to *listen* might submit to their universities for travel funds. Miller, who was to speak, had to pay his own way.

It is important to be specific about the needs of a scholar such as Miller, because to most of us, who are not accustomed to such work, it might seem that studies of Milton could be conducted with one's private collection of works by the master, biographies, and commentaries. But Miller's list of immediate needs in pursuing his project reveals why serious, basic research in the humanities does require financial support.

- photocopying a thousand pages of manuscript in Oldenburg, Germany; photocopying and microfilming about the same quantity in archives in the Hague, the British Library, Bodleian Library, and other depositories of unprinted, manuscript material
- hiring an expert to pick out the passages I have designated to be photocopied at the Public Record Office in England, so that they can be photocopied, because it is a government office without a budget for such services
- having prints made from the microfilms of originals that are so rare or fragile that they cannot be photocopied, but only microfilmed
- consulting rare books: at the Newberry Library there is the *only copy in the United States* of George Richter's *Letters* (published in 1612); one either goes to Chicago for a week—it is a thousand-page book in Latin—or pays over $125 for microfilms; the generous Newberry has no provision for me, only a bill; at the Huntington Library, in California, there is the *only copy in the United States* of Bernardi's *Letters from London to Genoa,* printed in 1882, and, until I asked for it last January, never opened by a soul: They had to cut the pages open for me. It is in Italian, and I had a choice of staying in California a week to read and take notes, or paying for photocopying
- locating rare books (many of the books I need are available *only* at Heidelberg or at Leiden or Uppsala; it may be necessary to write to thirty

libraries in Europe just to find out if they have a copy, before even getting to the question of copying; and postage rates keep climbing)

The process of gathering my material stretches over many months, so that I have to work simultaneously on several projects: otherwise I would be often at a total standstill while waiting for materials to become available. Try to explain to a "grant" reviewer that I am not in need of X dollars for project X, but for continuing funds to carry out a series of projects, evidenced by the continuing flow of new publications.

Is it all worth it? "In business," says Miller,

it was a matter of satisfaction to create an organization, invent products, develop a market, without a cent of capital, with no backing from anyone, to succeed in a field conspicuous for its number of failures—to succeed as an *independent.*

Similarly, to do, late at night, after working hours, and on odd weekends, what others are paid to do full-time in the universities, is not easy—but it can be very satisfying.[2]

CHAPTER TEN

Interdependence among Independent Scholars

If it were only possible to contrive a continuing fellowship among people who are trying to resolve some riddle, unravel a mystery, deal with a perennial issue of public concern. . . .

Frank Tannenbaum
A Community of Scholars

The dark side of independence is isolation. The scholar working on their own can suffer from lack of contact with peers or even with people in any field who are engaged in serious intellectual work. The consequence can be loneliness, but there is a significant *intellectual* danger too.

There is a classic publishing story about this danger, and I happen to have my own personal version. One morning the receptionist at the publishing house where I worked as one of the most junior editors called me to say that a gentleman in the waiting room was asking to see one of the editors in order to personally hand over a manuscript. He turned out to be a middle-aged, slightly scruffy, intense, deferential man clutching a manuscript contained in not one but two typing-paper boxes and bound together with twine. "It's a new system of philosophy based on mathematics," he declared. "It will revolutionize our understanding of the universe. I've been working on it for thirteen years. You're the first publisher to see it."

I listened to as much as he wanted to tell me about his book, made sure his name and address were on it and that he had retained a copy, gave him a receipt to assuage his apprehension at letting the manuscript leave his hands and disappear beyond the door leading into our offices, and told him the work would get prompt attention.

"You're the first person to see it since I started work on it," he said as we waited for the elevator. The words rang in my ears as I made my way back to my desk. I had heard them before, and their import was ominous.

The manuscript was Greek to me; it consisted almost entirely of mathematical formulas. After leafing through it for half an hour, I took it around to the science editor and asked him if he could take the first few chapters home with him and look them over on the train so that we could see what we had here. Intrigued, he turned a few pages, then skipped a few, then turned a few more. A frown began to furrow his forehead. "What's wrong?" I asked. "Is it gibberish?"

"Maybe worse than that," he said. "I'll take a look and get back to you tomorrow."

The next day the manuscript was lying on my desk when I arrived at the office. On it was a note from the science editor—four words that I never will forget. "He's reinvented the calculus."

The problem is widespread, as members of one independent scholars' roundtable were told by Erwin Knoll, the editor of *The Progressive* magazine.

We get hundreds of manuscripts every year from both academic and independent scholars, as most magazines do. The two biggest categories of manuscripts we reject are, first, from academics, and second, from independents. (Of course, a *few* from each of these categories are wonderful, and we publish them with joy!) The ones from academics have *their* characteristic vices, of course: jargon, obfuscation, pedantry, the mystification which comes from being part of a priesthood-of-sorts in which people write mainly for each other.

But the manuscripts from the independent scholars also have their characteristic flaws, and they tend to revolve around these researchers' isolation. They'll become enchanted by some odd idea, and come to see it as the solution to all problems in their field. I've come to notice the word "only" in titles of articles from some of them—"Vegetarianism: The Only Solution to World Hunger."

Independent scholars do tend to be loners. Many of them are rightly suspicious of being organized. "If you belong to a club which goes in for lectures, resign," advises Cornelius Hirschberg. "They are for people who distinctly do not wish to lay out a plan of self-education for their entire lifetime. They wish to lay out cheese rings, cookies, and canapés. You can find for yourself the difference between Keats and Yeats."

The last thing one wants is to see the independent scholar enlisted by some group purporting to do him or her good. Yet more and more independent scholars are seeing the truth in C. Wright Mills's insistence on some form of association: "I do not know the full social conditions of the best intellectual workmanship, but certainly surrounding oneself by a circle of people who will listen and talk—and at times they have to be imaginary characters—is one of them."

Howard Lewis, who is an independent scholar, puts it more positively: "There's an excitement that research freaks generate when they meet their own number. I have friends who share with me principally their enjoyment in delving into arcane areas." Whatever the mix of motivations, more and more independent scholars are benefiting from "interdependence." They are coming together in a variety of ways.

Loose networks or Special Interest Groups (SIGs) are perhaps the least formal. These are simply clubs or societies or associations of independent researchers and enthusiasts in a particular subject or topic. For example, in many cities there are Civil War roundtables that bring together the thousands of buffs throughout the nation who love the lore of that period. Astronomers usually have a loose organization in any major city, organizing activities for themselves and often for the general public when there is a notable celestial event to observe and explain. In these two fields, and quite a few others, the locus of SIGs often will be the local bookstores that specialize in the subject. Often the groups will meet regularly in a back room; in some cases, such as the field of war games, that's where they do what they do. SIGs have been organized in fields ranging from microscopy (the Philadelphia Microscopical Society) to cartographic studies (the Chicago Map Society).

Sometimes regional organizations are *inter*disciplinary: Independents in a given community meet together regularly for what I call "independent scholars' roundtables" in Washington, Wichita, Boston, New York, Madison, Atlanta, and Providence. Many national membership organizations have started (or in some cases existed for some time) in fields ranging from general semantics, psychohistory, and littoral (shoreline) studies, to futuristics, astronomy, and Richard III. Independents also are forging new kinds of alliances with mainline academic institutions, such as research libraries and universities. Both benefit as the enthusiasm and diverse interests of nonaffiliated scholars refresh the research agendas of the established institutions. Clearly, these new relationships and organizations spring out of needs felt by their members. Otherwise they could not sustain themselves. They have no other purpose than to be of use. As the late Paul Goodman wrote about one of them: "Without money, publicity, or organization . . . the movement seems to have no other strength than that it is a good idea."

Why do they do it? What might such organizing mean to *your* independent scholarship? To find out, let's visit a few oases of interdependent scholarship around the country. Schmoozing around the kitchen table at Basic Choices, in Madison, Wisconsin, made me realize how heartening it can be just to share a cup of coffee with people struggling with the problems of researching on one's own. Sitting in on one of the study groups at the Institute for Research in History or one of the monthly evening sessions at the New York Microscopists Society in the basement of the American Museum of Natural History in New York showed me how much there is to share among advanced researchers in allied fields. Joining an ongoing Columbia University seminar composed of practicing professionals and faculty members, I saw how the real world and the academic can be yoked together. Hearing independents and academic scholars discuss the problems and gratifications of research at the Newberry Library's weekly colloquium, which is open to anyone working at the library, I understood how much we have to learn from one another.

"This looks like *it*!" said John Ohliger as he rummaged through the day's mail spread on the kitchen table at Basic Choices, a "Midwest center for clarifying political and social options." And it was. The notice from the Internal Revenue Service announced that the homey think tank had been approved for tax-exempt status, making it a suitable recipient of foundation grants. Ohliger regarded the simple but significant IRS form for a moment as he sipped his coffee, then commented dryly: "Now, all we need is a foundation that wants to give us some money."[1]

Situated in a former parsonage in Madison, Wisconsin, Basic Choices is dwarfed by towering University of Wisconsin buildings on a street filled with students rushing to classes or jobs. The location nicely symbolizes its role in the community—to practice and promote a kind of knowledge development and knowledge dissemination that is different from the university's. "We call it 'action-oriented education,'" Ohliger explains. "We encourage people to explore alternatives to our present ways of thinking and living."

Ohliger and a few friends were exploring just such an alternative for themselves when they founded Basic Choices over a decade ago. The founders knew one another through comradeship in political and academic struggles, and three of the four were just leaving, or had just left, their positions in traditional institutions. Ohliger had been a professor, Art Lloyd, an Episcopal campus chaplain, and John Hill, the founder of the first priests' union in the United States and of a large community organization in Chicago, the Alliance Against Repression, had married and therefore left the priesthood. These men shared concerns about the retreat from the struggle for social justice, both on the campus and in the churches. "People have backed off [from] the university as they have seen it to be just as susceptible to corruption, self-interest, and institutional problems as every other institution," Lloyd observed at the time. But Lloyd and others agreed that, as he put it, "When you leave one institution, you need to replace it with something."

The founders' planning for their new venture was a model of thoughtfulness in initiating an organization for independent inquiry. They met regularly for a year to discuss goals and possible forms of organization, writing up their tentative plans and getting feedback from other political activists, educators, and religious workers. "Don't be just another brain trust or think tank," was a representative comment. "If you go to the nonprofit tax-exempt route, you'll be in danger of being co-opted," was another.

Concurrently, each of them also wrote up a list of what he could contribute to the undertaking (time, space, knowledge, contacts, study, research, writing, action). They decided that they did indeed want to work together and support one another in research and action in the broadly defined area of radical education. They also decided that they wanted to set up a Materials Center around the works and ideas of Ivan Illich, Paulo Freire, and the issue of mandatory continuing education.

Space for the fledgling institute was provided in 1977 by the Madison Campus Ministry, in a building divided among several struggling social change groups. Since then, Basic Choice's activities have included:

➤ operating the Materials Center, which constitutes a unique learning environment for other independent scholars in the community

➤ putting on conferences to focus on pressing social problems such as poverty and political change

➤ study groups

➤ a Community Scholars' Roundtable, which brings together a wide range of independent investigators for regular forums and presentations

➤ special projects

➤ a quarterly newsletter, *Second Thoughts*

➤ members' research, writing, and speaking, individually and collectively, on issues that relate to radical education

The Materials Center is perhaps the least well known of these activities, but it best illustrates the spirit of Basic Choices. Chris Wagner, a board member who has worked with many of the Center's users, explains its operations:

Our collection seems uniquely useful because "alternative" materials—radical, often suppressed or neglected materials—aren't buried among tons of traditional texts and books. Furthermore, people who use our library frequently use *us* as resources, too—to dialogue with us about their special interests and concerns, soliciting our comments on and responses to their ideas and writing as well as giving us feedback on *our* ideas and work. And often, their experience with our Materials Center leads a person from writing a paper for a class to concrete action in conjunction with the topic being studied. For example, one woman applied information she'd gathered from our materials concerning alternative education for children in setting up one of the alternative schools in Madison. One man recently spent considerable time working with our materials on Paulo Freire, as well as in dialogue with some Basic Choices members, in writing a paper to share with his co-professionals at a conference as well as in relation to his work as a member of a Freire study group. Based on research in our Materials Center, another woman working for the Department of Regulation and Licensing of the state of Wisconsin, compiled a report on whether or not mandatory continuing education should be required for relicensure/continued licensure. (Her conclusion, incidentally, was that it should not be.) Our Materials Center is designed to encourage people to research topics of concern to themselves—personally, politically, or professionally—*themselves*—rather than to rely on the words of experts. It is also designed to encourage persons to apply their research in a practical sense in their own lives and the life of the community.

The term "independent scholarship" was itself problematical for the people at Basic Choices, for good reasons that clarify essential points about public interest research in general. "Until you met with us," Wagner told me,

we had never used the term "independent scholarship" to label any of our activities although many of them would certainly fall under that rubric. Even now, we admit that we have some reservations about the use of the term, as people frequently interpret "independent" as "individual" and "scholarship" as a very narrow realm of activity devoid of subjectivity and politics.

We came across this problem when we were setting up our own roundtable for independent scholars in Madison; we mailed out a questionnaire to potential participants and stated that we were particularly interested in promoting collective, collaborative, independent scholarship. One respondent answered, "Collaborative independent scholarship really isn't independent scholarship, is it? It's group scholarship."

It is very important for us at Basic Choices that "independent" be interpreted as "free from university, large corporation or big government control," NOT independent from other co-workers, activists, thinkers, and community members. . . . Basic Choices wants to support scholarship which is practical in the real world and politically significant. It is therefore imperative to get beyond ivory-tower definitions of scholarship. Too often, scholars have been engaged in useless erudition instead of careful thinking about some problem linked to politically meaningful action; too often, "scholarship" has meant "learning more and more" about "less and less." These reservations, of course, account for the fact that we named our roundtable "The Community Scholars' Roundtable," in an attempt to make it clear that the scholar we wish to work with is very much a part of a community and his/her scholarship is, in some way, linked to that community.

Significantly, the single most notable subject addressed by Basic Choices is not an academic discipline or the usual kind of "researchable topic," but an *issue*. Basic Choices has led a campaign, within the profession of adult education and to some extent in the wider political arena, *against* mandatory continuing education (MCE)—the enforced, compulsory administration of education to adults. (Many adult educators as well as state professional licensing agencies have pushed this idea with considerable success.) Basic Choices believes that adults should be free to learn what, when, and how they want to, and that attempts to *compel* them to learn do not really work, and are inferior to alternative ways of encouraging people to keep up-to-date and to care about their minds.

To adult educators looking for customers, MCE seems to be a dream come true: a constantly renewed supply of people to teach. Quipped one skeptical professor: "To most people in the field, MCE means 'More Careers for Educators.'"

Basic Choices wanted to confront adult educators and educational policy-makers with the disadvantages of MCE, and prompt them to have second thoughts. To do so required all the skills of research and investigation—and more. To find out what was actually going on, amass the evidence, organize it, make connections, and draw conclusions was only the first step. That scholarly and scientific part was done, and done well. But more was involved in achieving the kinds of results sought by Basic Choices. So it also:

> ➤ convened national conferences on the issue
> ➤ made presentations at major conferences to the profession and also advocated and agitated at such conferences
> ➤ created the newsletter *Second Thoughts* to cover the issue and promoted it to some five hundred subscribers
> ➤ introduced legislative resolutions on the issue to the professional association in the field
> ➤ started the National Alliance for Voluntary Learning to carry on the fight

Basic Choices takes its stand as an alternative to the university, and we certainly need such alternatives in an era when higher education has come to monopolize the quest for knowledge, which should be diffused throughout society. Whenever this has happened, historically, new kinds of knowledge have had to originate outside the dominant institution. One thinks of the wandering scholars of the twelfth century, the sixteenth-century scientific societies that arose outside the classical universities of their time, and the counter-culture institutions of our own day.

But for many independent scholars, the university still provides a touchstone and a reservoir of knowledge and skills. For them, a relationship with the university, on equal terms, can yield benefits. And there is a well-tested model for such a relationship.

It is a snowy, miserable afternoon throughout the Northeast, and the prospect for the evening is worse. Yet after an arduous day pushing the piles of paper characteristic of any government bureaucracy, an assistant secretary of commerce in Washington takes the four o'clock shuttle flight to New York's La Guardia Airport, then rushes into Manhattan and up to Columbia University to make a seven o'clock meeting. There he finds fifteen people who have made similar treks: an urban planner consultant from Boston, an insurance executive from Philadelphia, and from the New York area, a dozen men and women including authors, business people, labor leaders, officials of governmental and voluntary organizations, and professors from Columbia and half a dozen other institutions. Once settled into its comfortable seminar room, this self-selected company turns eagerly to the evening's business: an intense discussion of a topic of mutual concern. Their purpose: to share information and understanding. Their means: vigorous, informed, disciplined, imaginative *talk*.

I have not specified the subject of this seminar because it is merely one of a congeries of such groups that have existed throughout the country. "Alumni" of The University Seminars at Columbia University, for example, include the late Margaret Mead, Paul Goodman, and Hannah Arendt. The subjects of the seminars range widely; at present, seminars are running in areas ranging from politics, history, and education to literature, religion, the arts, and science.

These seminars have great significance for independent scholarship. They demonstrate how fruitfully independent and academic scholars can consort, with mutual advantage and pleasure. They show what a real community of scholars looks like, when colleagues come together outside those institutional roles that customarily burden academic scholars. They demonstrate a simple, low-cost, potent way in which any university or major college can involve independent scholars in its intellectual life, and thereby enrich itself and its community.

What kind of communities do these seminars develop into? There are as many answers as there are seminars, as each is a group of strong individuals and also quickly attains its own collective character and direction.

The seminar I am most familiar with is the one I belong to, of course: Innovations in Higher Education. I was invited to join in October 1980, through an initial phone call from a member. "We're turning toward some new topics," he said, "and the seminar needs some fresh blood. From what I've told the other members about your work, they think you'd be able to make a contribution."

"What are the new directions?" I asked.

"We want you to look at developments outside higher education," he replied, "such as in business and industry, government, the military, labor unions, professions, and community centers. We expect to learn a lot from a study of these programs, to see what is applicable to colleges and universities. We've called our theme New Learning in New Places."

Naturally, I was intrigued—and flattered. The theme was particularly engaging to me because it paralleled the two major themes of my book *The Lifelong Learner*: the new role of learning in the lives of adults, and the "invisible university" of resources that permeates our society.

At my first meeting, I saw at once that the members came from a wide range of backgrounds. As participants introduced themselves for the new members, I could identify a career counselor, a foundation official, an association executive, a corporate planning officer, a sociologist, a dean of students, a management consultant, and several professors whose subjects ranged from management to English literature.

At each session of our seminar we have as a guest speaker someone who has done or discovered something extraordinary in this field. The guests are listened to with close attention and respect, of course. But when they finish speaking, it is open season—and the seminar audience is not an easy one. From a dozen different perspectives the speakers are challenged, not with hostility but with disinterested intellectual passion. Seminar participants attend because they really want to understand the topic of discussion, not because it is part of a doctoral program or something they are paid to do.

They want to go deeper than the surface facts. Often guests will remark that they have gotten as much out of the session, in terms of thinking freshly about their findings and experiences, as the participants have.

The colleagueship of the seminar extends beyond the meetings. For example, at one session the subject of concentrated study aroused great interest in the group. It is a subject quite relevant to independent scholarship: the notion that college students should be offered the option of studying *one subject at a time*, in great depth, for all of their time, rather than spreading their effort over five or six subjects simultaneously. I recalled that an interesting experiment along these lines had occurred at MIT, and participants expressed keen interest in what had been learned from it, whether or not it was still going on, and so forth. So prior to the next session I researched the matter, found the professor at MIT who had conducted the study, found out that it was just then being revived, and obtained his current views on its promise and problems, all of which I wrote up in a brief paper for distribution at the next month's meeting. This in turn impelled two other participants to get in touch with the MIT project, to the benefit of their own work.

Soon after, I was repaid handsomely. Invited to write a paper on independent scholarship for the *Chronicle of Higher Education*, the "trade paper" of academe, I distributed copies of my draft to members of the seminar and received prompt, courteous, thoughtful, eminently helpful advice. How many independent scholars, I could not help wondering, would be able to get such feedback on their work as they developed it for publication?

Of course, different seminars will produce different benefits for their members. For example, Theodore Spaet, chair of the Seminar on Biomaterials, describes his "community" this way.

> This ongoing group is unique in biomedical information interchange. Although many conferences have been held to bring different disciplines together, I know of no other that produces sustained interaction. . . . The Biomaterials Seminar has enabled its members from varied disciplines to generate a common vocabulary and to achieve a unique insight into the mysteries of the unfamiliar activities of their colleagues.

For Frank Tannenbaum, the founder, independent scholarship was an integral part of his germinal vision in 1945 of what the Columbia University seminars were to become.

We draw no distinction between the practicing and the academic world. All the necessary facts of any ongoing activity are important, and the whole is the sum of what goes on inside and outside the university. . . . [A University Seminar] has only one reason for being—the belief that collectively it can better pursue the aim of each of its members: to understand and untangle the hidden mysteries of an ongoing activity we call an institution, complex, area, or period. The group is held together by supporting each other's curiosities and the desire to open vistas hidden in the unknown experience of another profession or another's venture into the unexpected. . . .

You do not have to go far to find this basic idea in action at other colleges and universities. New York University, for example, established an Institute for the Humanities, accomplishing some of the same purposes. It mixes independent scholars and academics, it is interdisciplinary, it focuses on fundamental problems and issues rather than on narrow scholarly topics, and most important, it generates the same kind of vitality through colloquy.

"We're based on two principles," said co-director Aryieh Neier, a nonacademic who came to the Institute after directing the American Civil Liberties Union for many years. "First, that an intellectual community is more than an academy—that it includes thoughtful business people, lawyers, labor leaders, architects. Second, that people practice the humanities when they are self-critical and reflective about their own work. The fundamental purpose of the Institute is to create an intellectual culture that is urban in the best sense—diverse, open, and complex."

The Institute appoints fellows from a wide range of academic disciplines as well as from various professions and arts. Through these fellows it sponsors programs that bring people together from inside and outside the academy. Characterizing itself as a "collegial body," the Institute accepts no students in the bureaucratic sense and awards no degrees. Here, knowledge is pursued and shared for its own sweet sake and for its utility in understanding basic human questions.

Obviously the Institute is highly selective in appointing its fellows; it frankly acknowledges itself to be an elitist institution. But local independent scholars can benefit greatly even if they are not members, because the Institute leans over forward, unlike most departments or programs in American universities, to share its resources. "It offers poets and historians, economists and sociologists, critics and journalists a chance to interact," Richard Goldstein, the journalist, wrote after a visit. "This opportunity is so clearly lacking elsewhere in academic life that, simply by existing, the Institute expands the venue for intellectual discourse." Regarding non-affiliated scholars, Goldstein put the need even more dramatically. "Were it not for sex," he noted, "New York intellectuals might never have inter-course."

The Institute holds open lectures given by international and American humanists, cooperates with other New York City institutions in exhibits, conferences, and symposia, sponsors discussions of work-in-progress by Institute fellows and visitors, and explores the humanistic implications of current public issues. These programs are aimed at a general, intelligent audience in the city. Thousands of people have attended them and from some, such as Susan Sontag's lecture, "Illness as Metaphor," and Richard Wollheim's lecture, "On Persons and Their Lives," articles and books have developed.

These activities "draw," evidencing the need they fill. One, by Michel Foucault, drew a crowd of fifteen hundred. "The need for the Institute is bottomless," said co-director Richard Sennett, "There are so many really first-class people who crave the intellectual stimulation they don't get through their normal work."

Other major research institutions, outside academe, are moving to welcome independent scholars as never before. In Chicago, the Newberry Library's unparalleled collections in such fields as the Renaissance, American Indian history, historical maps, and local and family history used to be available only to certified academic scholars. But that has changed. As the director, Richard Brown, put it, "Today, we have nonaffiliated scholars working alongside professors in virtually every field. It's enriched our whole environment, helping the academics just as much as the 'independents.'"

Brown explained the change:

> We found ourselves faced with the question: Could we justify the possession of collections valued at approximately $200 million, simply by opening the doors to a public that might or might not come? We decided that, on the contrary, the possession of those materials gave us an obligation to make sure they were used, and well used. The Library has not been the same since.

The Newberry accepted an educational mission that includes being a center for nontraditional adult education. Brown believes that libraries have some advantages over universities in serving serious researchers. "We are not limited in what we do by degree programs or a credit structure," he points out. "We have no dead academic horses to ride, no pecking orders to sustain, no departmental turfs to protect. Here, scholars can relate on neutral ground, simply on the basis of shared interests and concerns."

The Institute for Research in History, in New York City, displayed most of the advantages that a full-fledged self-organization can yield for its members.*

Dorothy Heily described its origins. "Many of us used to think that history has to be a very lonely business. You went off to the archives, and eventually you came up with an idea that someone might be willing to read. But here we've discovered that you can get a great deal of thinking done, fast, if you toss ideas around with others who are keenly [interested] in the same topic."

The Institute was organized around research groups that constituted the center of its activity. Members would run notices in the Institute's *Memorandum* indicating that they were interested in forming a group to study a certain topic. Most groups were fairly small, composed of between two and fifteen members who shared a common scholarly interest, some as traditional as the translation of medieval Latin texts, others as topical as women's history. A commitment to membership in the Institute was a commitment to working within a research group. Some groups were reading groups; others involved the presentation of papers.

Much of the Institute's time and effort was devoted to working on members' grant proposals. During the nine months that it usually took between the initial idea for a grant and its final receipt, members read one another's proposals and offered ideas and advice according to their expertise. Each proposal was examined from a scholarly point of view and compared with work in a similar area that had already been undertaken. Various funding agencies were contacted and the process of matching a proposal with a potential source of support began. The Institute received 14 percent of each grant to

* The Institute closed several years after a report of its activities and aspirations appeared in the first edition of this book (1981). The account of its activities has been retained nonetheless: organizations may founder but still yield useful lessons.

cover administrative costs, although, as the executive director, Marjorie Lightman, suggested, there was a tremendous amount given and taken that had nothing to do with money.

Among the Institute's projects were a two-year program to develop a secondary school curriculum on the history of women and American law, and a photographic exhibition entitled "Places of Origin" that documented the European background of several large immigrant groups. Of particular interest to the observer of independent scholarship was a two-day conference, entitled "Research Institutions and Scholarly Life in the 1980s," that the Institute sponsored in October 1979. The conference examined the future of independent institutions and humanities scholarship and was funded by a grant from the Ford Foundation.

The activities of individual members of the Institute varied tremendously. Some worked only in research groups; others pursued their scholarship on a full-time basis. All members could contribute to the Institute's quarterly journal *Trends in History*, a review of current periodical literature. Articles on the history of medieval science, recent Soviet historiography, and the history of the American South were published. The Institute also published a monograph series entitled *Women and History*.

Lightman's comments on the Institute's contribution to the future of independent scholarship are still valid.

> I think that we are more in tune with the times than anyone gives us credit for. The way to see this is not to look at the scholarly journals, but at the literature of economics and sociology, the theories of leisure time and mid-life crises in particular: a society in which people will change careers two or three times in their lifetime.
>
> In a sense what we are saying is that graduate training is the gift of a lifetime. Some years you may write books. In others you may just enjoy the pleasure of reading them. Certainly someone holding a nine-to-five job doesn't have the same time during the summer that a professor does. Perhaps such a person will only write a book every ten years rather than every four or five. Someone who does that must be very highly motivated. Perhaps that is the only kind of scholarship worth nurturing.

The Institute demonstrated, if briefly, that scholarship of a high quality can not only flourish outside the academy, but also enrich the life of the surrounding community. "I think that we are the true idealists of our profession," said Lightman. "We are taking an ideal—the value of the humanities in society—at its face value. We are saying that if the ideal is valid in society, it *can* find a way to exist in the marketplace." Regrettably, she was proved wrong in the instance of her own institution—it died of penury anyway. But the fact that it existed at all makes one optimistic about the viability of independent scholarship.

Dozens of other cases of interdependence dot the map of independent scholarship in America, each of them illuminating some of the ways in which we can be of use to one another.

> The Open Network in Denver helps independent scholars to find the resources they need and to solve whatever problems they have, through sophisticated application of networking techniques.
> The International Society for General Semantics in San Francisco brings together local theorists and practitioners in communications, who share their researches, conduct workshops and conferences, issue a newsletter, and participate in the advance of this interdisciplinary field.
> The Monterey Institute for Research in Astronomy thrives by capitalizing on the fact that it is independent of academic norms and expectations. Founded by a group of young astronomers who despaired of being able to do the kind of advanced research they wanted to, because of the lack of jobs in the field, the Institute has won a respected place in its field.
> The Staten Island Institute of Arts and Science provides encouragement and some support service for independent scientists in the area.
> In virtually every state Public Interest Research Groups (PIRGs) press their inquiries into social, economic, and political areas.
> The Institute for Food and Development Policy in San Francisco carries out studies on the effects of American foreign policy on emerging nations.
> The Easalen Institute in Big Sur, California, has established itself as a world center of serious study of a wide variety of ideas and techniques related to human growth and well-being.

➤ The Naropa Institute in Denver is a center of inquiry into Eastern modes of thinking and analysis.

➤ The Worldwatch Institute in Washington, like other think tanks ranging from the Institute for Policy Studies on the left to the American Enterprise Institute on the right, provides a base of operations for independent scholars in the policy sciences.

➤ The National Coalition of Independent Scholars provides services to members, an annual membership directory, a grants handbook, and a quarterly newsletter (see Appendix VII).

How to Start a Roundtable for Independent Scholars

There is a simple, inexpensive, effective way to offer independent scholars in your community an opportunity to come together. I call it the independent scholars' roundtable. It has been tried, and has worked, in a variety of communities around the country, ranging from major cities to small university towns. One interested and committed person can get a roundtable going with a minimum investment of time and energy. Thereafter, the participants who find it of most use provide the energy and resources needed to keep it going. Such regularly scheduled occasions may be set up

➤ to provide a regular, visible opportunity for independent scholars and researchers to *convene*

➤ to offer useful *information* and understanding to independent scholars through presentations by resource people, dissemination of materials, and informal contacts

➤ to provide the opportunity for mutual psychological and intellectual *support* amongst independent scholars

➤ to provide a *launching place for self-organization* by discipline or other special interest

➤ to foster *collaborative* and *collective* action to obtain needed support and resources for independent research, such as access to required materials, eligibility for financial support, and so forth

➤ to foster *interdisciplinary discussion*

➤ to encourage wider *public awareness* of the accomplishments and problems of independent scholarship

➤ to function as a *contact point* within the community for the transmission of useful information developed by other roundtables and organizations

"Participants in our roundtable help one another locate resources for their work, plan their projects, and find the time and space in which to work," says Chris Wagner, who started the Madison, Wisconsin, Community Scholars' Roundtables under the aegis of Basic Choices.

Because of our interest in social change, our roundtable takes that special thrust. We have guest speakers like Erwin Knoll, editor of *The Progressive* magazine, published here in Madison, to talk about how to write about social and political issues. But mostly we've drawn from the members themselves, like Vince Kavaloski, who talked on his problems in pursuing serious research as an independent.

At its first meeting, the Madison roundtable addressed the basic issues that any such group must face.

➤ Who are the independent scholars, and what fields are they in?
➤ What kinds of services are being provided for independent scholars by different organizations and institutions?
➤ What are the needs and problems of independent scholars?
➤ What are the distinctive aspects of independent scholarship in Madison?
➤ How might independent scholars be better recognized, aided, and supported in their disciplines, in the intellectual life of the country, and in their communities?
➤ What are the larger implications, problems, and potentials of independent scholarship?

Subsequently a questionnaire was circulated to elicit the needs of the initial participants. A number of priorities emerged. The roundtable was:

1. To be a support group for the members
2. To develop networks of independent scholars and others involved in social change in Madison
3. To compile or obtain a list of grants and other resources available for independent scholars

4. To send letters to grant agencies that should (but at the time did not) fund independent scholars
5. To find out how individuals could tap into group medical insurance plans such as those offered by health maintenance organizations
6. To investigate legitimate ways to work one's income taxes to one's advantage and use existing resources creatively
7. To form a study group to look at theory in adult education

One participant spoke eloquently about what the initial sessions meant to her.

> The colloquium gave me an opportunity to get acquainted with other areas and problems people encounter in independent research and gave me a sense of fellowship with other scholars. It allowed me an opportunity to articulate some of my own needs and concerns and gave me a chance to get input on resources. . . . It has changed my rather gloomy outlook and given me encouragement to pursue my own work. Now, I need to know more about resources, networks of independent scholars, and funding.

Once the Madison roundtable gained momentum, new members were attracted through imaginative public events: a call-in radio show on a local station, WORT, a lecture at the university by an expert in the field, a newspaper story in the campus paper. "We've drawn quite a few people from the campus," Wagner reports. "They have faculty positions but they don't feel they get much of a chance in their departments to talk about their work and get the supportiveness and responsiveness which our group seems to generate."

Other roundtables around the country have gone in diverse directions. "Here in Boston, our roundtable has taken a different tack," said Frank Cantanzaro, the futurist, who leads the group there.

> Our first session, hosted by nontraditional Beacon College, drew about twenty people, including an expert in sixteenth-century French intellectual history, a political journalist, a Ph.D. in German, the founder of the local Alliance of Independent Scholars, a lawyer engaged in several projects in philosophy and literature centering on the topics of memory and imagination, and a member of the Harvard Center for International Affairs. The group came up with a novel programming formula: To involve a wide range of people—and also to

have a good time together—we're holding each of our meetings at the head-quarters of a different independent scholars' organization hereabouts: think tanks, small scholarly and quasi-scholarly societies. We're still feeling our way, and it's great fun. Our spirits are high and there seems to be a distinct sense of mission developing.

In Denver and Wichita, roundtables have gained momentum under the aegis of the local free universities, Denver Free University and Wichita Free University, respectively.

In Denver, Susan Spraggs, columnist for *The Learning Connection*, has enlisted the public library as an appropriate meeting ground.

> News of the Roundtable appeared in the DFU catalog, in the fall newsletters of organizations like Solar Energy Associates, Mycologists, MENSA, Historic Denver, and the amateur archaeologists. Fliers were put in each library, and we mailed to about ninety individuals whose names came from Open Network, a local computer linkage agency.
>
> We used the motto "Scholarship Is Their Joy, Not Their Job." To start things going, we put together a three-session series this fall, one session each month. At the opener, Richard Haight, who was a professor for fourteen years but had been doing his scholarship independently for several years, talked and led a discussion on problems and prospects in the field. In November, we had Philip Gordon, director of the Boulder Institute, which is a group of social scientists who find opportunities to use their skills outside academe. He talked on "Grantsmanship." At the latest meeting we talked about future planning to continue the Roundtable in directions chosen by the participants.

Spragg appeared on KVOD's noon-hour interview show to boost participation.

In Wichita, Rick Childers of WFU also used the public library to convene a small but spirited group through a notice in his summer catalog: "What's an independent scholar? It could well be you, if you research any area and aren't affiliated with a university. Learn what others are doing, and what can be done to help your efforts." Rick said, after the initial session, "I feel that common ground was reached quickly, and those wanting to continue the group are willing to assume the responsibility for its success. The group plans to actively promote participation beginnings with a class listing, a poster and public-service announcement campaign."

Each roundtable naturally capitalizes on its distinctive internal resources—the special people and organizations available locally. For example, a typical meeting of the New York roundtable was on "Finding Funding" (a favorite topic at virtually all sites!) and featured a speaker from the Foundation Center, the information library on grants and grant getting. The session was held at a facility in the same building as the Center, and after the meeting the participants could go right upstairs to use what they had learned to find possible funding sources for their work. (The Center has local outlets in major cities, so such a program is feasible elsewhere.)

Reinhold Aman:
The Meaning of Abuse

> People are killed and injured every day because of insults, but academe refuses to study them because the subject is disreputable. To me, it's the most riveting pursuit in the world. I've spent fourteen years on it, day and night, working like a demented (but usually orgasmic) beaver, because there's so much that's fascinating and worth doing.
>
> Reinhold Aman

Reinhold Aman, like many independent scholars, is a man seized by a subject that is beyond the ken—indeed, beyond the pale—of academe. Its pursuit has given him some of his keenest joys, and it has cost him his academic career.

The subject is offensive language: insults, curses, swearwords, slurs, blasphemy, racial and ethnic stereotypes, and other forms of what he calls "verbal aggression." "All cultures use verbal aggression," he points out, "from the very peaceful Dani tribe in New Guinea to those whose languages are know for it: German, Yiddish, Arabic, Greek, Hungarian, all the Slavic languages, French, Spanish, and Italian." Freud made an observation that illustrates the importance of having a highly structured "filthy" language as an alternative to the one considered "proper." "The first human being who hurled a curse against his adversary instead of a rock was the founder of civilization."

Despite a Ph.D. and a panoply of publications credits, Aman was driven out of academe (which he now calls "cacademe"). When he came up for tenure at the University of Wisconsin in 1972, his record as a teacher and researcher was strong. Rated among the five best teachers by students for the Annual Standard Oil Teaching Excellence Award, Aman had published a lexicon of abusive terms, had read papers at the prestigious annual meetings of the Modern Language Association and the International Linguistics Association, and had performed creditably for his department and the college.

"All that became too dangerous for the tenured schmucks who had power," he tells interviewers. "I was deviating from their country-club attitude towards their profession. So, at the first chance, they got rid of me. When I fought it legally, I was blacklisted nationally—there's an unofficial blacklist of 'troublemakers' who have the guts to sue the university for justice. That was the end of my academic career."

Aman still regrets that his own facility at swearing was not finely honed at the time he left. The best he could manage as he cleared off his desk was to call his department chairman "a boring ass," but he managed to sharpen that up some before leaving the campus, remarking to him that "when I see you my feet fall asleep."

"At that point," Aman recalls, "I knew that I had to sink, dragging down my wife and fourteen-year-old daughter, or swim as an independent scholar despite all the obstacles. So, after learning all there is to learn about typesetting, publishing, buying paper, postage rates, etc., I went into the scholarship as not just a vocation, but as an entrepreneurial *business*. It's been murder, both financially and emotionally—and worth every agony."

Aman initiated his own scholarly journal, *Maledicta*, for subscribers in fifty-two countries, including major national libraries such as the British Museum and the Sorbonne, and he has published books in the field through his International Research Center for Verbal Aggression. An important part of his income has come from lecturing on campuses.

"At the start it was murder, financially," Aman admits.

I had no income check from mid-1974 to 1977. About one hundred private foundations have turned down my request for support. As a nonaffiliated scholar, the usual grant sources won't touch me.

But now the journal is generating some income, the books are selling, and we are getting on our feet. My wife and daughter have been very understanding about my doing this work, which I consider such an important subject for research, and the one in which I feel I can make my major scholarly contribution.

At this point I've made it, and I have no interest in returning to cacademia. Conditions for getting onto some major campus would be too hard to swallow. Those people who run universities—chancellors, deans, etc.— are among the most stupid people I've ever met. Their only strength is politicking, back-stabbing, and brownnosing with the higher-ups. This kind of immorality goes against my grain. I'd rather work as a garbage collector than in such a corrupt system.

Aman's accomplishment is respected by some leaders within academe. Richard Brod of the Modern Language Association, while noting that the association as such does not pass judgment on scholarly work, asserts that "personally, I admire what he's accomplished. His journal certainly meets the objective criteria of scholarship, and his subject matter is as much a part of the human experience as any other aspect of the world of letters. I hope his success might embolden other independent scholars to find ways to do their own work."

As for his journal *Maledicta,* one academic reviewer wrote, "It is unique among scholarly journals, a delight to read, and almost impossible to put down. The journal provides a welcome respite from the tedium often produced by more typical academic annals." *Library Journal* said that *Maledicta's* "ribald wit is nicely matched with scholarship . . . the journal is a real find," and the usually staid *Booklist* of the American Library Association reveled in its "bawdy folk-talk, X-rated invective, poetic scurrility, scatology, [and] name-your-blasphemy."

Among articles from a handful of issues were such enticing items as "The Origin of Our Strongest Taboo-Word," "Aggression in Children's Jokes," "Common Patient-Directed Pejoratives Used by Medical Personnel," "He Show Her with Great Stones: Prominent Sexual Metaphors in the Non-Shakespearean Drama of Renaissance England," "How to Become a Cacademic Scribe; Or, Publish and Perish the Thought," and "How to Hate Thy Neighbor: A Guide to Racist Maledicta."

Beyond such delectable specifics, Aman and his colleagues throughout the world have begun to draw some illuminating and useful generalizations from their studies. Verbal aggression, they find, can be categorized according to its use by three groups:

> a WASP group that "primarily uses body parts, body functions, sex and excretion"
> a Roman Catholic group "that uses blasphemy, especially the name of the Lord, references to the saints, and references to Church implements"
> the group found mainly in Africa, Asia, and Polynesia whose verbal aggression is centered on family relationships, including derogatory—often sexual—references to the father, mother, grandparents, or siblings of one's adversary

The findings even have begun to suggest practical applications in understanding our behavior. Aman is convinced that aggressive language releases pent-up emotions and that it reveals crucial information about each culture and society.

Independent scholars, Aman believes, have got to take the initiative in making known the interest, importance, and possible uses of their research. Although few can rival Aman's resourcefulness in doing that, his success may be useful to others. He actively promotes lecture engagements and media appearances and has appeared on hundreds of radio and television shows. *Time* magazine wrote of him as "the only American who makes a full-time living out of insults . . . with the possible exception of Don Rickles." Aman has even created a persona, Uncle Maledictus, under which he pursues these promotional endeavors.

Having experienced both sides of the scholarly street—academic employment and the state of being "independent, free, and struggling"— Aman on the whole feels fortunate in his nonaffiliated position. "Operating as an independent scholar I can cultivate my own style, focus on my own interests, follow my research wherever it leads, and be bolder in my speculations about what we're learning in this field. We live on relatively little, but this is my mission in life, and the labor I put into it is all for love. I wouldn't want to be taking time out constantly for committee work, faculty socializing, or even teaching that wasn't directly related to my prime concerns. Being an independent scholar isn't an easy road—but you can make it on your *own*." [2]

Postscript:
Unfinished Business

Toward the end of my search for independent scholars, I had four encounters that did not yield the same kind of clear-cut lessons as those portrayed earlier. These were unsettling conversations, but it befits this book that it should end with the words of independent scholars themselves.

"Why don't more Americans ever find the kind of intellectual excitement which these people have discovered?" The speaker was Tom Adams, an expert microscopist and himself a sharp observer of other independent scholars in many fields. We were crammed into a corner booth of a bar in midtown Manhattan. Tom's eyes wandered around the shadowy interior of the bar while he sought the best way to explain what he meant.

> Maybe it has to do with barstools, and security. A guy without a job, he's not necessarily in trouble in this country. A guy without a woman, or a truck, is not in big trouble either, necessarily. But a guy who can't stride into a local bar, grunt his way onto a stool, and become an instantaneous and viable member of the group—that guy is beyond hope. It doesn't need to be a local bar either—he can be a thousand miles from home. The rules of acceptance are complex, but everyone knows them. One of the requirements is a certain purposeful stupidity.
>
> Many businesses are run with that same safe-but-limited perception of the world. This universal safety is an overwhelmingly important part of America. Almost every one overrates his own limitations, and seeks a safe job, a safe home, a safe family.

Now, what I'm wondering is whether we can find a chink in all this "a-intellectual" armor. Think beyond New York and the Northeast. Think about the depths of the Midwest. A majority of Americans are not anti-intellectual, they are a-intellectual.

What would be their potential, *if* thinking for yourself, about what you find most important even if no one else does, even if it's unsafe or crazy, became as acceptable as owning a recreational vehicle. . . .

Halfway around the world, another vista of intellectual barrenness and potential opened before me. I had been dispatched by the United Nations Children's Fund to observe innovative programs in the Far East, specifically in Bangladesh, which was then generally regarded as the world's worst "basket case." The last thing I expected to encounter in a nation with 80 percent illiteracy, grievous problems of survival, and a decimated culture was a lesson in independent scholarship.

This time the speaker was Naresh Chakraborty, a self-taught social reformer championing the boldest ideas in community development in one of the world's least developed nations. Our conversation took place in surroundings dramatically different from those of Max Schuster's book-lined study on Fifth Avenue, or Tom Adams's favorite Manhattan saloon. We tramped around the grounds of his school at Rudrupur, which has earned the sobriquet "miracle school" among Third World educators. As we walked and watched the students farming, running the school store, and making tools, Chakraborty flashed his dazzling white-toothed smile, fixed me with eyes that glowed like an Old Testament prophet's, and expounded his quietly astonishing educational philosophy.

He began by confessing his lack of "proper" training for what he was doing with such evident success.

There is a dearth of books in Bangladesh, so even if one has the time to learn, one lacks the resources. For example, my first awareness of principles of progressive education came when I visited one of our few teacher training institutes and saw a wall chart summarizing in two sentences some of the key ideas of Socrates, Rousseau, Montessori, Dewey. Those sentences resonated with my experience about how humans learn. I realized in a flash, too, that if those masters could find their own way, just by working with the children and their parents and *thinking* about what they were seeing, then each of us can, too.

> Each person has a natural urge to learn. Awakening that urge is the function of the schoolmaster and teacher. That is what we try to do here at the school.

He did not have to say more: The school spoke for the relevance of his philosophy to the lives of his students and their parents, and his penetrating eyes proclaimed his passionate commitment.

Such an approach to education does not sit well with officials in a nation where the standard pattern of primary education is to teach children to memorize obsolete British textbooks. Chakraborty has suffered the familiar fate of a prophet in his own country. For years government bureaucrats ignored or rejected his ideas, forcing him to call the most enlightened part of the program at his school "the extracurriculum." All schools in the country must follow the government-ordained conventional syllabus, which is largely irrelevant to the current and future real needs of students.

When it came time to take my leave from Naresh, both of us knowing that it was unlikely we would ever see each other again, I expressed concern for his safety. He had been arrested recently, on suspicion of carrying a gun, but his opponents had backed off at his spirited defense that "education is my only weapon."

"Do not be concerned for me—though I will be grateful for your concern about the school. *I* do only what I *must* do: This urge to learn feeds my own life. I must do this discovering, this creation with the people, or I will die spiritually."

These lessons from independent scholars continued right up to the final days of work on this book. "George has disappeared from the Newberry," wrote Dorothy Welker in response to my query about a fellow independent scholar. "For the moment he seems to have disappeared. He left no address, and the Library has no idea where he is. From what he told me shortly before he departed, he found the going as an independent scholar just too rough, and he had not, he said, received the kind of support he expected. . . ."

"George" is not his real name, but the haunting sense of a broken heart that hovers behind this report is all too real. "George" himself foreshadowed it publicly. I had gone to the Newberry early in this project for the happy reasons described earlier—this institution has done as much as any in the country to welcome, encourage, and aid independent scholars. At noontime I spoke to the monthly colloquium of all the scholars, affiliated and nonaffiliated, who work in the library. They come together to share a glass of wine, comradeship, and some talk of the joys and problems of their often solitary lives. At the conclusion of my talk and after a number of the usual sorts of questions and comments, I noticed one person in the back whose hand was only half-raised, as if he were not sure he wanted to speak. I asked whether he had a question, and he rose awkwardly. "Mr. Gross, it's wonderful to hear you speak so inspiringly and helpfully about the work I and others here are trying our hardest to do. But I have to say to all of you that this independent scholarship can break your heart. When you're onto something really important in your field, something that would be a real contribution to knowledge, and one that only you can make at this point, and you realize that you are probably never going to get the time, the support, or the resources to bring this key work to fruition—*that* can break your heart."

I knew at once that nothing I or anyone could say should follow that. As the meeting disbanded, the participants sobered by this statement of anguish, the speaker worked his way through the milling crowd, up to the front. He apologized to me for ending the session on such an emotional and "negative" note. I said it was the most important thing that I had heard on the subject so far, and that I shared his sadness. There were tears in both our eyes.

So, even as I routinely fact-checked the manuscript, there were still lessons to be learned—lessons sufficiently important to make me stop my checking long enough to type these pages into the book. I know that a work like this should not end on what George himself called "a negative note." But these sadnesses must be shared. The risks that independent scholars run, though risks mainly of the spirit, are real risks.

"Any book casually taken off the library shelf is likely to leave a hole through which another reality beckons. The more books I read, the larger the hole became, until finally I could walk through to look at history from the other side. I knew when I walked through that hole in the university to begin wandering around the world in search of Lindisfarne that I would not come back."

William Irwin Thompson, formerly a professor at MIT, believes that we have entered an era in which the individual can and must search out new truths independently of the established intellectual institutions. That one *can* do so, Thompson himself has demonstrated dramatically by "walking out on the university," as he puts it in one of his most famous essays. That one *must* do so, Thompson argues on the basis that the established institutions, the old culture, are moribund, and that the search for a fresh perspective, so necessary to personal and social renewal, must occur outside of them.

"Lindisfarne" is Thompson's name for that quest. The original Lindisfarne was established on a wind-swept primitive island off the coast of Northumberland in A.D. 635. Against the impending cultural darkness, a group of Celtic Christians founded a church and monastery to preserve the old Graeco-Roman knowledge and Celtic Christian practices. The monastery set up schools for scholars in the Dark Ages. Eventually sacked by the Vikings, Lindisfarne nevertheless seeded the emerging Western European civilization.

"We're headed for a new Dark Ages," Thompson insisted when I visited his new Lindisfarne on Long Island, New York (it has since been relocated to Colorado), "and we are setting down our roots." He calls Lindisfarne an "association," and it consists of a group of young people, students of a sort who, together with the "fellows," pursue their studies in an amalgam of fields and disciplines that they find relevant to their own needs and the present cultural crisis. Even when there were only five students at the Long Island facility, *The New York Times* called Lindisfarne "just possibly a very important new departure in American educational culture." And Bill Moyers, interviewing Thompson on public television, described Thompson's life as "a pilgrimage toward a humane environment where science, religion, and art merge in harmony, for life's sake."

Although Thompson is obviously an extraordinary individual, his importance for independent scholarship lies in suggesting the potential for many of us to do what he has done, but in our own fields and our own ways. "I've proved that there are other lives for the intellectual than being a civil servant in a bureaucracy," he says. He has thought through the possibility that each of us might set up as a small but significant center of independent inquiry, and has reported his conclusions in an essay that has served as a credo for many, "The Individual as Institution," which appears in his book *Passages About Earth*. Challenging the cliché that the individual intellect today is powerless against the giant universities, government agencies, and corporations, he argues and insists that "the individual has not been passed over—it is he who is passing over the institutions, to become an institution in himself." Citing many of the people already mentioned in these pages—such as Buckminster Fuller, Ivan Illich, and Ralph Nader—as well as many others, including Alan Watts, John Lilly, Paolo Soleri, and Edgar Mitchell, Thompson argues that with proper, and quite feasible, public support, "each individual could institutionalize himself in his own imaginative way."

The key question that I always want to ask each independent scholar is "What are you looking for?" It is a question that probes both inward and outward. It also usually stimulates the respondents to look both back toward their roots and forward to the prospect ahead. Asked that question, William Irwin Thompson gave an answer that captures much of my sense of what independent scholars are like at their best: serious but unsolemn, humble enough to learn from their experiences, but audacious enough to insist on making their own judgments, "chasers of horizons."

> When you become dissatisfied with the Catholic Church as a young person, you know that if you're going to leave the Church you're risking and wagering your immortal soul, and therefore if you decide to go ahead with it, then taking risks begin to be the nature of growth. And so at each point of your life you hear a voice saying, "Settle in, accept the way things are."
>
> You know, it's like the lines of Faust, "Remain a while, You are so sweet." And that's when you sell out to the Devil. And the other voice says, "No, keep pushing on, keep changing the horizons," that none of these places has been the perfect place, that it's almost like the archetype of the search for the Holy Grail, the ultimate integration that brings the fragments together.
>
> And so I've been looking. But in all the places I've been I've learned, even from the things that I've eventually rejected. . . . And at every point of my life someone has said, "Things aren't so bad, relax." And that's just not the way I am.
>
> I'm a chaser of horizons. And the chasing of horizons and the living of myth is a delight, you know, that the pursuit and the journey itself is its own reward; that ultimately you realize that the thing you're looking for at the end of the horizon, this Valhalla or whatever, has been with you all along.

Appendixes

I: Maxims for the Life of the Mind

Several years ago I noticed that the independent scholars whom I interviewed in their workplaces very often had about them, on walls or bulletin boards or under a glass top on their desks, favorite maxims on the life of the mind. It took a while before I realized that this was significant. Montaigne, I recalled, had surrounded himself in his tower study at his family estate in Périgord with a collection of "sayings" that he found fortifying and stimulating. "Terse advice, one man to another, on the discipline of life," is the way Professor Robert McClintock characterizes these sayings, commenting that these self-selected mottos "helped direct and sustain (Montaigne's) formation of self; they reinforced a regimen of self-culture, speaking to him sagely as he cut his quill, shelved a book, stoked his stove, or gazed in silent introspection."

I have asked the independent scholars I know to share with me their favorite such sayings. Among these maxims you will find, as I have, some profound, some practical, and some witty insights into the life of the mind. Some may touch upon your own aspirations (as well as upon your own weakness, bad habits, and self-delusions). They also may spur you to start your own collection, remembering always that, as the Zen proverb says, "The way of the masters was to find their own way."

> I don't see how you can write anything of value in social science if you don't offend someone. —*Marvin Harris*

> Lay off the muses—it's a very hard dollar. —*S. J. Perelman*

If we had a law that anybody who drilled a dry oil well would be shot, very few wells would be drilled. Our tolerance of dry wells does not seem to extend to research projects, which are always expected to gush. . . .
   —*Kenneth Boulding*

No one is more triumphant than the man who chooses a worthy subject and masters all its facts. . . .   —*E. M. Forster*

Que sais-je?   —*Montaigne's motto*

A little learning is *not* a dangerous thing to one who does not mistake it for a great deal.   —*William Allen White*

You can live longest and best and more rewardingly by attaining and preserving the happiness of learning.   —*Gilbert Highet*

A learned blockhead is a greater blockhead than an ignorant one.
   —*Benjamin Franklin*

Nobody who spends her time on the edge ever gets fat.   —*Cynthia Heimel*

Let nothing come between you and the light.   —*Thoreau*

The gods send thread for the web begun.   —*Leif Smith*

Some people will never learn anything, for this reason, because they understand everything too soon.   —*Alexander Pope*

To measure the quality of a scholar's work by the length of his bibliography is like measuring a man's capacity as a father by counting his children.
   —*Kathleen Spaltro*

My own way, or none at all. I am a stubborn little autodidact.
   —*Paul Goodman*

Work smarter, not harder.   —*Alan Lakein*

It is not the truth that a man possesses, or believes that he possesses, but the earnest effort which he puts forward to reach the truth, which constitutes the worth of a man. For it is not by the possession, but the search after the truth that he enlarges his power, wherein alone consists his ever-increasing perfection.   —*Gotthold Lessing*

They called him *dumkopf,* which means dope.
That's how we got the microscope.
   —*Maxine Kumin, from a poem about Anton Leeuwenhoek*

He who is not in some measure a pedant, though he may be wise, cannot be a very happy man.   —*Hazlitt*

We are like dwarfs that sit on the shoulders of giants.   —*Bernard of Chartres*

Yet all experiences is an arch wherethro'
Gleams that untravelled world, whose margin fades
For ever and for ever when I move, . . .

To follow knowledge like a sinking star,
Beyond the utmost bound of human thought.
   —*Alfred, Lord Tennyson*
   "Ulysses"

The brighter you are, the more you have to learn.   —*Don Herold*

It is surely harmful to souls to make it a heresy to believe what is proved.
   —*Galileo*

The best intelligence test is what we do with our leisure.
   —*Dr. Laurence J. Peter*

He not only overflowed with learning, but stood in the slops.   —*Sidney Smith*

Grow or die.   —*George Lock Land*

To each man is reserved a work which he alone can do.   —*Susan Blow*

II: Specialized Bookstores:
Gourmet Shops for Scholars

There is a bookstore in Kensington, Connecticut, that specializes in entomology, and in the same village is a shop that deals primarily in Scottish nonfiction. You can find books on foxhunting in "Horse and Hounds" in nearby Plainville, while Frances Edwards in Suffield sells works on Africa and slavery. Specialty bookstores can be found in cities and towns across the country, and they are to the scholar what gourmet shops are to a fine food aficionado.

A specialty bookstore is the place where all the latest materials in your field as well as many old and unknown ones can be found. It is the place where casual browsing can create that marvelous "serendipity" effect of opening up new or unexpected areas of exploration. It is the place where you come across the very thing you have been hunting down for ages. A bookstore owner who is familiar with your needs can be a gold mine, contacting you when something new or special comes to his attention and performing special orders or search services to find that special book.

A specialty bookstore convenient to home can become a favorite haunt of the independent scholar. Even one miles away can work for you, because many such stores provide catalogs and lists as well as mail-order services. But how can you find those that specialize in *your* field?

The most comprehensive listing of North American bookstores can be found in the *American Book Trade Directory*, which is edited and compiled by the Jacques Cattell Press and published annually by the R. R. Bowker Company. It is on the reference shelves of most large libraries. This massive volume lists almost twenty-five thousand retail outlets in the United States and Canada, as well as wholesalers, foreign language book dealers, exporters, importers, and the like. The *ABTD* is arranged geographically by city, and each entry includes the store name, address, telephone number, owner, manager, and buyer as well as information about store size, number of volumes stocked, date of establishment, types of books carried, subject specialities, and sidelines and services offered—such as antiquarian, college, educational, religious, paperback—is shown. Booksellers specializing in a subject to the extent of 50 percent of their stock have that subject designated as their major category. More than seventeen hundred of these specialty stores are listed in the directory. To find one specializing in your area of interest, you need only look through the stores listed in cities convenient to you.

In the course of research, I found that several specialty bookstore directories that had been published a few years ago were no longer in print. Could it be that the role of the specialty bookstore and its directories has given way to the age of electronic information and database searching?

III: Foundation Funding

For a description of The Foundation Center's network of foundation reference collections, see page 121.

Foundation Center Cooperating Collections

Free Funding Information Centers

The Foundation Center is an independent national service organization established by foundations to provide an authoritative source of information on private philanthropic giving. The New York, Washington, D.C., Cleveland, and San Francisco reference collections operated by the Foundation Center offer a wide variety of services and comprehensive collections of information on foundations and grants.

Cooperating Collections are libraries, community foundations, and other non-profit agencies that provide a core collection of Foundation Center publications and a variety of supplementary materials and services in areas useful to grantseekers. The core collection consists of:

Foundation Directory 1, 2, and *Supplement*
Foundation 1000
Foundation Fundamentals
Foundation Giving
Foundation Grants Index
Foundation Grants Index Quarterly
Foundation Grants to Individuals
Literature of the Nonprofit Sector
National Data Book of Foundations
National Directory of Corporate Giving
Selected Grant Guides
User-Friendly Guide

Many of the network members have sets of private foundation information returns (IRS Form 990-PF) for their state or region that are available for public use. A complete set of U.S. foundation returns can be found at the New York and Washington, D.C., offices of the Foundation Center. The Cleveland and San Francisco offices contain IRS Form 990-PF returns for the Midwestern and Western states, respectively.

Because the collections vary in their hours, materials, and services, it is recommended that you call each collection in advance. To check on new locations or current information, call toll-free (800) 424-9836.

Reference Collections Operated by the Foundation Center

The Foundation Center
79 5th Ave., 8th Floor
New York, NY 10003
(212) 620-4230

The Foundation Center
312 Sutter St., Rm. 312
San Francisco, CA 94108
(415) 397-0902

The Foundation Center
1001 Connecticut Ave., NW
Washington, DC 20036
(202) 331-1400

The Foundation Center
Kent H. Smith Library
1422 Euclid, Ste. 1356
Cleveland, OH 44115
(216) 861-1933

The Cooperating Collections Network

Participants in the Cooperating Collections Network are libraries or nonprofit information centers that provide fundraising information or other funding-related technical assistance in their communities. Cooperating Collections agree to provide free public access to a basic collection of Foundation Center publications during a regular schedule of hours, offering free funding research guidance to all visitors. Many also provide a variety of special services for local nonprofit organizations, using staff or volunteers to prepare special materials, organize workshops, or conduct orientations.

Alabama

Birmingham Public Library Government
Documents*
   2100 Park Place
   Birmingham 35203
   (205) 226-3600

Huntsville Public Library
   915 Monroe St.
   Huntsville, 35801
   (205) 532-5940

University of South Alabama
   Library Building
   Mobile 36688
   (205) 460-7025

Auburn University at Montgomery Library*
   7300 University Dr.
   Montgomery 36117-3596
   (205) 244-3653

Alaska

University of Alaska at Anchorage Library*
   3211 Providence Dr.
   Anchorage 99508
   (907) 786-1848

Juneau Public Library
   292 Marine Way
   Juneau 99801
   (907) 586-5267

Arizona

Phoenix Public Library Business &
Sciences Unit*
   12 E. McDowell Rd.
   Phoenix 85004
   (602) 262-4436

Tucson Pima Library*
   101 N. Stone Ave.,
   Tucson 85726-7470
   (602) 791-4010

Arkansas

Westark Community College—Borham
Library*
   5210 Grand Ave.
   Ft. Smith 72913
   (501) 785-7133

Central Arkansas Library System
   700 Louisiana
   Little Rock 72201
   (501) 370-5952

Pine Bluff-Jefferson County Library System
   200 E. 8th St.
   Pine Bluff 71601
   (501) 534-2159

California

Ventura County Community Foundation*
Funding and Information Resource Center
   1355 Del Norte Rd.
   Camarillo 93010
   (805) 988-0196

California Community Foundation Funding
Information Center*
   606 S. Olive St., Ste. 2400
   Los Angeles 90014-1526
   (213) 413-4042

Community Foundation for Monterey
County*
   177 Van Buren
   Monterey 93940
   (408) 375-9712

*Information available on private foundation returns for the state.

Grant & Resource Center of Northern
California
    2280 Benton Dr., Bldg. C, Ste. A
    Redding 96003
    (916) 244-1219

Riverside City & County Public Library
    3581 7th St.
    Riverside 92502
    (714) 782-5201

California State Library Information &
Reference Center
    914 Capitol Mall, Rm. 301
    Sacramento 95814
    (916) 654-0261

Nonprofit Resource Center
Sacramento Public Library
    828 I St., 2nd Fl.
    Sacramento 95812-2036
    (916) 522-8817

San Diego Community Foundation*
Funding Information Center
    101 W. Broadway, Ste. 1120
    San Diego 92101
    (619) 239-8815

Nonprofit Development Center Library*
    1762 Technology Dr., No. 225
    San Jose 95110
    (408) 452-8181

Peninsula Community Foundation*
Funding Information Library
    1700 S. El Camino Real, Rm. 301
    San Mateo 94402-3049
    (415) 358-9392

Volunteer Center of Greater Orange County
Nonprofit Management Assistance Center
    1000 E. Santa Ana Blvd., Ste. 200
    Santa Ana 92701
    (714) 953-1655

Santa Barbara Public Library*
    40 E. Anapamu St.
    Santa Barbara 93101
    (805) 962-7653

Santa Monica Public Library
    1343 6th St.,
    Santa Monica 90401-1603
    (310) 458-8600

Colorado
Pikes Peak Library District
    20 N. Cascade

    Colorado Springs 80901
    (719) 473-2080

Denver Public Library*
Social Sciences & Genealogy
    1357 Broadway
    Denver 80203
    (303) 640-8870

Connecticut
Danbury Public Library
    170 Main St.
    Danbury 06810
    (203) 797-4527

Hartford Public Library*
    500 Main St.
    Hartford 06103
    (203) 293-6000

D.A.T.A.
    70 Audubon St.,
    New Haven 06510
    (203) 772-1345

Delaware
University of Delaware*
Hugh Morris Library
    Newark 19717-5267
    (302) 451-2432

Florida
Volusia County Library Center
    City Island
    Daytona Beach 32014-4484
    (904) 255-3765

Nova University*
Einstein Library
    3301 College Ave.
    Fort Lauderdale 33314
    (305) 475-7050

Indian River Community College
Charles S. Miley Learning Resource Center
    3209 Virginia Ave.
    Fort Pierce 34981-5599
    (407) 468-4757

Jacksonville Public Libraries*
Business, Science & Documents
    122 N. Ocean St.
    Jacksonville 32202
    (904) 630-2665

Miami-Dade Public Library*
Humanities/Social Science
    101 W. Flagler St.

Miami 33130
(305) 375-5575

Orlando Public Library*
Social Sciences Dept.
101 E. Central Blvd.
Orlando 32801
(407) 425-4694

Selby Public Library
1001 Blvd. of the Arts
Sarasota 34236
(813) 951-5501

Tampa-Hillsborough County Public Library*
900 N. Ashley Dr.
Tampa 33602
(813) 223-8865

Community Foundation of Palm Beach &
Martin Counties
324 Datura St., Ste. 340
West Palm Beach 33401
(407) 659-6800

Georgia

Atlanta-Fulton Public Library*
Foundation Collection—Ivan Allen Dept.
1 Margaret Mitchell Sq.
Atlanta 30303-1089
(404) 730-1900

Dalton Regional Library
310 Cappes St.
Dalton 30720
(404) 278-4507

Hawaii

University of Hawaii
Hamilton Library
2550 The Mall
Honolulu 96822
(808) 956-7214

Hawaii Community Foundation*
Hawaii Resource Center
222 Merchant St., 2nd Floor
Honolulu 96813
(808) 537-6333

Idaho

Boise Public Library*
715 S. Capitol Blvd.
Boise 83702
(208) 384-4024

Caldwell Public Library*
1010 Dearborn St.

Caldwell 83605
(208) 459-3242

Illinois

Donors Forum of Chicago*
53 W. Jackson Blvd., Ste. 430
Chicago 60604-3608
(312) 431-0265

Evanston Public Library*
1703 Orrington Ave.
Evanston 60201
(708) 866-0305

Rock Island Public Library
401 19th St.
Rock Island 61201
(309) 788-7627

Sangamon State University Library*
Shepherd Rd.
Springfield 62794-9243
(217) 786-6633

Indiana

Allen County Public Library*
900 Webster St.
Ft. Wayne 46802
(219) 424-0544

Indiana University Northwest Library
3400 Broadway
Gary 46408
(219) 980-6582

Indianapolis-Marion County Public Library*
Social Sciences
40 W. St. Clair
Indianapolis 46206
(317) 269-1733

Iowa

Cedar Rapids Public Library*
Foundation Center Collection
500 1st St., SE
Cedar Rapids 52401
(319) 389-5123

Southwestern Community College*
Learning Resource Center
1501 W. Townline Rd.
Creston 50801
(515) 782-7081

Public Library of Des Moines*
100 Locust
Des Moines 50309-1791
(515) 283-4152

Kansas

Topeka Public Library*
    1515 W. 10th St.
    Topeka 66604
    (913) 233-2040

Wichita Public Library*
    233 S. Main St.
    Wichita 67202
    (316) 262-0611

Kentucky

Western Kentucky University
Helm-Cravens Library
    Bowling Green 42101-3576
    (502) 745-6125

Louisville Free Public Library*
    301 York St.
    Louisville 40203
    (502) 561-8617

Louisiana

East Baton Rouge Parish Library*
Centroplex Branch Grants Collection
    120 St. Louis
    Baton Rouge 70802
    (504) 389-4960

Beauregard Parish Library
    1201 W. 1st St.
    De Ridder 70634
    (318) 463-6217

New Orleans Public Library*
Business & Science Div.
    219 Loyola Ave.
    New Orleans 70140
    (504) 596-2580

Shreve Memorial Library*
424 Texas St.
    Shreveport 71120-1523
    (318) 226-5894

Maine

University of Southern Maine*
Office of Sponsored Research
    246 Deering Ave., Rm. 628
    Portland 04103
    (207) 780-4871

Maryland

Enoch Pratt Free Library*
Social Science & History
    400 Cathedral St.
    Baltimore 21201
    (301) 396-5430

Massachusetts

Associated Grantmakers of Massachusetts*
    294 Washington St., Ste. 840
    Boston 02108
    (617) 426-2606

Boston Public Library*
Humanities Reference
    666 Boylston St.
    Boston 02117
    (617) 536-5400

Western Massachusetts Funding Resource
Center
    65 Elliot St.
    Springfield 01101-1730
    (413) 732-3175

Worcester Public Library*
Grants Resource Center
    Salem Sq.
    Worcester 01608
    (508) 799-1655

Michigan

Alpena County Library*
    211 N. 1st St.
    Alpena 49707
    (517) 356-6188

University of Michigan-Ann Arbor
Graduate Library*
Reference & Research Services Dept.
    Ann Arbor 48109-1205
    (313) 664-9373

Battle Creek Community Foundation*
Southwest Michigan Funding Resource Center
    2 Riverwalk Centre
    34 W. Jackson St.
    Battle Creek 49017-3505
    (616) 962-2181

Henry Ford Centennial Library Adult Services*
    16301 Michigan Ave.
    Dearborn 48126
    (313) 943-2330

Wayne State University*
Purdy/Kresge Library
    5265 Cass Ave.
    Detroit 48202
    (313) 577-6424

Michigan State University Libraries*
Social Sciences/Humanities
    Main Library
    East Lansing 48824-1048
    (517) 353-8818

Farmington Community Library*
32737 W. 12 Mile Rd.
Farmington Hills 48018
(313) 553-0300

University of Michigan—Flint Library*
Flint 48502-2186
(313) 762-3408

Grand Rapids Public Library*
Business Dept.—3rd Floor
60 Library Plaza NE
Grand Rapids 49503-3093
(616) 456-3600

Michigan Technological University*
Van Pelt Library
1400 Townsend Dr.
Houghton 49931
(906) 487-2507

Sault Ste. Marie Area Public Schools*
Office of Compensatory Education
460 W. Spruce St.
Sault Ste. Marie 49783-1874
(906) 635-6619

Northwestern Michigan College*
Mark & Helen Osterin Library
1701 E. Front St.
Traverse City 49684
(619) 922-1060

Minnesota
Duluth Public Library*
520 W. Superior St.
Duluth 55802
(218) 723-3802

Southwest State University
University Library
Marshall 56258
(507) 537-6176

Minneapolis Public Library*
Sociology Dept.
300 Nicollet Mall
Minneapolis 55401
(612) 372-6555

Rochester Public Library
11 First St. SE
Rochester 55904-3777
(507) 285-8002

St. Paul Public Library
90 W. 4th St.
St. Paul 55102
(612) 292-6307

Mississippi
Jackson/Hinds Library System
300 N. State St.
Jackson 39201
(601) 968-5803

Missouri
Clearinghouse for Midcontinent Foundations*
University of Missouri
5110 Cherry St.
Kansas City 64113-0680
(816) 235-1176

Kansas City Public Library*
311 E. 12th St.
Kansas City 64111
(816) 221-9650

Metropolitan Association for
Philanthropy, Inc.*
5615 Pershing Avenue, Ste. 20
St. Louis 63112
(314) 361-3900

Springfield-Green County Library*
397 E. Central
Springfield 65802
(417) 869-9400

Montana
Eastern Montana College Library*
Special Collections—Grants
1500 N. 30th St.
Billings 59101-0298
(406) 657-1662

Bozeman Public Library
220 E. Lamme
Bozeman 59715
(406) 586-4787

Montana State Library*
Library Services
1515 E. 6th Ave.
Helena 59620
(406) 444-3004

Nebraska
University of Nebraska—Lincoln*
Love Library
14th & R Streets
Lincoln 68588-0410
(402) 472-2848

W. Dale Clark Library*
Social Sciences Dept.
215 S. 15th St.

Omaha 68102
(402) 444-4826

Nevada
Las Vegas-Clark County Library District*
833 Las Vegas Blvd. N.
Las Vegas 89101
(702) 382-5280

Washoe County Library*
301 S. Center St.
Reno 89501
(702) 785-4010

New Hampshire
New Hampshire Charitable Fund*
1 South St.
Concord 03302-1335
(603) 225-6641

Plymouth State College*
Herbert H. Lamson Library
Plymouth 03264
(603) 535-2258

New Jersey
Cumberland County Library
New Jersey Room
800 E. Commerce St.
Bridgeton 08302
(609) 453-2210

Free Public Library of Elizabeth
11 S. Broad St.
Elizabeth 07202
(908) 354-6060

Support Center of New Jersey
Resource Library
17 Academy St., Ste. 517
Newark 07102
(201) 643-5774

County College of Morris
Learning Resource Center
214 Center Grove Rd.
Randolph 07869
(201) 328-5296

New Jersey State Library*
Government Reference Services
185 W. State St.
Trenton 08625-0520
(609) 292-6220

New Mexico
Albuquerque Community Foundation
3301 Menual, NE, Ste. 22

Albuquerque 87176-6960
(505) 883-6240

New Mexico State Library*
Information Services
325 Don Gaspar
Santa Fe 87503
(505) 827-3824

New York
New York State Library*
Humanities Reference
Cultural Education Center
Empire State Plaza
Albany 12230
(518) 474-5355

Suffolk Cooperative Library System
627 N. Sunrise Service Rd.
Bellport 11713
(516) 286-1600

New York Public Library
Fordham Branch
2556 Bainbridge Ave.
Bronx 10458
(212) 220-6575

Brooklyn In Touch Information Center, Inc.
1 Hanson Place, Rm. 2504
Brooklyn 11243
(718) 230-3200

Buffalo & Erie County Public Library*
History Dept.
Lafayette Sq.
Buffalo 14203
(716) 858-7103

Huntington Public Library
338 Main St.
Huntington 11743
(516) 427-5165

Queens Borough Public Library
Social Sciences Division
89-11 Merrick Blvd.
Jamaica 11432
(718) 990-0700

Levittown Public Library*
1 Bluegrass Lane
Levittown 11756
(516) 731-5728

New York Public Library
Countee Cullen Branch Library
104 W. 136th St.
New York 10030
(212) 491-2070

SUNY at Old Westbury Library
223 Store Hill Rd.
Old Westbury 11568
(516) 876-3156

Adriance Memorial Library
Special Services Dept.
93 Market St.
Poughkeepsie 12601
(914) 485-3445

Rochester Public Library*
Business, Economics & Law
115 South Ave.
Rochester 14604
(716) 428-7328

Onondaga County Public Library*
447 S. Salina St.
Syracuse 13202-2494
(315) 448-4636

Utica Public Library
303 Genesee St.
Utica 13501
(315) 735-2279

White Plains Public Library*
100 Martine Ave.
White Plains 10601
(914) 422-1480

North Carolina
Asheville-Buncombe Technical
Community College*
Learning Resources Center
340 Victoria Rd.
Asheville 28801
(704) 254-4960

The Duke Endowment*
200 S. Tryon St., Ste. 1100
Charlotte 28202
(704) 376-0291

Durham County Public Library
301 N. Roxboro
Durham 27702
(919) 560-0110

State Library of North Carolina*
Government and Business Services
Archives Bldg., 109 E. Jones St.
Raleigh 27601
(919) 733-3270

Winston-Salem Foundation*
310 W. 4th St., Ste. 229
Winston-Salem 27101-2889
(919) 725-2382

North Dakota
North Dakota State University Library*
Fargo 58105
(701) 237-8886

Ohio
Stark County District Library
Humanities
715 Market Ave. N.
Canton 44702
(216) 452-0665

Public Library of Cincinnati &
Hamilton County*
Grants Resource Center
800 Vine St.—Library Sq.
Cincinnati 45202-2071
(513) 369-6940

Columbus Metropolitan Library
Business and Technology
96 S. Grant Ave.
Columbus 43215
(614) 645-2590

Dayton & Montgomery County Public
Library*
1st Floor, East Side
215 E. Third St.
Dayton 45402
(513) 227-9500 x211

Toledo-Lucas County Public Library*
Social Sciences Dept.
325 Michigan St.
Toledo 43624-1614
(419) 259-5245

Ohio University—Zanesville
Community Education Dept.
1425 Newark Rd.
Zanesville 43701
(614) 453-0762

Oklahoma
Oklahoma City University*
Dulaney Browne Library
2501 N. Blackwelder
Oklahoma City 73106
(405) 521-5072

Tulsa City-County Library*
400 Civic Center
Tulsa 74103
(918) 596-7944

Oregon
Oregon Institute of Technology Library
3201 Campus Dr.

Klamath Falls 97601-8801
(503) 885-1773

Pacific Non-Profit Network*
Grantsmanship Resource Library
33 N. Central, Ste. 211
Medford 97501
(503) 779-6044

Multnomah County Library*
Government Documents
801 SW 10th Ave.
Portland 97205
(503) 248-5123

Oregon State Library
State Library Building
Salem 97310
(503) 378-4277

Pennsylvania
Northampton Community College
Learning Resources Center
3835 Green Pond Rd.
Bethlehem 18017
(215) 861-5360

Erie County Library System*
27 South Park Row
Erie 16501
(814) 451-6927

Dauphin County Library System
Central Library
101 Walnut St.
Harrisburg 17101
(717) 234-4961

Lancaster County Public Library
125 N. Duke St.
Lancaster 17602
(717) 394-2651

Free Library of Philadelphia*
Regional Foundation Center
Logan Sq.
Philadelphia 19103
(215) 686-5423

Carnegie Library of Pittsburgh*
Foundation Collection
4400 Forbes Ave.
Pittsburgh 15213-4080
(412) 622-3114

Pocono Northeast Development Fund
James Pettinger Memorial LIbrary
1151 Oak St.

Pittston 18640-3755
(717) 655-5581

Reading Public Library
100 S. 5th St.
Reading 19602
(215) 478-6355

Rhode Island
Providence Public Library*
150 Empire St.
Providence 02906
(401) 521-7722

South Carolina
Charleston County Library*
404 King St.
Charleston 29403
(803) 723-1645

South Carolina State Library*
1500 Senate St.
Columbia 29211
(803) 734-8666

South Dakota
Nonprofit Grants Assistance Center
Business & Education Institute
Washington St., East Hall
Dakota State University
Madison 57042
(605) 256-5555

South Dakota State Library*
800 Governors Dr.
Pierre 57501-2294
(605) 773-5070
(800) 592-1841 (SD residents)

Sioux Falls Area Foundation
141 N. Main Ave., Ste. 500
Sioux Falls 57102-1134
(605) 336-7055

Tennessee
Knox County Public Library*
500 W. Church Ave.
Knoxville 37902
(615) 544-5700

Memphis & Shelby County Public Library*
1850 Peabody Ave.
Memphis 38104
(901) 725-8877

Nashville Public Library*
Business Information Division

8th Ave., N. & Union
Nashville 37203
(615) 862-5843

Texas
Community Foundation of Abilene*
Funding Information Library
500 N. Chestnut, Ste. 1509
Abilene 79604
(915) 676-3883

Amarillo Area Foundation*
700 First National Place
801 S. Fillmore
Amarillo 79101
(806) 376-4521

Hogg Foundation for Mental Health*
Will C. Hogg Bldg., Rm. 301
Inner Campus Dr.
University of Texas
Austin 78713
(512) 471-5041

Corpus Christi State University Library*
Reference Dept.
6300 Ocean Dr.
Corpus Christi 78412
(512) 994-2608

Dallas Public Library*
Urban Information
1515 Young St.
Dallas 75211
(214) 670-1487

El Paso Community Foundation*
1616 Texas Commerce Bldg.
El Paso 79901
(915) 533-4020

Funding Information Center of Fort Worth*
Texas Christian University Library
2800 S. University Dr.
Ft. Worth 76129
(817) 921-7664

Houston Public Library*
Bibliographic Information Center
500 McKinney
Houston 77002
(713) 236-1313

Longview Public Library
222 W. Cotton St.
Longview 75601
(903) 237-1352

Lubbock Area Foundation, Inc.
502 Texas Commerce Bank Bldg.
Lubbock 79401
(806) 762-8061

Funding Information Center*
530 McCullough, Ste. 600
San Antonio 78212-8270
(512) 227-4333

North Texas Center for Nonprofit
Management
624 Indiana, Ste. 307
Wichita Falls 76301
(817) 322-4961

Utah
Salt Lake City Public Library*
209 E. 500 South
Salt Lake City 84111
(801) 524-8200

Vermont
Vermont Dept. of Libraries*
Reference & Law Info. Services
109 State St.
Montpelier 05609
(802) 828-3268

Virginia
Hampton Public Library*
4207 Victoria Blvd.
Hampton 23669
(804) 727-1312

Richmond Public Library*
Business, Science & Technology
101 E. Franklin St.
Richmond 23219
(804) 780-8223

Roanoke City Public Library System*
Central Library
706 S. Jefferson St.
Roanoke 24016
(703) 981-2477

Washington
Mid-Columbia Library
405 S. Dayton
Kennewick 99336
(509) 586-3156

Seattle Public Library*
Science, Social Science
1000 4th Ave.

Seattle 98104
(206) 386-4620

Spokane Public Library*
Funding Information Center
W. 811 Main Ave.
Spokane 99201
(509) 838-3364

Greater Wenatchee Community
Foundation at the Wenatchee Public Library
310 Douglas St.
Wenatchee 98807
(509) 662-5021

West Virginia
Kanawha County Public Library*
123 Capitol St.
Charleston 25304
(304) 343-4646

Wisconsin
University of Wisconsin-Madison
Memorial Library*
728 State St.
Madison 53706
(608) 262-3242

Marquette University Memorial Library*
Foundation Collection
1415 W. Wisconsin Ave.
Milwaukee 53233
(414) 288-1515

Wyoming
Natrona County Public Library*
307 E. 2nd St.
Casper 82601-2598
(307) 237-4935

Laramie County Community College*
Instructional Resource Center
1400 E. College Dr.
Cheyenne 82007-3299
(307) 778-1206

Teton County Library
320 S. King St.
Jackson 83001
(307) 733-2164

Rock Springs Library
400 C St.
Rock Springs 82901
(307) 362-6212

Australia
Australian Association of Philanthropy
20 Queen St., 8th Floor
Melbourne 3000
(03) 614-1491

Canada
Canadian Centre for Philanthropy
Resource Center
1329 Bay St., Ste. 200
Toronto, Ontario M5R 2C4
(416) 515-0764

England
Charities Aid Foundation
114/118 Southampton Row
London WC1B 5AA
(71) 831-7798

Japan
Foundation Library Center of Japan
Elements Shinjuku Bldg. 3F
2-1-14 Shinjuku, Shinjuku-ku
Tokyo 160
(03) 350-1857

Mexico
Biblioteca Benjamin Franklin
American Embassy, USICA
Londres 16
Mexico City 6, DF 06600
(905) 211-0042

Puerto Rico
University of Puerto Rico
Ponce Technological College Library
Box 7186
Ponce 00732
(809) 844-8181

Universidad del Sagrado Corazon
M. M. T. Guevara Library
Santurce 00914
(809) 728-1515 x357

The Foundation Center welcomes inquiries from libraries or information centers in the United States that are interested in providing this type of public information service. If you are interested in establishing a funding information library for the use of nonprofit organizations in your area, or in learning more about the program, please write to Judith Margolin, Vice President for Public Services, The Foundation Center, 79 Fifth Avenue, New York, NY 10003-3076.

IV: Tax Deductions for Independent Scholarship as a Business

If you can show the IRS that your scholarly activities meet its criteria, you can take advantage of tax breaks available for business-related expenses. After all, like anyone else in a business or profession, you may make tax-deductible payments for equipment, supplies, books and journals, entertainment, conferences, and courses. Here is a run-down of just some of these:

- using your home in your business
- legal and professional fees that have to do with your business
- heat, light, and power
- incidental supplies and materials such as office supplies
- advertising expenses
- licenses and regulatory fees for your trade or business
- penalties for nonperformance of contract
- payments to charitable, religious, educational, or scientific organizations that are not, in fact, contributions or gifts
- donations to business organizations
- franchises, trademarks, trade names
- educational expenses

If you produce income from your scholarly activities, you will more than likely be required to pay taxes on that income. Moreover, you may be required to maintain certain kinds of business records to file quarterly declarations of estimated tax, and to pay special taxes such as the self-employment tax, a social security tax for people who work for themselves. So if you are going to have to "pay up" anyway, you might as well use the tax laws to your best advantage.

Unfortunately, the definition of a business and the qualifications regarding business expenses and deductions are not always as straightforward as they may at first seem. Indeed, the hundreds of special laws and rulings relating to business taxes and deductions that may affect you are often very complex. Because they may work to your advantage as well as to your disadvantage, it might be wise to consult a professional tax accountant.

To help you if you are a do-it-yourselfer (or just want to check the accuracy of the person you hire to fill out your return), those friendly folks at the IRS provide a broad variety of services without charge. For starters, get a free copy of the agency's annual best-seller, *Tax Guide for Small Businesses* (also known to the tax people as Publication No. 334). Number 334 can be of invaluable assistance because it furnishes far more information about specific situations than is supplied in the instructions that accompany your return. It contains numerous examples, as well as sample filled-out forms that take you on a line-by-line journey through the perplexities of Form 1040 and other "schedules." In the front are highlights of important changes in the tax laws over the past year so that you can take these changes into account before filling out your return.

The IRS also issues many other free publications that may be useful to you. Among them are:

- ➤ *Business Expenses* (No. 535)
- ➤ *Business Use of Your Home* (No. 587)
- ➤ *Educational Expenses* (No. 508)
- ➤ *The Withholding and Estimated Tax* (No. 505)
- ➤ *Miscellaneous Deductions* (No. 529)
- ➤ *Taxpayers Starting a Business* (No. 583)
- ➤ *Recordkeeping for Individuals* (No. 552)
- ➤ *Self-Employment Tax* (No. 533)
- ➤ *Scholarships and Fellowships* (No. 520)
- ➤ *Taxable and Nontaxable Income* (No. 525)
- ➤ *Travel, Entertainment, and Gift Expenses* (No. 463)

The publication *Your Federal Income Tax* (No. 17) is an excellent general guide for all taxpayers. For free copies of publications, stop by an IRS office or telephone (800) TAX-FORM.

The Small Business Administration also issues a number of publications which may be helpful to you. Lists of its free items (SBA 115A) and inexpensive booklets (SBA 115B) can be obtained from the Small Business Administration, Washington, D.C. 20416, or from its local field offices.

Among the most popular nongovernment tax guidebooks is *J. K. Lasser's Your Income Tax*, which is published annually in paperback and is available in most libraries and bookstores.

One of the best sources of advice that combines filing tips with understandable advice on tax planning is *Julian Block's Year-Round Tax Strategies* by Julian Block, an attorney in Larchmont, New York. It explains how to take advantage of often-overlooked, perfectly legal breaks that lower taxes for even persons of modest means. For a postpaid copy, send fourteen dollars (three dollars off the regular price for independent scholars) to Julian Block, 3 Washington Square, Larchmont, NY 10538-2032.

V: University Presses in North America

The following is a list of university presses in the United States and Canada and the cities and states or provinces where they are located.

University of Alabama Press
University, AL

University of Alberta Press
Edmonton, Alberta

University of Arizona Press
Tucson, AZ

Brigham Young University Press
Provo, UT

University of British Columbia Press
Vancouver, British Columbia

Bucknell University Press
Lewisburg, PA

University of California Press
Berkeley, CA

Cambridge University Press
New York, NY

Catholic University of America Press
Washington, D.C.

University of Chicago Press
Chicago, IL

Colorado Associated University Press
Boulder, CO

Columbia University Press
New York, NY

Cornell University Press
Ithaca, NY

University of Delaware Press
Newark, DE

Duke University Press
Durham, NC

Duquesne University Press
Pittsburgh, PA

Fairleigh Dickinson University Press
Madison, NJ

University Presses of Florida
Gainsville, FL

Fordham University Press
Bronx, NY

University of Georgia Press
Athens, GA

Harvard University Press
Cambridge, MA

University Press of Hawaii
Honolulu, HI

Howard University Press
Washington, D.C.

University of Illinois Press
Champaign, IL

Indiana University Press
Bloomington, IN

Inter American University Press
San Juan, PR

University of Iowa Press
Iowa City, IA

Iowa State University Press
Ames, IA

Johns Hopkins University Press
Baltimore, MD

Regents Press of Kansas
Lawrence, KS

Kent State University Press
Kent, OH

University Press of Kentucky
Lexington, KY

Les Presses de l'Université Laval
Quebec, Quebec

Louisiana State University Press
Baton Rouge, LA

Loyola University Press
Chicago, IL

McGill-Queen's University Press
Montreal, Quebec

University of Manitoba Press
Winnipeg, Manitoba

University of Massachusetts Press
Amherst, MA

M.I.T. Press
Cambridge, MA

Memphis State University Press
Memphis, TN

University of Miami Press
Coral Gables, FL

University of Michigan Press
Ann Arbor, MI

Michigan State University Press
East Lansing, MI

University of Minnesota Press
Minneapolis-St. Paul, MN

University Press of Mississippi
Jackson, MS

University of Missouri Press
Columbia, MO

Les Presses de l'Université de Montreal
Montreal, Quebec

Naval Institute Press
Annapolis, MD

University of Nebraska Press
Lincoln, NE

University of Nevada Press
Reno, NV

University Press of New England
Hanover, NH

University of New Mexico Press
Albuquerque, NM

New York University Press
New York, NY

University of North Carolina Press
Chapel Hill, NC

Northeastern University Press
Boston, MA

Northern Illinois University Press
DeKalb, IL

Northwestern University Press
Evanston, IL

University of Notre Dame Press
Notre Dame, IN

Ohio State University Press
Columbus, OH

Ohio University Press
Athens, OH

O.I.S.E. Press
Toronto, Ontario

University of Oklahoma Press
Norman, OK

Oregon State University Press
Corvallis, OR

Editions de l'Université d'Ottawa
Ottawa, Ontario

Oxford University Press
New York, NY

University of Pennsylvania Press
Philadelphia, PA

The Pennsylvania State University Press
University Park, PA

University of Pittsburgh Press
Pittsburgh, PA

The Pontifical Institute of Medieval Studies
Toronto, Ontario

Princeton University Press
Princeton, NJ

Purdue University Press
West Lafayette, IN

Rockefeller University Press
New York, NY

Rutgers University Press
New Brunswick, NJ

University of South Carolina Press
Columbia, SC

Southern Illinois University Press
Carbondale, IL

Southern Methodist University Press
Dallas, TX

Stanford University Press
Stanford, CA

State University of New York Press
Albany, NY

Syracuse University Press
Syracuse, NY

Teachers College Press
New York, NY

Temple University Press
Philadelphia, PA

University of Tennessee Press
Knoxville, TN

University of Texas Press
Austin, TX

Texas A&M University Press
College Station, TX

Texas Christian University Press
Fort Worth, TX

Texas Western Press
El Paso, TX

University of Toronto Press
Toronto

Troy State University Press
Troy, AL

University of Utah Press
Salt Lake City, UT

Vanderbilt University Press
Nashville, TN

University Press of Virginia
Charlottesville, VA

University of Washington Press
Seattle, WA

University Press of Washington, D. C.
Riverton, VA

Wayne State University Press
Detroit, MI

Wesleyan University Press
Middletown, CT

Wilfrid Laurier University Press
Waterloo, Ontario

University of Wisconsin Press
Madison, WI

Yale University Press
New Haven, CT

VI: Copyrighting Your Work

Copyright is a form of protection provided by the laws of the United States (title 17, U.S. Code) to the authors of "original works of authorship" including literary, dramatic, musical, artistic, and certain other intellectual works. This protection is available to both published and unpublished works. Section 106 of the Copyright Act generally gives the owner of copyright the exclusive right to do and to authorize others to do the following:

> ➤ *to reproduce* the copyrighted work in copies or phonorecords
> ➤ to prepare *derivative works* based upon the copyrighted work
> ➤ *to distribute copies or phonorecords* of the copyrighted work to the public by sale or other transfer of ownership, or by rental, lease, or lending

➤ *to perform the copyrighted work publicly,* in the case of literary, musical, dramatic, and choreographic works, pantomimes, and motion pictures and other audiovisual works

➤ *to display the copyrighted work publicly,* in the case of literary, musical, dramatic, and choreographic works, pantomimes, and pictorial, graphic, or sculptural works, including the individual images of a motion picture or other audiovisual work

It is illegal for anyone to violate any of the rights provided by the Act to the owner of copyright. These rights, however, are not unlimited in scope. Sections 107 through 119 of the Copyright Act establish limitations on these rights. In some cases, these limitations are specified exemptions from copyright liability. One major limitation is the doctrine of "fair use," which is given a statutory basis in section 107 of the Act. In other instances, the limitation takes the form of a "compulsory license" under which certain limited uses of copyrighted works are permitted upon payment of specified royalties and compliance with statutory conditions. For further information about the limitations of any of these rights, consult the Copyright Act or write to the Copyright Office.

Who Can Claim Copyright

Copyright protection subsists from the time the work is created in fixed form; that is, it is an incident of the process of authorship. The copyright in the work of authorship *immediately* becomes the property of the author who created it. Only the author or those deriving their rights through the author can rightfully claim copyright.

In the case of works made for hire, the employer and not the employee is presumptively considered the author. Section 101 of the copyright statute defines a "work made for hire" as:

➤ a work prepared by an employee within the scope of his or her employment

➤ a work specially ordered or commissioned for use as a contribution to a collective work, as a part of a motion picture or other audiovisual work, as a translation, as a supplementary work, as a compilation, as an instructional text, as a test, as answer material for a test, or as an atlas, if the parties expressly agree in a written instrument signed by them that the work shall be considered a work made for hire. . .

The authors of a joint work are co-owners of the copyright in the work, unless there is a an agreement to the contrary.

Copyright in each separate contribution to a periodical or other collective work is distinct from copyright in the collective work as a whole and vests initially with the author or the contribution.

Two General Principles

Mere ownership of a book, manuscript, painting, or any other copy or phonorecord does not give the possessor the copyright. The law provides that transfer of ownership of any material object that embodies a protected work does not of itself convey any rights in the copyright.

Minors may claim copyright, but state laws may regulate the business dealings involving copyrights owned by minors. For information on relevant state laws, consult an attorney.

Copyright and National Origin of the Work

Copyright protection is available for all unpublished works, regardless of the nationality or domicile of the author.

Published works are eligible for copyright protection in the United States if *any* one of the following conditions is met.

➤ on the date of first publication, one or more of the authors is a national or domiciliary of the United States or is a national, domiciliary, or sovereign authority of a foreign nation that is a party to a copyright treaty to which the United States is also a party, or is a stateless person wherever that person may be domiciled

➤ the work is first published in the United States or in a foreign nation that, on the date of first publication, is a party to the Universal Copyright Convention; or the work comes within the scope of a Presidential proclamation

➤ the work is first published on or after March 1, 1989, in a foreign nation that, on the date of first publication, is a party to the Berne Convention; or, if the work is *not* first published in a country party to the Berne Convention, it is published (on or after March 1, 1989) within thirty days of first publication in a country that is party to the Berne Convention; or the work, first published on or after March 1, 1989, is a pictorial, graphic, or sculptural work that is incorporated in a permanent structure located in the United States; or, if the work, first published on or after March 1, 1989, is a published audiovisual work, all the authors are legal entities with headquarters in the United States

What Works Are Protected

Copyright protects "original works of authorship" that are fixed in a tangible form of expression. The fixation need not be directly perceptible, so long as it may be communicated with the aid of a machine or device. Copyrightable works include the following categories:

> literary works
> musical works, including any accompanying words
> dramatic works, including any accompanying music
> pantomimes and choreographic works
> pictorial, graphic, and sculptural works
> motion pictures and other audiovisual works
> sound recordings
> architectural works

These categories should be viewed quite broadly: for example, computer programs and most "compilations" are registrable as "literary works"; maps and architectural plans are registrable as "pictorial, graphic, and sculptural works."

What Is Not Protected by Copyright

Several categories of material are generally not eligible for statutory copyright protection. These include among others:

> works that have *not* been fixed in a tangible form of expression; for example: choreographic works that have not been notated or recorded, or improvisational speeches or performances that have not been written or recorded
> titles, names, short phrases, and slogans; familiar symbols or designs; mere variations of typographic ornamentation, lettering, or coloring; mere listings of ingredients or contents
> ideas, procedures, methods, systems, processes, concepts, principles, discoveries, or devices, as distinguished from a description, explanation, or illustration
> works consisting *entirely* of information that is common property and containing no original authorship, for example: standard calendars, height and weight charts, tape measures and rulers, and lists or tables taken from public documents or other common sources

How to Secure a Copyright

The way in which copyright protection is secured under the present law is frequently misunderstood. No publication or registration or other action in the Copyright Office is required to secure copyright. There are, however, certain definite advantages to registration.

Copyright is secured *automatically* when the work is created, and a work is "created" when it is fixed in a copy or phonorecord for the first time. "Copies" are material objects from which a work can be read or visually perceived either directly or with the aid of a machine or device, such as books, manuscripts, sheet music, film, videotape, or microfilm. "Phonorecords" are material objects embodying fixations of sounds (excluding, by statutory definition, motion picture sound-tracks), such as audio tapes and phonograph disks. Thus, for example, a song (the "work") can be fixed in sheet music ("copies") or in phonograph disks ("phono-records"), or both.

If a work is prepared over a period of time, the part of the work that is fixed on a particular date constitutes the created work as of that date.

Excerpted from Copyright Basics, *Copyright Office, Washington, D.C., 1991.*

VII: The National Coalition of Independent Scholars

The National Coalition of Independent Scholars (NCIS) was founded in January 1989 by members of local organizations of independent scholars from many different parts of the country. A first step toward the creation of a national organization was a conference sponsored by one of the local groups, the San Diego Independent Scholars, in the fall of 1986. The conference had been inspired by the work of Ronald Gross and James Bennett, whose publications in the early 1980s brought attention to independent scholarship as a national phenomenon. After the conference, another local group, the Institute for Historical Study, began publishing a quarterly newsletter, *The Independent Scholar*, which served to inform both local groups and isolated individuals of the existence and activities of independent scholars elsewhere. Through *The Independent Scholar*, plans for the creation of a national organization were publicized, and nominations for the first board of directors were announced in 1988.

Although the impetus for NCIS came from local groups, and it does support those as well as encourage the formation of new ones, the organization also serves independent scholars as individuals and offers to people who are not themselves independent scholars, a way of supporting their colleagues' activities. Three purposes are accomplished with the three categories of membership: Affiliate (groups), Member (individuals), and Associate (supporters).

One of the coalition's main services to its members is its set of publications. Thus far, these include an annual membership directory, useful for reference by outsiders and for networking by members; a grants handbook, with a brief listing of government agencies and private foundations that have programs for individuals; and *The Independent Scholar*, a quarterly newsletter that carries information about NCIS itself, about the local groups, and about individuals. Longer articles on general topics of interest to independent scholars, such as interviews about publishing procedures, profiles of independent scholars, or reviews of trends in academic fields, are also published in the newsletter.

Members join upon giving evidence of some serious scholarly interest or ongoing project. Many have advanced degrees, but such credentials are not required. Although most of the members fall loosely into the humanities as broadly considered, many have an interdisciplinary bent, often bringing the social sciences to bear on their topics. A small number are scientists, including mathematicians, biologists, and astronomers.

Affiliate Members

> Alliance of Independent Scholars
> 6 Ash St., Cambridge, MA 02138

> Association of Independent Historians of Art
> 30 West 61st St., Ste. 29A, New York, NY 10023

> Center for Independent Study
> Box 3193 Yale Station, New Haven, CT 06520

> Five College Associates
> P.O. Box 740, Amherst, MA 01004

> Independent Scholars' Association/North Carolina Triangle
> 307 Estes Dr., Chapel Hill, NC 27514

> Institute for Historical Study
> 1791 Pine St., San Francisco, CA 94109

> Northwest Independent Scholars Association
> 2513 N.E. Skidmore, Portland, OR 97211

> Princeton Research Forum
> P.O. Box 497, Princeton, NJ 08540

> San Diego Independent Scholars
> 5027 Campanile Dr., San Diego, CA 92115

VIII: How Independent Scholars Can Organize: Five Case Studies

How might you join other independent scholars in your area to launch and run a group for mutual support and other purposes? Profiles of five such groups were assembled by Georgia Wright, the editor of *The Independent Scholar Newsletter*, and published in the winter of 1987. Since then much has changed in these organizations. Nevertheless, these accounts of their origins are inspiring and instructive.

The Institute for Historical Study

The Institute was the brainchild of two women, Paula Gillett and Francesca Miller, who first met at a hospitality session run by the Institute for Research in History at the 1978 meeting of the American Historical Association. Marjorie Lightman, executive director of that organization, described the New York Institute for them. The two then reached out to interested historians and held several small meetings in preparation for the large organizational meeting in October of 1979. This all-day meeting on the U.C. Berkeley campus attracted sixty people. A few people, who had come up from Southern California and from other sites outside the Bay Area, wished to form a statewide organization. But most of those at the meeting were worried about the administrative problems entailed in such a vastly spread-out group.

At the meeting, committees were formed to write the bylaws and constitution and to apply for 501(c)3 status. (The Management Center, which offers all sorts of services to nonprofits, was extremely helpful with these tasks.) The West Coast Association of Women Historians, several of whom were among the founders of the Institute, had given the new organization two hundred dollars. This was supplemented by a collection taken up at the meeting and some funds were voted to send Paula Gillett to New York to confer again with Marjorie Lightman. Paula, at the time finishing her Ph.D., was an incredible recruiter, and everyone seemed to know her. If you called Paula, as I did, to ask about something entirely different, you heard the pitch for the Institute—and joined! She was the first president of the new organization, and it was to her credit that her board was also strong.

While it was intended that the Institute be modeled upon the New York Institute, it was soon clear that members lived too far apart to support a program of seminars that worked in densely settled Manhattan. Nor did the board wish to take a strong feminist stance as the New York group did. From the beginning the Institute has had a good number of men, one-third or more of the members, as well as at least two men on the board.

The younger Institute stresses work-in-progress sessions. It has two long-running study groups, occasional minicourses taught by members for members, and workshops and conferences, usually mounted with the help of an institutional cosponsor. It has never had an advisory board nor more than one membership category. These were particularly hard-fought issues; those who felt rejected by academe did not want to ask for academic validation nor did they want to establish a hierarchy of membership on academic lines. Nevertheless, the Institute has attracted a large number of faculty and librarians from Bay Area colleges and universities, and the mix seems both natural and good.   —*Georgia Wright*

Independent Scholars' Association of the North Carolina Triangle (ISA/NCT)

The following description was offered in response to questions about the association between continuing education offices and independent scholars' groups.

Our organization has its origins firmly in the Duke Office of Continuing Education. In 1981 I wrote a grants proposal to our state humanities council for a statewide project using independent scholars. I was at that time the humanities coordinator for the Office of Continuing Education and an independent scholar myself who regularly taught literature to adults through that office and wrote grant proposals for special projects. The idea for the statewide project was not mine, I should add—it was either my boss's or the council's itself. At any rate, to help support my proposal I attached an article by Ron Gross about independent scholarship. The project was funded and successfully served North Carolina for over a year. Meanwhile I became the director of Continuing Education.

In 1983 one of my co-workers and I read an article about how Ron Gross had visited a campus and kicked off an independent scholar's group. We decided to have him come to Durham for the same purpose. In November of 1983 Gross delivered two lectures on the Duke campus and about eighty-five people came to the one that specifically launched the local group. To get people to that meeting, we advertised heavily, put up flyers, phoned people we thought would be interested, and had a feature article published on Ron Gross. . . . He is a master at publicity, and he gave us many tips on drumming up business as well as on forming the group itself. He stayed overnight and we carefully orchestrated the foundation of what would become the ISA/NCT. Several of the people who attended that original meeting are still active in the group.

In my estimation there is no particularly natural fit between an independent scholars' group and an office of continuing education unless the personnel at the latter are independent scholars. The "natural" aspect of the connection is that independent scholars often teach courses through continuing education operations.

I doubt that, unless a director [of continuing education] had a personal interest in independent scholarship, he or she would be willing to invest what I do in such a group. I float the duplication and the mailing of our monthly newsletter, either wholly (if my budget permits) or largely. My secretary puts in several hours a month for the group. My postage, stationery, and duplication add up to a significant amount in the course of a year. Yet I believe in the purposes of such an organization and I publish an account of its activities in our office's annual report every year. Because I have been the president until now (in January, I will give up that office and become secretary), and because my office has provided goods and services, we say that the ISA/NCT is "loosely affiliated" with Duke Continuing Education.

—*Judith Ruderman*

Alliance of Independent Scholars

The idea for establishing a community of women with Ph.D.s originated with Simone Reagor (now a dean at Harvard Law School), who was working at Radcliffe in 1979, and became aware of how little the Harvard-Radcliffe community offered women scholars in the way of social community or encouragement for ongoing work. A Ph.D. in history herself, Reagor had redefined her own position to become an administrator. Deciding to call an organizational meeting, she telephoned a few other women in the area who seemed in need of support, and each of these called one or two others working on a book or dissertation, looking for a job, or simply yearning to discuss new ideas. Over thirty of us assembled as an interdisciplinary group—and we have remained so—a distinction that from the first has made us different from the Institute for Research in History in New York, which we used as a model as much as we could. Indeed, Marjorie Lightman generously spent an evening with us in Boston to describe how the Institute functioned.

But conditions in Boston have always remained different from those in New York: The intellectual climate is much less democratic and there is less money. Several of us have gotten grants as individuals, but we have not been successful in funding group projects. But, like the New Yorkers, we are incorporated as a not-for-profit organization, and we have written a constitution and defined the goals we want to support. We have always been committed to feminism, for example, though we now have several male members who play an active role in the administration of group activities.

Our aims have been flexible enough to allow us to mount a series of colloquia to test and develop our own scholarly work—and to drop the series of outside speakers we originally invited to steer us into work outside academe. We now also have regular group meetings every other month, which include a couple of purely social potluck suppers or cheese and wine parties.

Operating on a shoestring budget, we have a file drawer at the Radcliffe Seminars Office and we use a meeting room provided by the Radcliffe Graduate Center—a reminder of our women's college origins. The twenty-five dollars in dues we collect (five dollars for graduate students) manages to cover the expenses of our newsletter and the renting of larger meeting rooms.

We are a loose group in general, always wishing that new members would play more active roles. But our strength comes from the fact that we provide what is needed at the moment. A "book-finishing" group, for example, enabled four of us to produce four books—and get them published. As a group our publication rate is extremely good, although our work is often outside the academic mainstream.

Now that there is a national network of independent scholars, who share dreams of library cards and beds-and-breakfasts near research centers, we may all agree that serious scholarly work has often been done outside academe. But we continue to acknowledge that women particularly, and many retired academics, often need ego boosting and constructive criticism to enable them to continue scholarly projects. It is hard for anyone to work in a vacuum. We feel that we fill an important need in this society.   —*Eugenia Kaledin*

San Diego Independent Scholars (SDIS)

SDIS got started in 1981 somewhere between Texas and California. I drove west, leaving behind a teaching position in Washington, D.C., and cognizant that I would probably encounter difficulties finding another position. I found I welcomed the chance to pursue my own research unfettered by class preparations or papers to grade, but I was only too aware that I would miss the stimulation of colleagues, and I wondered if there might be others in the San Diego area in similar circumstances.

Shortly after settling in, I proposed the formation of an independent scholars' group to Mary Stroll, whom I had known for some time and who was engaged in independent research. She responded positively and offered to contact prospects. Three of us next met to compile a list of people who might be interested. About a dozen people turned out for the organizational meeting. In presenting my ideas for the formation of an independent scholars' organization, I used the model of the Princeton Research Forum. Having originally come from Princeton, I had contacted my friends who belonged to that group and gleaned all the information that I could from them.

We determined that, like the Princeton Research Forum, ours would be an interdisciplinary group. We decided to meet monthly in order to encourage the cohesiveness of the group, and we were able to secure a community room in a local bank as a regular meeting place, preferring to meet in a public space rather than in a private home. In addition to the monthly meetings, we held informal brown-bag lunch sessions in a bookstore, where we hotly debated issues such as the criteria for membership, in particular whether full members should hold the Ph.D. Until the Board of Directors was in place and bylaws enacted, all decisions were arrived at by consensus. We recruited members almost exclusively by word of mouth.
—*Joy Frieman*

Princeton Research Forum

In the autumn of 1979 a philosopher and two historians who were not then teaching, an anthropologist, and a freelance writer discussed the idea of founding a group for intellectual exchange. Throughout the winter three of them met to study the subject of intellectual communities and to formulate a plan for their own community of independent scholars in the Princeton area. The Institute for Research in History (IRH) and the New Haven Center for Independent Study were the only known examples of the type of organization that has become so familiar to us since then.

The founding mothers wanted an interdisciplinary organization, which meant that the structure would have to be different from that of IRH; but the specifically scholarly orientation imagined for the group seemed at the same time to require a structure somewhat different from the one chosen by the New Haven group. The winter of 1979–1980 was dedicated to investigating these structural problems, to canvassing possible members, and to discussing purposes and activities. Organizational meetings were held, the structure of governance was devised by a bylaws committee, and the group was incorporated under New Jersey law as a nonprofit corporation.

The Princeton Research Forum (PRF) was launched in the spring of 1980, and in the autumn it began to publish a newsletter to inform members of the group's activities, of specific research groups formed, and of the work of individual members. Research groups in women's studies, urban history, translation, and poetry were formed, as well as a work-in-progress seminar. PRF held a grants workshop and a meeting on computers, and set up a regular informal lunch group. A membership committee met regularly to consider new members according to the criteria established in the bylaws. A committee explored problems of library access. Budgets were developed and dues were levied as the financial stability of the group became a concern, and a board was elected at the end of the first year.

The founders felt that to launch an interdisciplinary group without a solid organizational structure was to invite disintegration after the first wave of enthusiasm ebbed. PRF's seven years of active development have demonstrated that there is a continuing need for such a group, and that even when old members are no longer active, new independent scholars will come forward to avail themselves of the group's resources. Almost all of the research groups are still functioning, and the larger membership still supports the goals of the organization. The three founders are no longer in executive positions, a proof of PRF's autonomy and resilience.

—*Sonya Rudikoff*

Notes

Prologue

1. Max Schuster spelled out his advice on becoming an independent scholar at greater length in "Assignment: Success" in *A Treasury of Success Unlimited*, edited by Og Mandino (New York: Pocket Books, 1976), 212–15.

2. Jacob Bronowski's further reflections on the need to democratize scientific understanding can be found in *The Ascent of Man* (Boston: Little, Brown, 1973), Chapter 13.

Part I
Chapter 1. Risk Takers of the Mind

1. Loring Thompson's speculations on "avocational scholarship" are developed at length in "Higher Education: From Occupation to Way of Life," *Planning for Higher Education* 3 (August 1974): 2–6.

2. The work of Maurice Gibbons and his associates is reported in "Toward a Theory of Self-Directed Learning: A Study of Experts Without Formal Training," *Journal of Humanistic Psychology* 20, no. 2 (Spring 1980).

3. Robert Stebbins's studies of amateurs in several fields are reported in his book *Amateurs: On the Margin Between Work and Leisure* (Beverly Hills, Calif.: Sage, 1979).

4. Henry Doering's interviews with independent scholars and other enthusiasts are contained in *The World Almanac Book of Buffs, Masters, Mavens and Uncommon Experts* (New York: World Almanac, 1980).

5. Charles Kadushin, *The American Intellectual Elite* (Boston: Little, Brown, 1974).

6. Maurice Hungiville's reflections on the need for scholarship about recent events and issues appeared in the *Chronicle of Higher Education*, 31 October 1977.

7. The interviews on which the descriptions of the work of Emily Taitz and

Sondra Henry is based were conducted in Great Neck, New York, in the summer of 1981.

Chapter 2. From "Messy Beginnings" to the Fruits of Research

1. Eric Hoffer's experiment in "sluicing [his] mind" is described in his book *Before the Sabbath* (New York: Harper & Row, 1979), in which he also reports on the products of the experiment.

2. Buckminster Fuller's Chronolog is described by several of his biographers.

3. *The Morning Notes of Adelbert Ames, Jr.*, edited and with a preface by Hadley Cantril, Rutgers University Press (New Brunswick, NJ, 1960).

4. Ari Kiev's suggestion about how to plumb one's interests through newspaper clipping is from his helpful book *A Strategy for Daily Living* (New York: The Free Press, 1973).

5. Allen Tough's list of possible fields of study appears in his book *Expand Your Life* (New York: College Entrance Examination Board, 1980).

6. C. Wright Mills's observation about social scientists' only writing about their plans when they are seeking funding is from his essay on "Intellectual Craftsmanship."

7. From an interview with John Walter.

8. Loring Thompson's suggestions to generate "preliminary theories prior to scholarship" comes from his paper "Toward Creative Thinking," *Main Currents in Modern Thought* (September 1951): 89.

9. From an interview with Charles Kapral.

10. From an interview with Mark Overland.

11. Hoffer declared that he never would write an autobiography, but he did reveal himself interestingly to trusted friends and interviewers, and intermittently in his own writings. Two sympathetic sketches of his life and thought, both handsomely illustrated with many photographs of his homely face, are *Hoffer's America* by James D. Koerner (La Salle, Ill.: Library Press, 1973) and *Eric Hoffer: An American Odyssey* by Calvin Tomkins, based on a profile in *The New Yorker* (New York: Dutton, 1968). Unfortunately neither volume contains a bibliography. Among his own books two of my favorites, because they show the process of his mind at work, rather than merely presenting its conclusions, are *Before the Sabbath* (New York: Harper & Row, 1978), and *Working and Thinking on the Waterfront* (New York: Harper & Row, 1979). His writing career is a credit, too, to his publishers. Hoffer's first book, *The True Believer* (New York: Harper & Row, 1951), is warmly dedicated to Margaret Anderson, an editor at Harper & Row, "without whose goading finger which reached me across a continent this book would not have been written." Thereafter the house of Harper continued to publish Hoffer's works, presumably because they were worth making available to the reading public rather

than because they would match the sales of his breakthrough book. In such cases, sadly rarer today, editor and publisher serve nobly as the handmaidens of talent.

Part II

The epigraph is from Michael Rossman's *On Learning and Social Change* (New York: Random House, 1972).

1. The "loose parts" approach to problem solving was first suggested to me by Simon Nicholson of Britain's Open University.

2. The patchwork overcoat metaphor for one's assemblage of "loose parts" came from the humanist psychologist Richard Grossman.

3. The account of the effort to enable Helen Lane to translate Ernesto Sábato's *On Heroes and Tombs* appeared in *The New York Times Book Review*, August 30, 1981.

Chapter 3. Resources: Where? What? Who? How?

1. The section on special library collections was researched and written by Julie Klauber and updated by Ellen Berman. The text dealing with special libraries and interlibrary loan was kindly reviewed by Professor Patrick R. Penland (School of Library and Information Science, University of Pittsburgh) and Cynthia Randall (Nassau Library System). The text dealing with databases was kindly reviewed by Skip McAfee (American Society for Information Science).

2. Sometime after the interviews on which this section is based, Barbara Tuchman published a splendid account of her craft as the first ninety-page section of her book *Practicing History: Selected Essays* (New York: Knopf, 1981). There she spoke at length about the actual writing of history: the means, the techniques ("I do not invent anything, even the weather."), and the opportunities of her métier. There is a charming essay on libraries and the "rare thrill in research." I consider this book essential reading for independent scholars.

Chapter 4. Working with Others

1. The definitive book on learning networks is still *The Learning Exchange* by Robert Lewis and Diane Kinishi (Evanston, Ill.: The Learning Exchange, 1979).

2. So-called nontraditional college programs are listed and described in *College Degrees for Adults* by Wayne Blaze and John Nero (Boston: Beacon Press, 1979).

3. Robert Stebbins's *Amateurs: On the Margin Between Work and Leisure* (Beverly Hills, Calif.: Sage Publications, 1979).

4. David Riesman's proposal for enlisting amateur observers to strengthen social science research appears in "Observations on Social Science Research" in his book *Individualism Reconsidered and Other Essays* (New York: Free Press, 1954), 467–83.

5. The Delphi technique was developed by the RAND Corporation, to enable groups of experts in a given field to achieve increasing consensus in predicting the future. Key references are: O. Helmer and N. Rescher, "On the Epistemology of Inexact Sciences," *Management Science* 6, no. 1 (October 1959); and N. Dalkey and O. Helmer, "An Experimental Application of the Delphi Method to the Use of Experts," *Management Science* 9, no. 3 (April 1963).

6. William Wang's article, "The Unbundling of Higher Education," can be found in the *Duke Law Journal* 53 (1975).

7. The interviews on which this profile is based were conducted in the summer of 1981.

Chapter 5. Intellectual Craftsmanship

1. Betty Friedan has written eloquently about her motivation and methods, especially in the introduction to the tenth anniversary edition of *The Feminine Mystique*, and in her autobiographical *It Changed My Life*. I have drawn from both of these sources as well as from an interview I conducted with her. It should be noted that this profile was written before the publication and enthusiastic reception of her book *The Second Stage*, which testified to her leadership in the women's movement.

Chapter 6. Wherewithal

1. This section was researched and written by Julie Klauber and reviewed and updated by professional staff at the Foundation Center in New York City.

2. More information about the emergence of "public history" can be found in "The New Historian," a special issue of *The Maryland Historian* 10, no. 1 (Spring 1979); "History Goes Public," a special issue of the American Association for State and Local History's *History News* 34, no. 5 (May 1979); *Outside Academe: New Ways of Working in the Humanities*, a report on the conference "Independent Research Institutions and Scholarly Life in the 1980s," edited by Marjorie Lightman and William Zeisel (New York: The Institute for Research in History and The Haworth Press, 1981); and the journal *The Public Historian*, published by the Graduate Program in Public Historical Studies of the University of California at Santa Barbara.

3. William Ruddick, *Philosophers in Medical Centers* (New York: Society for Philosophy and Public Affairs, 1980).

4. The interview on which this profile is based was conducted in the spring of 1981. Snyder's key paper is "The Space Oblique Mercator Projection," *Photogrammetric Engineering and Remote Sensing* 44, no. 4 (May 1978): 585–96.

Part III

Chapter 7.   Sharing Your Work

1. For a full account of the free university movement, see William Draves, *The Free University: A Model for Lifelong Learning* (Chicago: Follett, 1980).

2. The best source of information and support for Study Circles is the Study Circles Resource Center, P.O. Box 203, Route 169, Pomfret, CT 06258, (203) 928-2616.

3. The materials for this profile were developed through correspondence during 1981.

Chapter 8.   "Play for Mortal Stakes": The Intellectual Pleasures of Your Work

1. The materials for the profile of Samuel Florman were developed through correspondence during 1981.

2. The chief sources for this profile are Fuller's own voluminous autobiographical writings and two of his many marathon lectures. Two good biographies are *Buckminster Fuller: At Home in the Universe* by Alden Hatch (New York: Crown, 1974), and *Pilot for Spaceship Earth* by Athena V. Lord (New York: Macmillan, 1978). More spirited and bolder in explicating his concepts is *Bucky: A Guided Tour of Buckminster Fuller* by Hugh Kenner (New York: Morrow, 1973). The place to start for Fuller's own account of his ideas is *Ideas and Integrities: A Spontaneous Autobiographical Disclosure* (Englewood Cliffs, N.J.: 1963). My favorite among his memoirs is the poem "How Little I Know," written for Norman Cousins's collection of comparable autobiographical essays from other brilliant thinkers, *What I Have Learned* (New York: Simon and Schuster, 1968).

Chapter 9.   Scholarship as Your Joy, if Not Your Job

1. Robert Everhart's observations on the tradition of independent scholarship appeared in his article "The Boundless Scholar" in *Change* (April 1978).

2. The materials for this profile were developed through correspondence during 1981.

Chapter 10.   Interdependence among Independent Scholars

1. The case studies reported in this chapter were developed through visits to the sites in 1980 and 1981.

2. The interviews on which this profile is based were conducted in 1980 and 1981.

Bibliography

A Basic Bookshelf for the Independent Scholar

Realms of Mind

Altick, Richard D. *The Art of Literary Research.*
New York: Norton, 1963.

In this brief, spirited volume, Richard Altick evokes the esprit of humanistic research and portrays the basic techniques common to all such inquiries instead of offering a systematic treatise on the materials and methods of literary research. He makes such inquiry immensely attractive with his image of the scholar as both explorer and detective, living partly in the past, yet struggling to make his discoveries meaningful for the present. His aim is "to suggest what it is like to be a scholar." But the book delves authoritatively into such scholarly regimens as textual study, solving problems of authorship, searching for origins, tracing reputation and influence, and cultivating one's sense of the past.

Barzun, Jacques. *The House of Intellect.*
New York: Harper & Row, 1959.

How is intellect different from mind, intelligence, "smarts"? Why is it useful to think of it as a "house"? What is it in our educational system, our culture, and our institutions, from the press to philanthropy, that obstructs and undermines intellect?

Barzun's cogent answers to such questions make this book still relevant after more than thirty years. "A powerful, welcome book, calculated to embarrass all of us at procedures and habits of our own minds," commented *The American Scholar* when it first appeared. Barzun's dissections of such habits as the "thought-cliché" are, once read, unforgettable. On a larger scale, his analysis of the forces within our society, against which any independent scholar must struggle, is illuminating.

He argues, for example, that the overprofessionalization of intellectual pursuits by academe has destroyed the general audience "willing, let alone eager, to attend to intellectual matters."

Anecdotes abound in this sharply personal book, as Barzun deftly discerns the meaning in such commonplace tribulations as having the title of one's article changed by an editor to make it more "appealing," or being asked to substitute the name of Newton for Descartes because the former is "better known." "The characteristics of Intellect—its scarcity and superiority, its eccentricity and intangibility—prevent the democratic public from entertaining about it a just view or a straightforward emotion."

I do not agree with Barzun's aristocratic point of view, and some parts of *this* book would doubtless appall him. But his contentions command attention by anyone concerned about, let alone personally involved in, the life of the mind.

Barzun, Jacques, and Graff, Henry F. *The Modern Researcher.* 4th ed.
New York: Harcourt Brace Jovanovich, 1983.

A standard in the field since it was first published, this is one of the most lucid and comprehensive how-to guides of its kind. The combined wisdom, experience, and wit of Barzun and Graff take the reader step-by-step through the preparation and composition of any essay, article, or book based on research. Together they illuminate and illustrate the principles by which facts are assembled, sifted, and organized into a readable finished product.

Although addressed primarily to students of history, the topics it covers apply to almost any field; indeed, it uses examples from music and literature, medicine and painting, science and journalism. Among the subjects covered are how to find the facts, select and verify data, handle ideas, choose the word you mean, write effective sentences, organize paragraphs, chapters and parts, avoid jargon and cliché, cite sources, quote quotables, write footnotes, build a bibliography, and revise for publication.

The fourth edition reflects contemporary innovations in the "mechanics and facilities" of research, such as data banks, joint repositories, microcollections, and the like, and its excellent bibliographies include many newer works. Its brief section on lecturing is one of the best of its kind.

Brim, Gilbert. *Ambition.*
New York: Basic Books, 1992.

Don't judge this one by its title. It is actually about the innate striving in each of us for growth and mastery. Independent scholarship is a species of this genus, of course.

Brim is director of the MacArthur Foundation Research Network on Successful Mid-Life Development and was president of the Russell Sage Foundation, so he is a master at distilling and interpreting the latest psychological and social research. He illustrates his arguments with fascinating real-life examples.

Bronowski, Jacob. *The Ascent of Man.*
Boston: Little, Brown, 1973.

Developed from the thirteen-part television series produced by the British Broadcasting Corporation, this book is a humanist's journey through intellectual history, celebrating those "great monuments of human invention" from the flint tool to the theory of relativity. "Man ascends by discovering the fullness of his own gifts . . . what he creates on the ways are monuments to the stages in his understanding of nature and of self."

From the moment in the first chapter when Bronowski reaches up and places his own hand over the imprint of a prehistoric ancestor in the caves of Altamira, we know we are in the hands of a writer who can reveal the personal dimension of cultural achievements. Throughout the book, the spirit of independent inquiry is evoked in incident after incident, era after era. And by the end we have achieved a vivid understanding of how, in each of us in a small but real way.

I know of no better book to refresh one's sense that the life of the mind transcends our present shriveled notions of academic learning.

Ghiselin, Brewster. *The Creative Process.*
New York: Mentor, 1952.

There has been a plethora of books on "creativity" in recent years, but most of them are not very creative. This little book is different, and sparkling. Rather than being a study of creativity by a researcher not notable for that faculty, it consists of thirty-eight self-explanations by brilliant men and women including Albert Einstein, Carl Jung, W. B. Yeats, Henry James, Henry Moore, Thomas Wolfe, and Paul Valéry. (Obviously, artistic, rather than scientific or mathematical creativity, is emphasized.)

In each selection, the focus is on how the creators actually begin and complete creative works. The writers tell in their own words, about such things as the form of expression they choose, how they acquire the background knowledge, how they master their technique. The intertwined roles of inspiration, will, patience, and play are revealed in intriguing ways.

The editor, Brewster Ghiselin, is more than a compiler: His substantial introduction is itself an eloquent evocation of the creative spirit (he is a poet). Most of the few things worth knowing about the creative process are here put tellingly. "Production by a process of purely conscious calculation seems never to occur," the editor notes. But he also points out that "the mind in creation and in preparation for it nearly always requires some management. . . . The larger objects of management are two: discovering the clue that suggests the development to be sought, that intimates the creative end to be reached, and assuring a certain and economical movement toward that end."

A shorter, more accessible treatment of creativity from a psychological and existential point of view is Rolo May's *The Courage to Create*. While focusing largely on artistic creativity, it illuminates the generic process, especially in an extended analysis of two scientific "breakthrough" experiences, one the author's, the other from the memoirs of the mathematician Poincaré.

Glazer, Myron.
The Research Adventure: Promise and Problems of Field Work.
New York: Random House, 1972.

This is the best book I know on the gut problems of doing field work in sociology. What actually happens when you get out on that streetcorner, onto that military base, into that executive suite, in that foreign country? What problems do you encounter, and how have peers solved them—or failed? Down-to-earth as they are, these are questions that few graduate students ever seriously consider. They engage the core methodological problems and ethical issues of the sociologist's craft. This is the next work to read after Mills's *On Intellectual Craftsmanship*.

The consulting editor for the series in which this book appeared describes it accurately:

> Glazer takes the reader through the stages of the field research process: deciding on the project and the method; considering the problem of gaining acceptance and establishing a legitimate identity (while facing the ever-present suspicions of those studied); learning one's way around; getting behind the scenes or, as Erving Goffman puts it, "backstage"; dealing with data, and, finally, considering the matter of what knowledge for whom.

What makes the book invaluable is that the author introduces you to a number of well-known and several less-well-known but intriguing studies from which insights and lessons are drawn that are about as candid as you will find anywhere in print. The process worked like this, as Glazer explains:

> Much of the material for the first draft of this volume was garnered from available books and journals. The draft was then sent to all those field workers whose experiences had been cited. They most generously responded with critical comments and provided further insights that I incorporated into subsequent revisions. Thus, while I have quoted very little from published sources, I have included statements from the many letters, telephone calls, and personal conversations that I had with these researchers. The willingness of the field workers to answer many sensitive questions merits my deep gratitude and warm personal thanks.

Ours, too. This book illuminates the difficulties and rewards of serious social inquiry.

A good companion volume, not as spirited or original, but solid and useful, is *The Research Experience*, edited by Patricia Golden (Itasca, Illinois: Peacock, 1976). It has helpful chapters (by diverse contributors) on field studies, experiments, surveys, using available data, and measurement.

Goleman, Daniel, and associates. *The Creative Spirit.*
New York: E. P. Dutton, 1992.

A grand tour of creativity around the world, packaged in a book that is authoritative (Goleman covers this subject for *The New York Times*), as well as a joy to read and look at (it is the book version of a PBS series and has wonderful graphics).

Creativity is a key knack for independent scholars who want to work smarter, not harder. Using it can provide independents with a keen edge over academic scholars, who are often trapped in an uncreative, overly critical, and excessively cautious academic culture.

Good, Carter V. and Scates, Douglas E.
Methods of Research: Educational, Psychological, Sociological.
New York: Appelton-Century-Crofts, 1954.

It's all here—just don't drop it on your foot. Topping out at almost one thousand pages, this grandaddy of all research manuals has nurtured generations of investigators. "The purpose of research is to serve man," it proclaims nobly within the first ten pages, and it is informed throughout by a confidence in progress through intelligence and knowledge that we can no longer fully share, but must respect.

The best way to suggest the contents is to simply run down the major chapter headings, each of which goes into detail within its category:

➤ Formulation and Development of the Problem
   Hundreds of researchers each year still come a cropper for want of some of the wisdom that can be found in the savvy sections on Hazards, Penalties, Handicaps, and on the Time Factor.
➤ Survey of Related Literature and Library Technique
   Still a sticky problem, with all our data banks—recall the case [page 113] of the professor and the high school teacher who did not know of each other's work.
➤ The Historical Method
➤ The Descriptive Method
➤ Descriptive-Survey and Normative Research; Illustrative Surveys and Procedures in Data-Gathering; Questionnaire and Interview Techniques; Observational, Small-Group, Content-Analysis, and Appraisal Techniques
➤ The Experimental Method
➤ Case and Clinical Studies

➤ Genetic, Developmental, and Growth Studies
➤ The Reporting and Implementing of Research

The spirit of this book transcends its technical virtuosity. "The goal of research is the good life," the authors conclude. A fitting motto for the independent scholar.

Gross, Ronald.
Peak Learning: A Master Course in Learning How to Learn.
Los Angeles, Jeremy Tarcher, Inc., 1991.

Building on my earlier book *The Lifelong Learner*, this book offers strategies and techniques for learning faster, easier, better, and more enjoyably. Among the topics covered are: discovering your personal learning style; getting "into flow"; breaking through learning blocks; brain-friendly techniques for reading, memorization, and note taking; tapping into the Invisible University; setting up your own learning space; and mobilizing your critical and creative powers to support your intellectual growth.

Hayes, Charles D. *Self-University.*
Wasilla, Alaska: Autodidactic Press, 1990.

The most inspiring book on self-education published in the last decade. Addressing topics from the search for meaning in life to how to create your own credentials, this book is a life-affirming experience.

Author Charles Hayes is a high school drop-out, ex-marine, and ex-Dallas police officer, who is now retired from working in the Arctic for Atlantic Richfield. He discovered self-education, educated himself, and now educates others in how to do it. "You can create your own university," declares this visionary writer. "One that empowers you for life."

Jones, Howard Mumford.
One Great Society: Humane Learning in the United States.
New York: Harcourt, Brace, 1959.

Prepared for the Commission on the Humanities of the American Council of Learned Societies, this volume still stands as the most readable and eloquent *apologia* for those subjects we loosely call "the humanities"—philosophy, history, literature, music, the arts, and languages. Through them, Jones demonstrates, we discover what being "human" really, fully means. For the individual and for the nation, he argues persuasively, humane learning is essential. His detailed discussions of exactly what a scholar in the humanities does, as well as how, why, and with what consequences, have never been expressed better. "The man of learning must exhibit as a matter of course the qualities of all sound intellectual workers, such as openness to ideas, readiness to make inquiry, objectivity . . . humility of mind, and a capacity to adhere to principles in the cause of truth."

Koestler, Arthur. *The Act of Creation.*
New York: Macmillan, 1964.

One of this century's premier independent scholars here analyzes the work and play of the human intellect operating at its best. This book is both an exemplification of, and a treatise on, much that I mean by independent scholarship.

Koestler's insight is that all creative activities, from scientific discoveries to dirty jokes, have a basic pattern in common. To illuminate that pattern he draws from a wide range of fields in the humanities and physical and life sciences. Much of his argument is summed up in a triptych that appears at the front of the volume: The Sage, representing Discovery, is flanked on either side by the Jester and the Artist. The diagram itself is a marvelously stimulating object of meditation.

This book is even more significant for independent scholars than its obviously relevant theme of creativity would suggest. For as the capstone of its author's career, it represents an important assertion about intellectual life in our time. Arthur Koestler struggled to meet the challenges posed by totalitarianism, experiencing personally, as well as documenting and analyzing, the loss of freedom. From *Darkness at Noon* on, his *oeuvre* has "hammered out by means of plot and rational argument . . . the possibilities of free action," as the critic George Steiner put it when *The Act of Creation* appeared: "It is in the speculative play of the mind, in the power of consciousness to alter the 'set' of existence, to surprise itself with revelation, that Koestler now locates the essence of freedom." Such a work belongs on the bookshelf of every independent scholar.

Medawar, P. B. *Advice to a Young Scientist.*
New York: Harper &Row, 1979.

A witty and irreverent peek under the scientist's lab smock by a Nobel Laureate. Medawar construes "science" broadly to mean "all exploratory activities of which the purpose is to come to a better understanding of the natural world. . . . What I say will bear upon sociology, anthropology, archaeology, and the 'behavioral sciences' generally, and not just upon the world of laboratories, test tubes, and microscopes."

A list of some of the topics he covers will convey how unorthodox and unstuffy is his approach. By page four he is telling you about "the most crooked scientist I know"; on page ten he touches on the pecking order within science ("a most complex *snobismus*"); halfway along he catalogs the "dirty tricks" that constitute "Scientmanship," the scientist's version of Potter's Oneupmanship; and by the end of his brief book he has covered such down-to-earth topics as "Hard Luck on Spouses," "Excess of Hubris," "Ambition," "What Shall I Do Research On?," and "Prizes and

Awards," as well as such heavies as "Scientific Meliorism versus Scientific Messianism" and "Sexism and Racism in Science."

Van Leunen, Mary-Claire. *A Handbook for Scholars.*
New York: Knopf, 1978.

The stylebook for people who hate stylebooks. Van Leunen is a witty, companionable guide to the mechanics of scholarly writing: citation, references, footnotes, bibliographies, format, styling, text preparation, and all related matters. Her made-up examples of wrong usage are brisk fun, and her opinions on such "scholarly peculiarities" as The Abstract, Acknowledgments, The Colonated Title, Hyperqualification, The Waffle, and Bending Over Backwards, constitute a painless purge for some of our worst offenses. For example: Why does scholarly prose bristle with *so* many footnotes? "The footnote permits the scholar to say another word, just one other word, just one word more, before he has to stop."

Woolf, Virginia. *A Room of One's Own.*
New York: Harcourt, Brace & World, 1929.

"Why don't women write fiction?" Virginia Woolf had been asked by the sponsors of the lectureship that resulted in this book. In the course of answering that question, she composed not only a classic feminist manifesto, but also one of the most stirring invitations to join the life of the mind. As we accompany her step by step on her quest, we share the struggles of an independent intelligence at work on a momentous problem.

"I propose making use of all the liberties and licenses of a novelist, to tell you the story of . . . how, bowed down by the weight of the subject which you have laid upon my shoulders [the text was originally delivered as lectures], I pondered it, and made it work in and out of my daily life." The problem was one we all face: creativity constrained by circumstance—not enough time, not enough leisure, not enough freedom. "A woman must have money and a room of her own if she is to write . . . five hundred [pounds] a year stands for the power to contemplate . . . a lock on the door means the power to think for oneself."

Invention abounds in these pages: you will meet Judith Shakespeare, William's equally talented but thwarted sister; Professor von X, author of *The Mental, Moral, and Physical Inferiority of the Female Sex*; and Mary Carmichael, whose *Life's Adventure* starts out "like a person striking a match that will not light," but works up to the unprecedented sentences "Chloe liked Olivia. They shared a laboratory together. . . ."

You will laugh a little and your eyes may fill with tears at certain points, as when the author finds herself, exhilarated with an idea she wants to pursue, blocked from entering the university library because "ladies are only admitted . . . if accompanied by a Fellow of the College or furnished with a letter of introduction." There is no other book like this.

Usable Knowledge

Feyerabend, Paul.
Against Method: An Outline of an Anarchistic Theory of Knowledge.
London: Verso, 1978.

Remember how you were taught "*the* scientific method" in school, college, or even graduate school? Since then, philosophers or science have taken another look—a more scientific one, focusing on how scientists actually *practice* science. Paul Feyerabend is the most radical of them. He argues that the most successful scientific inquiries have never proceeded according to the rational method at all.

"His book is quite unrestrained," wrote the British *Tribune*, "sparkling with ideas and philosophical sophistication, born of extensive scholarship." Indeed, it is an intellectual romp. Early on, he goes beyond even the word anarchism: "I now prefer to use the term *Dadaism.* . . . A Dadaist is utterly unimpressed by any serious enterprise and he smells a rat whenever people stop smiling and assume that attitude and those facial expressions which indicate that something important is about to be said."

Something important is said in this book: that intellectual progress is encouraged by exalting the creativity and individuality of the investigator. Feyerabend goes further than we may want to follow, in looking forward to the "withering away of reason." But no serious (but unsolemn) thinker will fail to benefit from playing with his basic idea that "the only principle which does not inhibit progress is anything goes."

Fuller, R. Buckminster. *Operating Manual for Spaceship Earth.*
New York: Dutton, 1973.

Operating Manual for Your Mind could be the alternate title of this brief, readable masterwork. "Because our spontaneous initiative has been frustrated, too often inadvertently, in earliest childhood, we do not tend, customarily, to dare to think competently regarding our potentials." Fuller welcomes us back to the exercise of our "comprehensive propensities" with a sweeping attack on intellectual specialization. "Specialization is . . . only a fancy form of slavery wherein the 'expert' is fooled into accepting his slavery by making him feel that in return his is in a socially and culturally preferred, ergo, highly secure, lifelong position."

Extreme? Of course. But to wrestle with Fuller's arguments is the best way I know to clarify your own position on this question. One of the independent thinker's greatest freedoms is to escape encapsulation in a narrow speciality: that is one of the reasons that, each in his or her own way, Barbara Tuchman, Eric Hoffer, Betty Friedan, and indeed Fuller himself, were able to make the contributions they made. The professor strays out of his "field" only at his peril; the independent scholar can cross over to different fields, disciplines, and intellectual turf.

Some eighty years ago Arnold Bennett urged that "the most important of all perceptions is the continual perception of cause and effect—in other words, the perception of the course of evolution." Invites Fuller: "Let us now exercise our intellectual faculties as best we can to apprehend the evolutionary patternings transcending our spontaneous cognitions and recognitions." Thus do a man of letters and a man of science concur over the generations.

Lindblom, Charles E. and Cohen, David K.
Usable Knowledge: Social Science and Social Problem Solving.
New Haven, Conn.: Yale University Press, 1979.

Only recently has academe itself begun to admit the narrowness of its definition of knowledge. This little knotty volume is one of a handful of iconoclastic self-reflections (the authors are notable academics, at Harvard and Yale, respectively). Here, the "imperial claims" of professional researchers in the social sciences are scored as false, misleading, and dangerous. Social scientists have greatly—and damagingly—exaggerated their own importance in helping to solve social problems.

The book argues that professional social science research is only one factor among several important ones in shaping solutions to social problems—and that others, including what they call "ordinary knowledge, negotiations, politics, etc.," are more important. In developing this case, the authors provide dynamite for the following myths promulgated by the professoriate in most fields: that the subject is co-terminous with our present definition of it; that the only legitimate investigators are professors; that the only suitable topics are the ones our journals are currently accepting. Lindblom and Cohen cite the embarrassing record of American social science in avoiding for so long such taboo subjects as black Americans, Third-World economies, inequalities in our society. (I hasten to add that this list of "myths" is mine, and should not be blamed on these authors.)

Independent Scholars at Work

The editors of *The World Almanac.* Edited by Henry Doering.
Book of Buffs, Masters, Mavens and Uncommon Experts.
New York: World Almanac Publications, 1980.

More than two hundred brief but vivid interviews with individuals who devote their spare time to an amazing array of subjects, topics, issues, and enthusiasms (some of them are mentioned on pages 8–9 of this book). The categories, not all of them representing what I would call independent scholarship, include Collectibles, Philately, Numismatics, Civil War, Militaria, Vehicles, People, History, Nature and Science, Arts and Crafts, and So Forth.

It is the lively direct quotes from the subjects that makes the book a delight to have at hand. "I enjoy these people's enthusiasm and their stories," says Doering. "They have something to tell us about how to live a full life." Indeed, they do, and the book captures much of it. It is the closest thing to being able to telephone a dozen vivacious independent scholars and tune in to their energy and resourcefulness whenever you need some psychological refreshment.

Jacoby, Russell. *The Last Intellectuals.*
New York: Basic Books, 1987.

The most important book on independent scholarship published in the last ten years. It chronicles the disappearance of the nonacademic intellectual from American cultural life. As the generation of Daniel Bell, William Buckley, Jr., C. Wright Mills, Lewis Mumford, Edmund Wilson, and Jane Jacobs leaves us, it appears that there are few younger successors in the generation to follow.

Jacoby is passionate, lucid, and compelling. His book exemplifies the virtues he finds endangered, and he himself is a model for what can be accomplished.

Kadushin, Charles. *The American Intellectual Elite.*
Boston: Little, Brown, 1974.

I have used this book's findings to point out that the majority of our most notable intellectuals are *not* college professors. But there is more here that will interest independent scholars—despite the datedness of the data. For Kadushin challenges the prevalent image of the American intellectual elite as an eastern establishment, a literary Mafia, "effete snobs," a homogeneous group of leftish persuasion radiating its influence and authority to the far corners of the nation.

This book reveals the "elite" to be in many ways not different from the rest of well-educated Americans—human, fallible, disorganized, and politically ineffective. The author examines the journals the elite write for—magazines such as *The New Yorker, The New Republic, The New York Review of Books, Commentary, Partisan Review*—and dissects the circles of fluctuating power that form around them. He traces the patterns of Who talks to Whom—and Why. He analyzes their religions, ages, social classes, sex, and politics, and uncovers quite a few startling facts about the elite's declared positions on social and economic problems.

Among Kadushin's provocative conclusions is that the central and "certifying" institutions for intellectuals are not universities but circles and journals.

Kostelanetz, Richard.
Master Minds: Portraits of Contemporary American Artists and Intellectuals.
New York: Macmillan, 1969.

"By looking at the fourteen remarkable individuals discussed in this book . . . we [can] acquire a rough sense of how genius develops in this country; for they comprise a viable sample of master minds in America today." Kostelanetz's claim is just: in fact, it is modest. His portraits are penetrating, sensitive, and detailed. Through them, we have the precious opportunity to enter the daily life of vibrant individuals doing the most with their minds. The book brims with energy and practicality. Once you read how Glenn Gould "takes the cue of Marshall McLuhan and Makes the telephone an extension of himself," thus being "constantly in touch with everyone important to him, at once, with minimum fuss," your own use of this tool will probably change.

The subjects of the book are the theologian Reinhold Niebuhr, the composer Elliott Carter, the management consultant Bernard Muller-Thym, the applied scientist John R. Pierce, the social philosopher Paul Goodman, the communications theorist Marshall McLuhan, the esthetic philosopher John Cage, the novelist Ralph Ellison, the composer Milton Babbitt, the historian Richard Hofstadter, the policy scientist Herman Kahn, the visual artist Robert Rauschenberg, the poet Allen Ginsberg, and the pianist Glenn Gould.

The joy of the book is in the journey, but Kostelanetz's conclusions matter. He concludes that, unlike European intellectuals of comparable eminence, most of whom come from the "right" families and go to the "right" schools, great American minds come from unlikely backgrounds and realize themselves in eccentric ways. "This analysis suggests simply that there are no 'right' parents to have, places to grow up in, schools to attend, schedules to follow: for the truth is that in a country where every [person] suffers disadvantages of one kind or another, as well as opportunities, each master mind makes [their] own eminence."

Lightman, Marjorie and Zeisel, William.
Outside Academe: New Ways of Working in the Humanities.
New York: The Institute for Research in History and the Haworth Press, 1981.

This report of a conference on "independent research institutions and scholarly life in the 1980s," supported by a grant from the Ford Foundation, contains a superb essay on the emergence of an independent scholarly sector in the field of history. For a glimpse of what has begun to happen in some of the major academic disciplines, this is the place to start.

McLeish, John A. B.
The Ulyssean Adult: Creativity in the Middle and Later Years.
Toronto: McGraw-Hill Ryerson, 1976.

This neglected volume proclaims, and documents, the principle that "the conditions required for the creative life are more available in the later years of adulthood than earlier in life." McLeish, a Canadian adult educator whose range of interests has embraced art, cinema, music, poetry, social causes, and athletics, takes the Ulysses of Tennyson's poem as his archetype: "To follow knowledge like a sinking star." He marshals data and dramatic case studies of people who "used the remarkable brain-and-mind which is their heritage without fretting about supposed declines and deficits, knowing that there is an abundance of power there, knowing it will serve them well." Usefully, McLeish explains in plain language the keys to fostering continued creativity in ourselves:

> These are the attitudes towards life and the later years which are typical of Ulysseans: that life is a process of continuous growth, as much through the later and the very late years as in any earlier period; that the capacity to learn is fully operative among human beings across the entire span of life; . . . that human creativity comprises, apart from the splendours of genius, thousands of manifestations of the mind and imagination which transform an individual's own self or his or her environment.

Stebbins, Robert A. *Amateurs: On the Margin Between Work and Leisure.*
Beverly Hills, Calif.: Sage Publications, 1979.

"The modern amateur is a serious participant in an avocation that impels him away from play and dilettantism toward necessity, obligation, and commitment as demonstrated by regimentation and systematization. He operates within a professional-amateur-public system of functionally interdependent relationships, where he is further differentiated from his professional counterpart by a characteristic set of attitudes." The word "serious" is central to Stebbins's definition, and his rigorous observational studies of the "amateur routine" in a variety of fields (he is a sociologist) confirm—indeed, they generated—this characterization. He sees his "amateurs" as standing out sharply from "professionals who work in the same field and from dabblers who merely play at it." They "are serious about their leisure and therefore misunderstood by those of their associates—friends, neighbors, relatives, workmates—who participate only in *popular leisure.*"

Independent investigators will be especially intrigued by three chapters on amateur archaeologists covering their "routine" (that is, their round of activities in the field), their relations with others as those relations are affected by their scientific pursuits, and their "perspective," including their rewards, thrills (the author is not afraid to use such words), disappointments, dislikes, and tensions.

Tannenbaum, Frank.
A Community of Scholars: The University Seminars at Columbia.
New York: Praeger, 1965.

Most colleges and universities fail as communities of scholars. They chop knowledge up into departmental "turfs," and sabotage intellectual comradeship with careerist competitiveness. Each professor finds himself or herself confined to one area, channeled into the acceptable modes of inquiry in that field, driven by the "publish or perish" imperative.

Is it possible to create a true community of scholars in such an environment? And if it is, could independent scholars from the community be involved on an equal basis? The University Seminars program at Columbia (described on pages 216–19) has succeeded, over many years, in doing those two things.

In this moving volume, eleven participants including such renowned intellectuals as Daniel Bell, Paul Goodman, Margaret Mead, Robert Theobold, and Paul Lazarsfeld, reflect on their experiences and on the significance of the seminar movement as a whole. Far more than a report of one project, the book presents the most powerful image in print of what authentic intellectual communion, at the highest level, is all about.

Index